Th

Vest
Pocket
Guide to IFRS

THE
VEST
POCKET
Guide to IFRS

 Steven M. Bragg

WILEY

John Wiley & Sons, Inc.

Published by John Wiley & Sons, Inc., Hoboken, New Jersey.
Published simultaneously in Canada.

For general information on our other products and services or for technical support, please contact our Customer Care Department within the United States at (800) 762-2974, outside the United States at (317) 572-3993 or fax (317) 572-4002.

Wiley also publishes its books in a variety of electronic formats. Some content that appears in print may not be available in electronic books. For more information about Wiley products, visit our web site at www.wiley. com.

Library of Congress Cataloging-in-Publication Data:
Bragg, Steven M.
  The vest pocket guide to IFRS/Steven M. Bragg.
    p. cm.
  Includes index.
  ISBN 978-0-470-61947-6 (pbk.); ISBN 978-0-470-88547-5 (ebk); ISBN 978-0-470-88563-5 (ebk) ; ISBN 978-0-470-88564-2 (ebk)
  1. Financial statements—Standards—Handbooks, manuals, etc.
  2. Accounting—Standards—Handbooks, manuals, etc. I. Title.
  HF5626.B73 2010
  657'.3—dc22   2010013502

Printed in the United States of America

10 9 8 7 6 5 4 3 2 1

CONTENTS

ABOUT THE AUTHOR

Steven Bragg, CPA, has been the chief financial officer or controller of four companies, as well as a consulting manager at Ernst & Young. He received a master's degree in finance from Bentley College, an MBA from Babson College, and a bachelor's degree in economics from the University of Maine. He has been two-time President of the Colorado Mountain Club and is an avid alpine skier, mountain biker, and certified master diver. Mr. Bragg resides in Centennial, Colorado. He has written the following books:

Accounting and Finance for Your Small Business
Accounting Best Practices
Accounting Control Best Practices
Accounting Policies and Procedures Manual
Advanced Accounting Systems
Billing and Collections Best Practices
Business Ratios and Formulas
Controller's Guide to Costing
Controller's Guide to Planning and Controlling Operations
Controller's Guide: Roles and Responsibilities
    for the New Controller
Controllership
Cost Accounting
Cost Reduction Analysis
Essentials of Payroll
Fast Close
Financial Analysis
GAAP Guide
GAAP Policies and Procedures Manual
GAAS Guide
Inventory Accounting
Inventory Best Practices
Investor Relations
Just-in-Time Accounting
Management Accounting Best Practices
Managing Explosive Corporate Growth
Mergers and Acquisitions
Outsourcing
Payroll Accounting
Payroll Best Practices

Revenue Recognition
Run the Rockies
Running a Public Company
Sales and Operations for Your Small Business
The Controller's Function
The New CFO Financial Leadership Manual
The Ultimate Accountants' Reference
The Vest Pocket Controller's Guide
The Vest Pocket Guide to IFRS
Throughput Accounting
Treasury Management

WHAT THIS BOOK WILL DO FOR YOU

This is a handy pocket problem solver for the accountant, controller, and chief financial officer. It provides complete coverage of all international financial reporting standards (IFRSs), using a question and answer format that provides concise explanations and hundreds of supporting examples for all IFRS topics. The layout is designed for quick comprehension of such questions as:

- What are the direct and indirect method layouts for the statement of cash flows?
- Should I consolidate a special purpose entity?
- What are the thresholds for segment reporting?
- How do I calculate diluted earnings per share?
- What related party information should I disclose?
- How do I account for adjusting events after the reporting period?
- How do I restate financial results in a hyperinflationary economy?
- How do I account for a joint venture?
- How do I account for an investment in an associate?
- What costs can I include in inventory?
- Can I adjust property, plant, and equipment to its fair value?
- How do I recognize intangible assets?
- When is an asset impaired, and how do I account for the impairment?
- What is a provision, and when do I recognize it?
- How do I recognize installment sales?
- How do I account for defined benefit plans?
- How do I account for a share-based payment?
- What types of leases are there, and how do I account for them?
- How do I account for a business combination?
- How do I account for discontinued operations?
- How do I determine an entity's functional currency, and how do I report transactions in that currency?

Vest Pocket IFRS is divided into sections, each dealing with four main categories of IFRS: the financial statements, assets and liabilities, revenue and expenses, and special transactions.

Part 1, The Financial Statements (Chapters 1–8), addresses IFRSs for the construction of financial statements. Part 1 is divided into separate chapters to address the basic form of the financial statements, how to consolidate them, and how to report on special situations. These special situations include the reporting of operating segments, earnings per share, and interim reporting, all of which are required for publicly held entities. Other chapters address special disclosures, including related party disclosures and the reporting of events occurring after the reporting period. Finally, Part 1 covers financial reporting in hyperinflationary economies.

Part 2, Assets and Liabilities (Chapters 9–16), addresses IFRSs for accounting issues related to assets and liabilities. There are separate chapters covering the accounting for investment property, interests in joint ventures, investments in associates, inventory, property, and intangible assets. A separate chapter addresses the key issue of asset impairment, and Part 2 concludes with a discussion of provisions and contingencies.

Part 3, Revenue and Expenses (Chapters 17–20), delves into a variety of revenue and expense topics. These include revenue recognition, employee benefits, share-based payments, and income taxes.

Part 4, Special Transactions (Chapters 21–31), addresses a broad range of accounting transactions. These include business combinations, changes in accounting estimates, discontinued operations, the effects of foreign exchange rate changes, financial instruments (such as derivatives), and the appropriate treatment of government grants, insurance contracts, leases, mineral exploration activities, and retirement benefit plans.

Throughout, *Vest Pocket IFRS* has been structured to provide concise answers to the IFRS questions that an accountant is most likely to encounter during a typical business day. Keep it handy for easy reference and daily use.

 ## Free On-Line Resources by Steve Bragg

Steve issues a free accounting best practices podcast. You can sign up for it at www.accountingtools.com, or access it through iTunes.

PART I

THE FINANCIAL STATEMENTS

CHAPTER 1

FINANCIAL STATEMENTS PRESENTATION

 What Is Profit or Loss?

Profit or loss is the total of an entity's revenue and expenses, not including any components of other comprehensive income (see the next question). It is also known as *net income*.

Total comprehensive income is the combination of profit or loss and other comprehensive income.

 What Is Other Comprehensive Income?

Other comprehensive income includes financial items that are not permitted in profit or loss. Items that you should insert in other comprehensive income include:

- ○ *Actuarial gains and losses on defined benefit plans* (see the Employee Benefits chapter)
- ○ *Available-for-sale gains and losses caused by remeasurement* (see the Financial Instruments: Recognition and Measurement chapter)
- ○ *Cash flow hedge gains and losses, effective portion only* (see the Financial Instruments: Recognition and Measurement chapter)
- ○ *Changes in the revaluation surplus* (see the Property, Plant, and Equipment chapter)
- ○ *Foreign currency translation gains and losses* (see the Effects of Foreign Exchange Rate Changes chapter)

Reclassification adjustments are amounts reclassified into profit or loss in the current period that had been recognized in other comprehensive income in either the current or previous periods.

What Information Is Included in a Complete Set of Financial Statements?

All of the following should be included in a complete set of financial statements for a reporting period:

Statement	Description
Statement of financial position	Contains all asset, liability, and equity items
Statement of comprehensive income	Contains all income and expense items
Statement of changes in equity	Reconciles changes in equity for the presented periods
Statement of cash flows	Displays all cash inflows and outflows from operating, financing, and investing activities
Notes	Summarizes accounting policies and explanatory information

You should clearly identify these financial statements and distinguish them from other information presented in the same report. It is important to do this, because International Financial Reporting Standards (IFRSs) apply only to financial statements; thus, users will be more likely to understand which documents within the report adhere to specific accounting standards.

You should include in the financial statements a prominent display of the name of the reporting entity (and note any change in it from the preceding reporting period), whether the statements are for a single entity or group of entities, the period covered by the statements, the presentation currency, and the level of rounding used to present amounts. This information usually is presented most easily in column and page headers.

It is not necessary, but useful, for management to also present a financial review that includes such items as the primary factors impacting financial performance, its investment policy, dividend policy, sources of funding, targeted financial ratios, and any other resources not recognized in the financial statements.

What Line Items Do I Include in the Statement of Financial Position?

You should include the following line items, at a minimum, in the statement of financial position:

Assets

- ○ Cash and cash equivalents
- ○ Trade and other receivables
- ○ Investments accounted for using the equity method
- ○ Other financial assets
- ○ Current tax assets
- ○ Investment property
- ○ Inventories
- ○ Biological assets
- ○ Property, plant, and equipment
- ○ Intangible assets
- ○ Assets held for sale
- ○ Deferred tax assets (do not classify as a current asset)

Liabilities

- ○ Trade and other payables
- ○ Provisions
- ○ Current tax liabilities
- ○ Other financial liabilities
- ○ Deferred tax liabilities (do not classify as a current liability)
- ○ Liabilities held for sale

Equity

- ○ Noncontrolling interests
- ○ Issued capital and reserves attributable to owners of the parent

You should add headings and subtotals to this minimum set of information if it will improve a user's understanding of the financial statements. You should add other line items when their size, nature, or function makes separate presentation relevant to the user.

EXAMPLE 1.1

Katana Cutlery presents its statement of financial position in the following format:

KATANA CUTLERY STATEMENT OF FINANCIAL POSITION

(000s)	as at 12/31/x2	as at 12/31/x1
ASSETS		
Noncurrent assets		
Property, plant, and equipment	€551,000	€529,000

(Continued)

(*Continued*)

Goodwill	82,000	82,000
Other intangible assets	143,000	143,000
Investments in associates	71,000	93,000
Available-for-sale financial assets	121,000	108,000
	968,000	955,000
Current assets		
Inventories	139,000	128,000
Trade receivables	147,000	139,000
Other current assets	15,000	27,000
Cash and cash equivalents	270,000	215,000
	571,000	509,000
Total assets	€1,539,000	€1,464,000
EQUITY AND LIABILITIES		
Equity attributable to owners of the parent		
Share capital	€500,000	€500,000
Retained earnings	425,000	350,000
Other components of equity	25,000	19,000
	950,000	869,000
Noncontrolling interests	57,000	38,000
Total equity	1,007,000	907,000
Noncurrent liabilities		
Long-term borrowings	85,000	65,000
Deferred tax	19,000	17,000
Long-term provisions	38,000	34,000
Total noncurrent liabilities	142,000	116,000
Current liabilities		
Trade and other payables	217,000	198,000
Short-term borrowings	133,000	202,000
Current portion of long-term borrowings	5,000	5,000
Current tax payable	26,000	23,000
Short-term provisions	9,000	13,000
Total current liabilities	390,000	441,000
Total liabilities	532,000	557,000
Total equity and liabilities	€1,539,000	€1,464,000

What Information Should I Disclose in the Statement of Financial Position?

You should provide additional subclassifications of the primary line items required for the statement of financial position, if needed to clarify an entity's operations, or to be in accordance with the various IFRSs. Examples of these additional classifications are:

- Separate property, plant, and equipment into different asset classifications.
- Separate accounts receivable into amounts receivable from trade customers, related parties, and prepayments.
- Separate inventories into merchandise, supplies, raw materials, work in process, and finished goods.
- Separate equity into paid-in capital, share premiums, and reserves.

For each class of share capital, you should disclose the following:

- *Internal holdings.* Any shares held by the entity or its subsidiaries or associates
- *Par value.* The par value per share or the fact that there is no par value
- *Reclassifications.* Any reclassifications of financial instruments between liabilities and equity, and the timing and reasons for the reclassifications
- *Reconciliation.* Reconciliation of the share totals at the beginning and end of the reporting period
- *Reserved shares.* Any outstanding share options or other contracts for the sale of shares, as well as the terms of these agreements
- *Reserves.* The nature of any equity reserves
- *Rights and restrictions.* Restrictions on dividend distribution and capital repayment, as well as any other rights, preferences, and restrictions
- *Shares.* The number of shares authorized, issued and fully paid, and issued but not fully paid

When Do I Present Information as Current or Noncurrent?

You should present current and noncurrent assets and liabilities within the statement of financial position, except when a presentation based on liquidity is more reliable and more relevant. If liquidity is the more relevant basis of presentation, then present all assets and liabilities sorted in order by level of liquidity.

Whether you present line items by current/noncurrent or by liquidity, you should separately disclose the amount you expect to recover or settle after more than 12 months for any line item that combines amounts that are expected to be recovered within 12 months of the reporting period and later than 12 months from the reporting period.

You should classify an asset as current when an entity expects to sell or consume it during its normal operating cycle or within 12 months after the reporting period, or if it holds the asset in order to trade it, or if it is a cash or cash equivalent (unless it is restricted from use). Current assets always include cash, inventories, and assets held for trading. You should classify all other assets as noncurrent.

You should classify a liability as current when the entity expects to settle it during its normal operating cycle or within 12 months after the reporting period, or if it holds the liability in order to trade it, or if it is scheduled for settlement within 12 months, or if the entity does not have the right to defer its settlement for at least 12 months. You should classify financial liabilities as current when they are scheduled for settlement within 12 months, even if the original term was for a longer period. Current liabilities always include trade payables and accruals for employee and other operating costs. You should classify all other liabilities as noncurrent.

If an entity reaches an agreement after the reporting period but before the financial statements are authorized for issuance, to reschedule payments or refinance so that payments are due *after* the 12-month period, you should still categorize them as current liabilities. If an entity expects and has the ability to refinance or roll over an obligation so that it is due more than 12 months after the reporting period, then you should classify the obligation as noncurrent.

If an entity breaches a provision of a long-term debt agreement during a reporting period and this effectively makes the agreement payable on demand, you should categorize it as a current liability, even if the lender agrees, before the financial statements are authorized for issuance, not to demand payment. However, if the lender agrees, by the end of the reporting period, to provide at least a 12-month grace period, then you can classify the debt as noncurrent.

An entity's operating cycle is the time required to acquire assets for processing and convert them into cash. If you cannot determine the operating cycle, assume that it is 12 months.

What Line Items Do I Include in the Statement of Comprehensive Income?

You should present all items of income and expense for the reporting period in a statement of comprehensive income. Alternatively, you can split this information into an income statement and a statement of comprehensive income.

You should include the following line items, at a minimum, in the statement of comprehensive income:

- ○ Revenue
- ○ Finance costs
- ○ Share of associates' and joint ventures' profit or loss recorded with the equity method
- ○ Tax expense
- ○ Post-tax profit or loss for discontinued operations and for the disposal of these operations
- ○ Profit or loss
- ○ Other comprehensive income, subdivided into each component thereof
- ○ Share of associates' and joint ventures' other comprehensive income recorded with the equity method
- ○ Total comprehensive income

A key additional item is to present an analysis of the expenses in profit or loss, using a classification based on their nature or functional area, maximizing the relevance and reliability of presented information. If you elect to present expenses by their nature, the format looks similar to Exhibit 1.1.

Exhibit 1.1 NATURAL EXPENSE PRESENTATION

Revenue		XXX
Expenses:		
Change in finished goods inventories	XXX	
Raw materials used	XXX	
Employee benefits expense	XXX	
Depreciation expense	XXX	
Telephone expense	XXX	
Other expenses	XXX	
Total expenses		XXX
Profit before tax		XXX

Exhibit 1.2 Functional Expense Presentation

Revenue	XXX
Cost of sales	XXX
Gross profit	XXX
Administrative expenses	XXX
Distribution expenses	XXX
Research and development expenses	XXX
Other expenses	XXX
Total expenses	XXX
Profit before tax	XXX

Alternatively, if you present expenses by their functional area, the format looks similar to Exhibit 1.2.

Of the two methods, presenting expenses by their nature is easier, since it requires no allocation of expenses between functional areas. Conversely, the functional area presentation may be more relevant to users of the information, who can see more easily where resources are being consumed. If you elect to use a functional area presentation, you also must disclose information about the nature of the expenses, at least including separate presentation of depreciation expense, amortization expense, and employee benefits expense.

In addition, you should disclose the profit or loss and total comprehensive income attributable to any noncontrolling interests and to the owners of the parent entity.

Taxes require additional disclosure to the line items noted above. You should disclose the amount of tax related to each component of other comprehensive income. This information can be included in the statement itself or in the associated notes. You should not present any components of other comprehensive income net of related taxes.

You should provide additional headings, subtotals, and line items to the items noted above if doing so will increase a user's understanding of the entity's financial performance.

EXAMPLE 1.2

Plasma Storage Devices presents its statement of financial position in two statements by the nature of the items, resulting in the following format, beginning with the income statement:

PLASMA STORAGE DEVICES INCOME STATEMENT FOR THE YEARS ENDED DECEMBER 31		
(000s)	20×2	20×1
Revenue	€900,000	€850,000
Other income	25,000	20,000
Changes in finished goods inventories	(270,000)	(255,000)
Raw materials used	(90,000)	(85,000)
Employee benefits expense	(180,000)	(170,000)
Depreciation and amortization expense	(135,000)	(125,000)
Impairment of property, plant, and equipment	0	(50,000)
Other expenses	(75,000)	(72,000)
Finance costs	(29,000)	(23,000)
Share of profit of associates	21,000	30,000
Profit before tax	167,000	120,000
Income tax expense	(58,000)	(42,000)
Profit for the year from continuing operations	109,000	78,000
Loss for the year from discontinued operations	(42,000)	0
PROFIT FOR THE YEAR	€67,000	€78,000
Profit attributable to:		
Owners of the parent	60,000	70,000
Noncontrolling interests	7,000	8,000
	€67,000	€78,000
Earnings per share:		
Basic	€0.13	€0.16
Diluted	0.09	0.10

Plasma Storage Devices then continues with the following statement of comprehensive income:

PLASMA STORAGE DEVICES STATEMENT OF COMPREHENSIVE INCOME		
(000s)	20×2	20×1
Profit for the year	€67,000	€78,000
Other comprehensive income:		
Exchange differences on translating foreign operations	5,000	9,000
Available-for-sale financial assets	10,000	(2,000)
Cash flow hedges	(1,000)	(3,000)
Gains on property revaluation	7,000	11,000
Actuarial losses on defined benefit pension plan	(2,000)	(2,000)
Share of other comprehensive income of associates	1,000	4,000

(Continued)

(*Continued*)		
Other comprehensive income, net of tax	20,000	17,000
TOTAL COMPREHENSIVE INCOME	€87,000	€95,000
Total comprehensive income attributable to:		
Owners of the parent	78,000	86,000
Noncontrolling interests	9,000	9,000
	€87,000	€95,000

What Information Should I Disclose in the Statement of Comprehensive Income?

You should ensure that the following information is included in either the statement of comprehensive income or its associated notes:

○ *Reclassification adjustments.* Disclose any reclassification adjustments related to components of other comprehensive income (arise when items previously recognized in other comprehensive income are shifted into profit or loss).

○ *Material items.* If an income or expense item is material, separately disclose its nature and amount. Examples of items that may require separate disclosure are inventory write-downs, restructurings, asset disposals, discontinued operations, provision reversals, and the settlement of litigation.

What Line Items Do I Include in the Statement of Changes in Equity?

You should include the following line items in the statement of changes in equity:

○ Total comprehensive income (with separate presentation of the amounts attributable to the owners of the parent entity and to noncontrolling interests)

○ Effects of retrospective applications or restatements on each component of equity (usually shown as adjustments to the opening balance of retained earnings)

○ Reconciliation of changes during the period for each component of equity resulting from profit or loss, each item of other comprehensive income, and transactions with owners (including contributions by and distributions to them)

○ Dividends recognized, and the related amount per share (alternatively, this item can be presented in the associated notes)

EXAMPLE 1.3

Musical Heritage Company presents its statement of changes in equity as follows to reflect changes in its equity over a two-year period:

	Share Capital	Retained Earnings	Total	Non-controlling Interests	Total Equity
Balance at Jan. 01, 20×1	350,000	50,000	400,000	40,000	440,000
Accounting policy change	—	(3,000)	(3,000)	—	(3,000)
Restated balance	350,000	47,000	397,000	40,000	437,000
Changes in equity for 20×1					
Dividends	—	(25,000)	(25,000)	—	(25,000)
Total comprehensive income	—	42,000	42,000	4,000	46,000
Balance at Dec. 31, 20×1	350,000	64,000	414,000	44,000	458,000
Changes in equity for 20×2					
Dividends	—	(18,000)	(18,000)	—	(18,000)
Issue of share capital	125,000	—	125,000	—	125,000
Total comprehensive income	—	37,000	37,000	4,000	41,000
Balance at Dec. 31, 20×2	475,000	83,000	558,000	48,000	606,000

 What Are the Main Components of the Statement of Cash Flows?

The statement of cash flows contains information about activities that generate and use cash. The primary activities are:

○ *Operating activities*, which are an entity's primary revenue-producing activities. Examples of operating activities are cash receipts from the sale of goods, as well as from royalties and commissions, and payments to employees and suppliers.

○ *Investing activities*, which involve the acquisition and disposal of long-term assets. Examples of investing activities are cash receipts from the sale of property, the sale of debt or equity instruments of other entities, and repayment of loans made to other entities, and from futures contracts, swap contracts, and forward contracts. Examples of cash payments that are investment activities include capitalized development costs, the acquisition of property, plant, and equipment, purchases of the debt or equity of other entities, and payments for futures contracts, swap contracts, and forward contracts.

○ *Financing activities*, which result in alterations to the amount of contributed equity and the entity's borrowings. Examples of financing activities include cash receipts from the sale of the entity's own equity instruments or from issuing debt, as well as cash payments to buy back shares and to pay off outstanding debt.

The statement of cash flows also incorporates the concept of *cash and cash equivalents*. A cash equivalent is a short-term (usually maturing in three months or less), very liquid investment that is easily convertible into cash, and which is at minimal risk of a change in value.

What Are the Direct and Indirect Method Layouts for the Statement of Cash Flows?

You can use the *direct method* or the *indirect method* to present the statement of cash flows. The direct method presents the specific cash flows associated with items that affect cash flow. Items typically affecting cash flow include:

○ Cash collected from customers
○ Interest and dividends received
○ Cash paid to employees
○ Cash paid to suppliers
○ Interest paid
○ Income taxes paid

Under the indirect method, the presentation begins with net income or loss, with subsequent additions to or deductions from that amount for noncash revenue and expense items, resulting in net cash provided by operating activities.

Examples of both methods are located in the answer to the next question.

 What Line Items Should I Include in the Statement of Cash Flows?

The statement of cash flows reports cash activities during a reporting period, subdivided into operating, investing, and financing activities. The information you should include in these activities is as follows:

○ *Operating activities.* Use either the direct method (disclosing major classes of gross cash receipts and payments) or the indirect method (adjusting profit or loss for changes in inventories, receivables, payables, and a variety of noncash items). The IFRS-recommended approach is to use the direct method.

○ *Investing activities.* Separately report the major classes of gross cash receipts and payments caused by investing activities.

○ *Financing activities.* Separately report the major classes of gross cash receipts and payments caused by financing activities.

There are a number of special situations that call for unique treatment within the statement of cash flows. They are as follows:

○ *Changes in ownership interests.* Separately report the aggregate cash flows from obtaining and losing control of subsidiaries in investing activities. When doing so, report the total consideration paid or received, the proportion of this consideration comprising cash and cash equivalents, the amount of cash and cash equivalents in the subsidiaries over which the entity has gained or lost control, and the major categories of assets and liabilities other than cash and cash equivalents in the subsidiaries over which the entity has gained or lost control.

○ *Components of cash and cash equivalents.* Disclose the components of cash and cash equivalents, and also reconcile the amount of cash and cash equivalents in the statement of cash flows with the amounts reported for these items in the statement of financial position. Also note the entity's policy for determining the composition of cash and cash equivalents, and the effect of any changes to this policy in the reporting period.

- ○ *Foreign currency cash flows.* If an entity has transactions in a foreign currency, record them in its functional currency (see the Effects of Foreign Exchange Rate Changes chapter) using the relevant exchange rate on the cash flow date. If an entity has a foreign subsidiary, it also should translate the cash flows of the subsidiary into its functional currency on the various cash flow dates. A weighted average exchange rate for the reporting period can be used for these translations.

- ○ *Income taxes.* Separately disclose cash flows from taxes on income and classify them within cash flows from operating activities. You should classify them within cash flows from financing or investing activities only if they are specifically identified with those activities.

- ○ *Interest and dividends.* Separately disclose cash flows from interest and dividends received and paid. You should disclose the total amount of interest paid during a period in the statement of cash flows, even if you have capitalized the interest expense. The categorization of interest and dividends is as follows:

  Interest paid: Operating cash flows or financing cash flows

  Interest received: Operating cash flows or investing cash flows

  Dividends paid: Operating cash flows or financing cash flows

  Dividends received: Operating cash flows or investing cash flows

- ○ *Investments in subsidiaries, associates, and joint ventures.* If you use the equity or cost methods to account for investments in associates or subsidiaries, then report only cash flows between the entity and the investee. If you use proportionate consolidation to account for investments in a jointly controlled entity, then report the entity's proportionate share of the jointly controlled entity's cash flows.

- ○ *Net reporting.* It is sometimes acceptable to combine cash receipts and payments into a single reported net number. Specifically, you can use net reporting for cash receipts and payments concerning items involving fast turnover, short maturities, and large amounts. Examples are payments and receipts related to credit card customers, investments, and short-term borrowings. You also can use net reporting for cash transactions on behalf of customers where the cash flows reflect the customer's activities rather than the entity's. Examples are funds held for customers by an investment fund, and rent collected on behalf of a property owner.

○ *Noncash transactions.* Exclude noncash investing and financing transactions from the statement of cash flows. Examples of such transactions are converting debt to equity, acquiring an entity through an equity issuance, and acquiring an asset by assuming the related finance lease.

○ *Restricted cash.* Note any significant amounts of cash and cash equivalents that are not available for use. For example, a subsidiary may have significant cash holdings, but be located in a country where exchange controls restrict the movement of the cash to the parent entity.

EXAMPLE 1.4

Afjord Defense and Aerospace constructs the following statement of cash flows using the direct method:

AFJORD DEFENSE AND AEROSPACE STATEMENT OF CASH FLOWS FOR THE YEAR ENDED 12/31/×1

Cash flows from operating activities		
Cash receipts from customers	€45,800,000	
Cash paid to suppliers	(29,800,000)	
Cash paid to employees	(11,200,000)	
Cash generated from operations	4,800,000	
Interest paid	(310,000)	
Income taxes paid	(1,700,000)	
Net cash from operating activities		€2,790,000
Cash flows from investing activities		
Purchase of property, plant, and equipment	(580,000)	
Proceeds from sale of equipment	110,000	
Interest received	12,000	
Dividends received	5,000	
Net cash used in investing activities		(453,000)

(Continued)

(Continued)

Cash flows from financing activities		
Proceeds from issuance of share capital	1,000,000	
Proceeds from borrowings	500,000	
Dividends paid	(450,000)	
Net cash used in financing activities		1,050,000
Net increase in cash and cash equivalents		3,387,000
Cash and cash equivalents at beginning of period		1,613,000
Cash and cash equivalents at end of period		€5,000,000

EXAMPLE 1.5

Gaelic Fire Candy constructs the following statement of cash flows using the indirect method:

GAELIC FIRE CANDY STATEMENT OF CASH FLOWS FOR THE YEAR ENDED 12/31x1

Cash flows from operating activities		
Profit before taxation		£3,000,000
Adjustments for:		
Depreciation	£125,000	
Foreign exchange loss	20,000	
Investment income	(80,000)	
Interest expense	40,000	
		105,000
Increase in trade receivables	(250,000)	
Decrease in inventories	325,000	
Decrease in trade payables	(50,000)	
		25,000
Cash generated from operations		3,130,000
Interest paid		(12,000)
Income taxes paid		(870,000)
Net cash from operating activities		2,248,000
Cash flows from investing activities		
Purchase of property, plant, and equipment	(500,000)	
Proceeds from sale of equipment	35,000	
Interest received	10,000	
Dividends received	8,000	
Net cash used in investing activities		(447,000)

Cash flows from financing activities		
Proceeds from issue of share capital	150,000	
Proceeds from borrowings	175,000	
Payment of finance lease liabilities	(45,000)	
Net cash used in financing activities		280,000
Net increase in cash and cash equivalents		2,081,000
Cash and cash equivalents at beginning of period		2,919,000
Cash and cash equivalents at end of period		£5,000,000

The following additional disclosure items are not required, but are encouraged for inclusion within the statement of cash flows or in the notes associated with it:

○ *Borrowing facilities.* The amount of borrowing facilities that may be available for future use, as well as any restrictions on their use
○ *Capacity related.* The aggregate cash flows associated with increases in operating capacity, reported separately from those cash flows associated with maintaining existing operating capacity
○ *Joint venture cash flows.* The aggregate cash flows from interests in joint ventures for which the entity is using proportionate consolidation
○ *Segment reporting.* The cash flows arising from the activities of each reportable segment (see the Operating Segments chapter)

EXAMPLE 1.6

Danish Energy reports the following cash flow information for its two segments:

	Geothermal Segment	Wind Farm Segment	Total
Cash flows from:			
Operating activities	€4,290,000	€28,430,000	€32,720,000
Investing activities	420,000	(3,750,000)	(3,330,000)
Financing activities	(100,000)	75,000	(25,000)
	€4,610,000	€24,755,000	€29,365,000

What Additional Information Should I Disclose with the Financial Statements?

You should present financial statement notes in the following sequence:

1. Statement of compliance with IFRSs
2. Summary of the entity's significant accounting policies
3. Supporting information for line items in the financial statements, in the order in which the various statements are presented
4. Other disclosures, such as for nonfinancial information

You should include the following information in the notes accompanying the financial statements:

- *Assumptions.* Information about major assumptions regarding the future.
- *Basis of preparation.* The measurement basis used to prepare the statements (e.g., historical cost, current cost, net realizable value, fair value, or recoverable amount), and other accounting policies used that are relevant to understanding the statements. If you use more than one measurement basis, then indicate which basis is used for general categories of assets and liabilities. It is especially important to disclose an accounting policy when an IFRS allows alternative treatment.
- *Capital management.* Description of capital the entity manages, how it meets its capital management objectives, the nature of any externally imposed capital requirements, and a summary of what it manages as capital, and how capital levels have changed during the period. Also note whether the entity has complied with any externally imposed capital requirements; if not, describe the consequences of noncompliance.
- *Dividends.* The amount of dividends not recognized as a distribution, but proposed or declared before the financial statements were authorized for issuance. Also, note the unrecognized amount of any cumulative preference dividends.
- *Domicile.* The domicile of the entity, its country of incorporation, and the address of its registered office.

○ *Estimation uncertainty.* Major sources of estimation uncertainty that may result in a significant material adjustment of the carrying amount of the entity's assets and liabilities within the next fiscal year. Note the nature and carrying amount of the potentially impacted assets and liabilities. For example, there may be estimation uncertainty about the future recoverable amounts of assets, the impact of technological obsolescence on inventories, and the requirements of defined benefit plans. This disclosure is not needed for those assets and liabilities already being measured at their fair values based on recent market prices.

○ *IFRS requirements.* Disclosures required by other IFRSs that are not already included in the financial statements.

○ *Legal form.* The legal form of the entity.

○ *Life.* If the entity has a limited duration, note the length of its life.

○ *Management judgments.* The judgments that management has made when applying accounting policies, and which have a significant effect on financial results. Examples are, the decision to classify an asset as held-to-maturity, whether sales are actually financing arrangements, and whether the entity exercises control over another entity.

○ *Name.* The name of the entity's parent and of the ultimate parent of the group.

○ *Operations.* The nature of the entity's operations.

○ *Puttable financial instruments.* The amount classified as equity; the objectives, policies, and processes for redeeming these instruments; the cash outflow caused by the expected redemption; and information about how you determined the redemption amount.

○ *Other information.* Other information not presented elsewhere in the financial statements, but that is relevant to understanding them.

You should cross-reference items in the various financial statements with these notes.

How Frequently Should I Issue Financial Statements?

An entity should issue a complete set of financial statements at least once a year. If it changes the end of its reporting period, so that the current year is less or longer than 12 months, you should disclose the reason for the altered period and state that the amounts included in the financial statements are not entirely comparable with those of previous years.

What Comparative Information Should I Report?

You should disclose comparative information for the previous period(s) for all amounts that an entity is reporting in its current-period financial statements. This may include narrative information if it improves users' understanding of the financial statements. Exhibit 1.3 reveals the extent of comparative information requirements for different situations.

Exhibit 1.3 COMPARATIVE PERIODS REQUIRED

Report Name	Minimum Scenario	For Retrospective Policy Change, Restatement, Reclassification
Statement of financial position	Ends of current period and preceding period	End of current period, end of preceding period, and beginning of the earliest comparable period
Statement of comprehensive income	Current period and preceding period	Current period and preceding period
Statement of changes in equity	Current period and preceding period	Current period and preceding period
Statement of cash flows	Current period and preceding period	Current period and preceding period
Notes	Current period and preceding period	Current period and preceding period

How Consistent Should the Financial Statement Presentation Be?

You should retain the presentation and classification of items shown in the financial statements across all presented periods. Exceptions are when an IFRS requires a presentation alteration, or when a significant change in an entity's operations makes a different presentation more appropriate. If the latter is the reason, then you should do so only if the significant change is likely to continue into the future.

 ## How Do I Aggregate Information in the Financial Statements?

You should separately present each material class of similar items. Conversely, do not aggregate items of a dissimilar nature, unless they are immaterial. If an item is not material enough to be separately presented in the financial statements, you may still consider separate presentation in the accompanying notes.

 ## What Are International Financial Reporting Standards?

International Financial Reporting Standards are standards and associated interpretations promulgated by the International Accounting Standards Board. IFRSs include International Accounting Standards and International Financial Reporting Standards. Also, Interpretations are created by the International Financial Reporting Interpretations Committee.

 ## Do I Have to Affirm Compliance with International Financial Reporting Standards?

Yes. You should make a statement of compliance with IFRSs within the notes accompanying the financial statements.

If an entity departs from IFRSs in its financial reporting, you must disclose that management has complied with applicable IFRSs, except for a specific departure that achieves a fair presentation of financial information. Also note the title of the IFRS from which the entity's financial statements have departed, describing the treatment required by the IFRS, the entity's alternative treatment, and the reason why using the IFRS would be misleading. Also state the impact of the departure for each period presented in the financial statements.

If an entity complies with the financial reporting requirements of IFRSs, but management feels that such compliance is misleading, it should disclose the title of the IFRS causing the issue, why management believes it to be misleading, and the adjustments needed in each period to achieve a fair presentation of the information.

However, before departing from IFRS reporting standards, consider whether the entity's circumstances differ markedly from those of other entities that are complying with the requirement.

 ## What Impact Does a Going Concern Issue Have on the Financial Statements?

Management should assess an entity's ability to continue as a going concern whenever it prepares financial statements, and should prepare them on a going concern basis unless there is an intent to liquidate the entity or management has no realistic alternative to doing so. This assessment should include a consideration of projections for at least the next 12 months, including such factors as profitability, debt repayments, and potential sources of replacement financing.

If management is aware of material uncertainties that cast doubt on the entity's ability to continue as a going concern, you should disclose the uncertainties. If you do not prepare the financial statements on a going concern basis, disclose that fact and why management does not consider the entity to be a going concern.

 ## Is the Accrual Basis of Accounting Required?

Yes. Under the accrual method of accounting, record revenue and expenses when they are incurred, irrespective of when cash is exchanged.

 ## Can I Offset Assets and Liabilities or Revenue and Expenses?

Not unless specifically authorized by an IFRS, which typically is only for a very restricted application. In nearly all situations, you should separately report assets and liabilities, and revenue and expenses. If you engage in offsetting these accounts, it detracts from the ability of users to understand the underlying transactions and to assess the entity's future cash flows.

You are not offsetting when you measure assets net of valuation allowances, which is a common and acceptable practice for accounts receivable and inventory.

Can I Present Any Income or Expense Items as Extraordinary Items?

No. You cannot designate any income or expense item as an extraordinary item, either in the statement of comprehensive income or in its associated notes.

How Do I Disclose a Financial Statement Reclassification?

When you reclassify or alter the presentation of an item in an entity's financial statements, you should reclassify comparable amounts in prior periods, unless it is impractical to do so. You should disclose the nature and amount of the reclassification, and the reason for making the change. If it is impractical to create a matching reclassification in prior periods, then disclose the reason for not doing so, and the type of adjustments that would have been made if you had presented a reclassification.

What Is a Material Omission or Misstatement?

An omission or misstatement is material if it could influence the economic decisions of the users of an entity's financial statements. Materiality is subjective, depending upon the size and nature of the omission or misstatement. Of importance, an omission or misstatement can be material either individually or collectively. Thus, a large number of small omissions can be considered a material omission.

CHAPTER 2

CONSOLIDATED AND SEPARATE FINANCIAL STATEMENTS

 What Are Consolidated Financial Statements?

Consolidated financial statements are the financial statements of a group of entities that are presented as being those of a single economic entity. A *group* is a parent entity and all of its subsidiaries. A *subsidiary* is an entity that is controlled by a parent entity.

 Who Should Present Consolidated Financial Statements?

A parent entity presents consolidated financial statements in which it consolidates the investments it has made in its subsidiaries.

An entity does not present consolidated financial statements if it is itself a subsidiary of another entity, the parent's financial instruments are not publicly traded, the parent has not filed and is not filing with a regulatory organization to issue any financial instruments in a public market, and the ultimate parent entity produces consolidated financial statements that comply with International Financial Reporting Standards (IFRS).

 When Must a Parent Include Another Entity in Its Financial Statements?

Consolidated financial statements must include all of the subsidiaries of the parent entity. These subsidiaries are entities over which the parent entity has:

- ○ More than half of the voting power of the entity (unless such ownership does not constitute control); or

- ○ Indirect voting power over more than half of the voting rights of the entity through an agreement with other investors; or
- ○ The power to govern the entity's financial and operating policies; or
- ○ The power to appoint or remove a majority of the entity's board of directors; or
- ○ The power to cast the majority of votes at the entity's board meetings

---

EXAMPLE 2.1

The Arona, Barranco, and Chamorga Companies each own 30 percent of the voting shares of Don Ventura Company. In addition, Barranco owns call options that it can exercise at any time at a fixed price; if it does so, Barranco will own a majority of the voting rights in Don Ventura. Even though Barranco's management does not intend to exercise the call options, the existence of the call options gives Barranco control over Don Ventura for consolidation purposes.

A parent entity must include a subsidiary in its consolidated financial statements even if the subsidiary's business activities are not similar to those of the other subsidiaries whose results are included in the consolidated financial statements.

A parent entity must still consolidate the financial results of its subsidiaries as defined here, even if the parent is a venture capital organization, unit trust, mutual fund, or some similar type of entity.

Should a Special Purpose Entity Be Consolidated?

A special purpose entity (SPE) is created to accomplish a specific objective, such as research and development activities, or the securitization of accounts receivable. The entity on whose behalf the SPE was created typically shifts assets to the SPE, may have the right to use the output of the SPE, and so may be considered to have control over it. A parent entity should consolidate an SPE when the substance of the relationship indicates a control situation, using the indicators noted in the answer to the previous question.

The following circumstances may indicate a control situation that would require consolidation:

○ The parent entity obtains benefits from the SPE's operations.
○ The parent entity has the power to obtain most of the benefits of the SPE, or originally set up the SPE with that objective.
○ The parent entity retains a majority of the ownership and operational risks of the SPE.

EXAMPLE 2.2

Saba Exploratory Consortium helps to create an SPE that researches new methods for deep-water mineral exploration. Part of the operating agreement of the SPE allows Saba to acquire any patents filed by the SPE in exchange for a minimum payment. Since Saba has the power to obtain the benefits of the SPE, it should include the results of the SPE in its consolidated financial statements.

What Is the Process for Consolidating Financial Statements?

The general process for consolidating the financial statements of a parent entity and its subsidiaries is to combine the statements line by line. More specifically:

1. Adjust the financial statements of any member of the group to conform to the accounting policies used by the parent for consolidating the financial statements.
2. Make adjustments for the effects of significant transactions or events occurring between the dates of the financial statements of the subsidiaries and the parent, if they differ.
3. Eliminate all intragroup balances, transactions, income, and expenses. This includes the elimination of profits and losses resulting from intragroup transactions.
4. Eliminate the carrying amount of the parent's investment in each subsidiary and the parent's portion of equity of each subsidiary.
5. Identify noncontrolling interests in the profit or loss of consolidated subsidiaries.

6. Separately identify the noncontrolling interests in the net assets of the consolidated subsidiaries. These noncontrolling interests include the amount of noncontrolling interests at the date of the original combination and the noncontrolling interests' share of any changes in equity since the date of combination.

7. Present noncontrolling interests in the consolidated statement of financial position within equity, separately from the equity of the parent entity's owners.

8. If there are outstanding cumulative preference shares at the subsidiary level that are held by noncontrolling interests, then compute the parent entity's share of profits or losses after adjusting for the dividends on these shares, irrespective of a dividend declaration.

9. Attribute profit or loss and each component of other comprehensive income to the owners of the parent entity and to noncontrolling interests, even if the result is a deficit balance for the noncontrolling interests.

If the financial statements prepared by a subsidiary for inclusion in consolidated statements are as of a different date than the date used for the statements of the parent, then the subsidiary should prepare additional financial statements that are as of the same date as those of the parent, unless it is impracticable to do so. It is not allowable to ever have a difference between the dates of the financial statements of the parent and its subsidiaries of more than three months.

As of What Date Do I Include the Revenue and Expenses of an Acquired Subsidiary?

You should include the revenue and expenses of a newly acquired subsidiary in the consolidated financial statements of the parent entity beginning on the acquisition date.

What Happens to a Consolidation If You Lose Control of a Subsidiary?

If the parent entity loses control of a subsidiary, it takes the following five steps as of the date of loss of control:

1. Derecognize the assets and liabilities of the subsidiary at their carrying amounts. This includes the derecognition of goodwill.

2. Derecognize the carrying amount of any noncontrolling interests in the former subsidiary. This includes any items of other comprehensive income attributable to the noncontrolling interests.

3. Recognize the fair value of any consideration received from the event resulting in the loss of control. This includes the fair value of any distribution of the subsidiary's shares to the owners.

4. Recognize any investment still retained in the former subsidiary at its fair value.

5. Account for all amounts recognized in other comprehensive income for the subsidiary as though the parent had disposed of the related assets or liabilities. For example, if a revaluation surplus recognized in other comprehensive income would have been transferred to retained earnings upon asset disposal, then do so when the parent loses control of the subsidiary.

EXAMPLE 2.3

Hospital Transport Services is an investor in and has significant influence over Plasma Collection Services. Plasma Collection has €100,000 of available-for-sale securities, for which Hospital Transport previously recognized a gain of €10,000 in other comprehensive income on its share of those securities. Hospital Transport loses significant influence over Plasma. On the date of its loss of significant influence, Hospital Transport should reclassify the €10,000 gain to profit or loss.

What Information Should I Disclose about Consolidated Financial Statements?

The parent entity should disclose the following information in its consolidated financial statements:

○ *Cash restrictions.* Any significant restrictions on the ability of subsidiaries to transfer funds to the parent entity.

○ *Control reasoning.* The reasons why the parent does not have control over an entity, despite having more than half of the voting power.

○ *Date differentials.* The date of the financial statements of a subsidiary if it varies from that of the parent entity, and the reason for allowing this different date.

○ *Joint control or associate investments.* If the parent entity has an interest in a jointly controlled entity or an associate and prepares separate financial statements, then disclose that the statements are reported separately, and why these statements are prepared. Also, list the parent entity's significant investments in subsidiaries, jointly controlled entities, and associates; its ownership interest in each one; their locations; and the method used to account for these investments.

○ *Loss of control.* The gain or loss recognized upon loss of control in a subsidiary, the portion of that amount attributable to recognizing investments retained in the subsidiary at their fair value, and where the gain or loss is recognized in the statement of comprehensive income.

○ *Nonconsolidation disclosures.* If the parent prepares nonconsolidated financial statements, then disclose that the statements are reported separately under an exemption from consolidation, and the name, address, and country of the parent entity that has made its IFRS-compliant consolidated financial statements available. Also, list the parent entity's significant investments in subsidiaries, jointly controlled entities, and associates; its ownership interest in each one; their locations; and the method used to account for these investments.

○ *Ownership changes.* A schedule revealing the effects of ownership changes in a subsidiary.

○ *Partial voting power.* The nature of the parent's relationship with a subsidiary when the parent does not own more than half of the voting power.

CHAPTER 3

OPERATING SEGMENTS

 What Is an Operating Segment?

An operating segment is a component of an entity that is a profit center, that has discrete financial information available, and whose results are reviewed regularly by the entity's chief operating decision maker for purposes of performance assessment and resource allocation. An operating segment generally has a segment manager who is accountable to the chief operating decision maker for the results of the segment.

An entity's corporate headquarters is not considered an operating segment, nor are an entity's post-employment benefit plans.

 What Type of Entity Must Report about Its Operating Segments?

An entity must disclose information about its operating segments if its debt or equity trades in a public market, or it files its financial statements with a regulatory organization so that it can issue debt or equity in a public market. An entity also must disclose information about its operating segments if its financial statements are consolidated into those of a parent entity having these characteristics.

 When Can I Aggregate Operating Segments?

You can aggregate two or more operating segments into a single segment if the segments have similar products, services, production processes, customers, distribution methods, and regulatory environments.

What Are the Quantitative Thresholds for Segment Reporting?

You must disclose an operating segment if it meets any of these thresholds:

○ *Revenue.* Its external and intersegment sales are at least 10 percent of the combined revenue of all segments.
○ *Profit.* Its absolute profit or loss is at least 10 percent of the greater of the combined profit of all segments not reporting a loss and the combined loss of all operating segments reporting a loss.
○ *Assets.* Its assets are at least 10 percent of the combined assets of all operating segments.

If the total external revenue reported by operating segments meeting these thresholds is less than 75 percent of the entity's revenue, then report on additional segments until you meet the 75 percent threshold, even if the extra segments are individually below the threshold criteria.

EXAMPLE 3.1

Bright Star Corporation has six operating segments. The following table shows the operating results of the segments:

Segment Name	Revenue	Profit	Loss	Assets
A	€ 101,000	€ 5,000	€ –	€ 60,000
B	285,000	10,000	–	120,000
C	130,000	–	(35,000)	40,000
D	500,000	–	(80,000)	190,000
E	440,000	20,000	–	160,000
F	140,000	–	(5,000)	50,000
Totals	€1,596,000	€35,000	€ (120,000)	€620,000

Because the total reported loss of €120,000 exceeds the total reported profit of €35,000, the €120,000 is used for the 10 percent profit test. The tests for these segments are itemized in the next table, where test thresholds are listed in the second row. For example, the total revenue of €1,596,000 shown in the preceding table is multiplied by 10 percent to arrive at the test threshold of €159,600 that is used in the second column. Segments B, D, and E all have revenue levels exceeding this threshold, so an "X" in the table indicates that their results must be separately reported. After conducting all three of the 10 percent tests, the table shows that segments B, C, D, and E must be reported, so their revenues are itemized in the last column. The last column shows that the total revenue of all reportable segments exceeds the €1,197,000 revenue level needed to pass the 75 percent test, so no additional segments must be reported.

Segment Name	Revenue 10% Test	Profit 10% Test	Asset 10% Test	75% Revenue Test
Test threshold	€159,600	€12,000	€62,000	€1,197,000
A				
B	X		X	$ 285,000
C		X		130,000
D	X	X	X	500,000
E	X	X	X	440,000
F				
			Total	€1,355,000

The decision tree in Exhibit 3.1 shows how to determine which segments must be separately reported, as well as which segments should be aggregated, and which ones can be summarized into the "all other" segments category.

If an operating segment that was reported separately in the immediately preceding period has now dropped below the threshold criteria, management can still separately report the segment's results if it believes the information is significant.

If a segment meets the threshold criteria for the first time, then report its results for any prior periods presented in the financial statements, unless the needed information is not available and would be excessively expensive to develop.

It is allowable to aggregate the results of smaller segments to create a reportable segment, but only if they

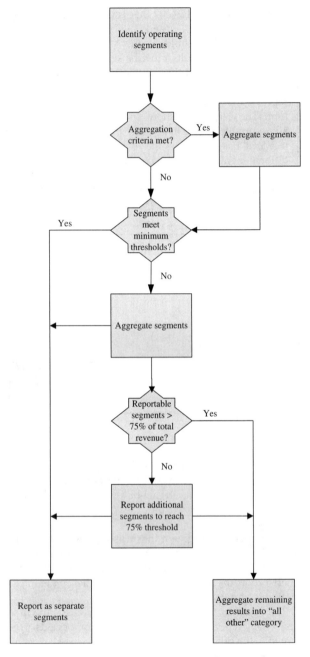

Exhibit 3.1 Decision Tree for Determination of Reportable Segments

share similar economic characteristics and a majority of the previously noted aggregation criteria.

 ## How Do I Report Segments That Are Not Separately Identifiable?

If an operating segment does not meet the threshold criteria just noted for separate reporting status, then combine them in an "all other segments" category.

 ## Is There a Limit to the Number of Reportable Segments?

There is no precise limit to the number of reportable segments, but consider a reduction if the number exceeds 10 segments.

 ## What Controls Should I Use for Segment Reporting?

The periodic closing procedures should include a step in which the information issued for segment reporting is compared with the internal segment reports. This information should match. Notify the controller of any variations between the two reports, which should be reconciled before the segment reports intended for external consumption are released.

 ## What Segment-Specific Information Do I Disclose?

In general, you disclose segment information that enables financial statement users to evaluate the entity's business activities and economic environment. In more detail, this requires the following disclosures:

- *General information.* The factors used to identify reportable segments, and the types of products and services sold by each segment. Also note the basis of organization, which shows whether the organization is organized around products or services, geographical regions, regulatory environments, or some combination thereof.
- *Profit or loss information.* Revenue from external customers, intersegment revenue, interest revenue, interest expense, depreciation and amortization,

material expense items, equity method interests in other entities, income tax expense or income, and other material noncash items, as well as the resulting profit or loss.

○ *Asset and liability information.* Equity method investments, and the amounts of additions to noncurrent assets (other than insurance contract rights, post-employment benefits, deferred tax assets, and financial instruments).

EXAMPLE 3.2

Consolidated Green Products owns a number of subsidiaries that focus on reduced carbon emissions. It reports the results of its identifiable segments as follows:

(000s)	Electric Motors	Furnaces	LED Lighting	All Other	Totals
Revenue from external customers	€2,700	€ 4,500	€ 8,100	€900	€16,200
Intersegment revenue		2,700	1,300		4,000
Interest revenue	400	650	230	50	1,330
Interest expense	100	120	90	10	320
Depreciation	180	80	40	20	320
Reportable segment profit	270	450	800	70	1,590
Reportable segment assets	1,800	3,200	3,700	800	9,500
Expenditures for reportable segment noncurrent assets	250	400	250	150	1,050
Reportable segment liabilities	900	1,600	2,000	400	4,900

These disclosures are required only if they are reported to the chief operating decision maker in order to make decisions about resource allocation and performance assessment.

What Additional Information Do I Disclose?

You must provide an explanation of the measurements used when deriving segment information, which includes:

- *Intersegment accounting.* The basis of accounting for any intersegment transactions
- *Measurement differences.* The reasons for any differences between segment-level profits and losses, assets and liabilities, and the same information in aggregate for the entire entity
- *Interperiod differences.* The reasons for any differences between the measurement of profits and losses, assets and liabilities, and the same information in prior periods
- *Asymmetrical allocations.* The reasons for using different allocations to different segments, such as the allocation of depreciation expense to one segment, but not to another

What Reconciling Information Do I Disclose?

You should disclose reconciling information, alongside the segment reporting, that includes the following:

- *Comparisons.* The total of the revenue, profit and loss, and assets and liabilities for the reported segments in comparison to the entity's totals for the same items
- *Other material items.* The total of any other material amounts for the reported segments in comparison to the entity's totals for the same items, with each material item separately identified and described

When Do I Restate Segment Information?

If the entity changes its organizational structure sufficiently that it changes the composition of its reportable segments, then restate the corresponding information for earlier periods. This is not necessary if the required information is not available for the earlier periods and the cost of developing it would be excessive. However, the ability to create earlier information is made at the line-item level, so you may provide information for some line items and not for others. If you restate information for earlier periods, then disclose this fact.

If it is not possible to restate information for prior periods to reflect a change in organizational structure, then disclose the year in which the organizational change occurs. Also, provide segment information for both the old and new organizational structures for the current period, unless this information is not available and would be excessively expensive to develop.

What Information Do I Disclose about Products and Services?

If you do not provide product and service information at the segment-reporting level, then do so for the entire entity. Do so for each product and service, or grouping thereof, unless this information is not available and would be excessively expensive to develop (in which case, disclose this fact).

EXAMPLE 3.3

The Company operates in the consumer products industry, in which the Company designs, manufactures, markets, and distributes footwear, apparel, and accessories. For the year ended December 31, 2010, the Company sold £168 million of footwear, £19 million of apparel, and £11 million of accessories.

What Information Do I Disclose about Geographical Areas?

If you do not provide geographical information at the segment-reporting level, then do so for the entire entity. This involves the disclosure of:

○ *Revenue.* External revenue for the entity's country of domicile and the total for all other countries. If the revenue for an individual country is material, then disclose it separately. Also note the basis for attributing revenue to individual countries.
○ *Assets.* Noncurrent assets located in the entity's country of domicile and the total for all other countries. If the assets in an individual country are

material, then disclose them separately. This disclosure does not include deferred tax assets, financial instruments, insurance contract rights, or post-employment benefit assets.

EXAMPLE 3.4

The Company operates a single business segment that includes the installation and servicing of oil rigs for independent oil exploration and production companies. The following table summarizes the Company's revenue and assets in different countries:

	2010	2009
Revenue:		
Iraq	£ 67,000,000	£61,000,000
Nigeria	31,000,000	26,000,000
Other foreign countries	11,000,000	9,000,000
Total	£109,000,000	£96,000,000
Assets:		
Iraq	£ 29,000,000	£28,000,000
Nigeria	17,000,000	13,000,000
Other foreign countries	4,000,000	4,000,000
Total	£ 50,000,000	£45,000,000

Do not disclose this information if it is not available and would be excessively expensive to develop (in which case, disclose this fact).

The entity also may provide subtotals of geographical information about groups of countries, at its option.

What Information Do I Disclose about Major Customers?

If you do not provide major customer information at the segment-reporting level, then do so for the entire entity. If revenue from a single customer is 10 percent or more of total entity revenue, then disclose that fact, as well as the total revenue for each such customer, and the identity of the segments reporting that revenue.

It is not necessary to disclose the identity of these major customers, or the amount of revenue that each segment reports from them.

A group of customer entities under common control should be considered a single customer. Similarly, a government and entities controlled by that government are considered a single customer.

EXAMPLE 3.5

The Company derives a significant portion of its net revenue from a limited number of customers. For the fiscal years ended December 31, 2010 and 2009, revenue from one client totaled approximately £15.7 million and £17.8 million, which represented 12% and 15% of total net revenues, respectively. For the fiscal year ended December 31, 2008, revenue from two clients totaled approximately £13.6 million and £10.9 million, which represented 16% and 12% of total net revenues, respectively.

CHAPTER 4

EARNINGS PER SHARE

 Which Entities Should Report Earnings per Share?

An entity should report its earnings per share if its shares are traded in a public market, or if it is filing its financial statements with a regulatory organization to issue ordinary shares in a public market. The same applies to a group with a parent whose shares are traded in a public market, or that is filing its financial statements with a regulatory organization to issue ordinary shares in a public market.

If an entity presents both individual and consolidated financial statements and it fits the preceding criteria, it has to report earnings per share only for the consolidated financial statements.

 What Is Dilution and Anti-Dilution?

Dilution is the reduction in earnings per share or increase in loss per share that results when one assumes that convertible instruments are converted, that options and warrants are exercised, or that ordinary shares are issued if specified conditions are satisfied. *Anti-dilution* is the increase in earnings per share or decrease in loss per share that results when one assumes the conversion of convertible instruments, the exercise of options and warrants, or the issuance of ordinary shares if specified conditions are satisfied.

 What Are Options and Warrants?

Options and warrants give their holders the right to purchase an entity's ordinary shares. A *put option* gives its holder the right to sell ordinary shares at a stated price for a stated period of time.

What Is an Ordinary Share?

An ordinary share is an equity instrument subordinate to all other equity classes. The holder of an ordinary share participates in an entity's profits only after all other types of shares have participated. There may be more than one class of ordinary shares. A *potential ordinary share* is a financial instrument or other contract that may give its holder the right to ordinary shares, such as options, warrants, and convertible preferred stock.

How Do I Calculate Basic Earnings per Share?

You calculate basic earnings per share as follows:

$$\frac{\text{Profit or loss attributable to ordinary equity holders of the parent entity}}{\text{Weighted average number of ordinary shares outstanding during the period}}$$

This calculation is further split into the profit or loss from continuing operations attributable to the parent entity, and total profit or loss attributable to the parent entity. You should adjust both of these items for the effects of preference shares classified as equity.

Also, incorporate the following adjustments into the numerator of the calculation of basic earnings per share:

- *Dividends.* For the calculation of basic earnings per share, deduct from the profit or loss in the numerator the after-tax amount of any dividends declared on noncumulative preference shares as well as the after-tax amount of any dividends for cumulative preference shares, even if the dividends have not been declared; this does not include the amount of such dividends paid or declared during the current period that relates to previous periods.
- *Increasing rate preference shares.* A share having a preference dividend with a low initial discount or an above-market dividend in later periods is called an increasing rate preference share. If there is an original issue discount or premium on such shares, amortize them using the effective interest method and include this discount or premium as a preference dividend when calculating basic earnings per share.
- *Share repurchases.* If an entity repurchases preference shares at an above-market price, deduct the excess of

the consideration paid over the fair value of the shares from the profit or loss in the numerator of the basic earnings per share calculation.

Also, incorporate the following adjustments into the denominator of the calculation of basic earnings per share:

○ *Contingent shares.* If shares are contingently issuable, treat them as outstanding as of the date when all necessary conditions are satisfied. If shares are contingently returnable, do not treat them as outstanding until the time the shares can no longer be returned.

○ *Issuance date.* Include shares in the denominator as of the date when cash is receivable for sold shares, when dividends are reinvested, when interest ceases to accrue on convertible debt instruments for which shares are issued, when a liability is settled in exchange for shares, when an acquisition is recognized in exchange for shares, and as services are rendered in exchange for shares. If there is a mandatorily convertible instrument, then include the related shares in the denominator as of the contract date.

○ *Issuances without resource change.* If shares are issued without a corresponding change in resources, include them in the denominator as of the issuance date. Examples of such issuances are stock dividends, share splits, and reverse share splits.

○ *Weighted average shares.* The calculation of the weighted average number of shares outstanding during the period is made to adjust the number of shares outstanding at the beginning of the period for the number of ordinary shares repurchased or issued during the reporting period, adjusted by the number of days that the shares are outstanding as a proportion of the total days in the period.

EXAMPLE 4.1

Ram-Jet International earns a profit of £10 million after tax in Year 1. In addition, Ram-Jet owes £250,000 in dividends to the holders of its cumulative preference shares, and there is also a £100,000 original issue premium on increasing rate preference shares. Ram-Jet calculates the numerator of its basic earnings per share as:

$$£10,000,000 \text{ profit} - £250,000 \text{ dividends} - £100,000 \text{ original issue premium} = £9,650,000$$

(Continued)

(Continued)

Ram-Jet had 8 million ordinary shares outstanding at the beginning of Year 1. In addition, it sold 500,000 shares on April 1 and 800,000 shares on October 1. It also issued 1,000,000 shares on July 1 as part of a share true-up transaction to the shareholders of a former acquisition. Finally, it bought back 100,000 shares on December 1. Ram-Jet calculates the weighted average number of shares outstanding as follows:

Date	Shares	Weighting (months)	Weighted Average
January 1	8,000,000	12/12	8,000,000
April 1	500,000	9/12	375,000
July 1	1,000,000	6/12	500,000
October 1	800,000	3/12	200,000
December 1	(100,000)	1/12	8,333
			9,083,333

Ram-Jet's basic earnings per share is £9,650,000 adjusted profits ÷ 9,083,333 weighted average shares, or £1.06 per share.

How Do I Calculate Diluted Earnings per Share?

The calculation of diluted earnings per share goes beyond the calculation of basic earnings per share to also include the effects of all dilutive potential ordinary shares. As a result, you increase the number of shares outstanding by the weighted average number of additional ordinary shares that would have been outstanding if all dilutive potential ordinary shares had been converted to ordinary shares. This dilutive change also may impact the profit or loss in the numerator of the earnings per share calculation. You calculate diluted earnings per share as follows:

$$\frac{\text{Adjusted profit or loss of the parent entity}}{\substack{\text{Weighted average number of ordinary} \\ \text{shares outstanding during the period,}}}$$

This calculation is further split into the profit or loss from continuing operations attributable to the parent entity, and total profit or loss attributable to the parent entity.

Also, incorporate the following adjustments into the numerator of the calculation of diluted earnings per share:

- ○ *Dividends.* Adjust for the after-tax effect of dividends or other dilutive potential ordinary shares.
- ○ *Interest expense.* Reverse any interest expense related to dilutive potential ordinary shares, since these shares are assumed to have been converted to ordinary shares, which eliminates the interest expense.

Also, incorporate the following adjustments into the denominator of the calculation of diluted earnings per share; these adjustments are *in addition to* those already noted for basic earnings per share:

- ○ *Contingent shares, general.* Treat contingently issuable ordinary shares as outstanding as of the beginning of the period, and therefore include them in the calculation of diluted earnings per share, as long as the conditions required to issue the shares have been satisfied.
- ○ *Contingent shares, future earnings.* If a contingent share issuance involves maintaining a specific earnings level past the current period, then assume that the related potential shares issued based on the amount of actual earnings at the end of the reporting period are the same as the amount at the end of the contingency period.
- ○ *Contingent shares, future prices.* If a contingent share issuance depends on the future market price of ordinary shares, then base the potential share issuance on the market price at the end of the reporting period. If the issuance depends on the average market price over a period that has already started and extends into the future, then use the average price just for the period of time that has elapsed.
- ○ *Contingent shares, other conditions.* If a contingent share issuance depends on a condition other than future earnings or future share prices, then assume that the present status of the condition remains unchanged through the end of the contingency period.
- ○ *Contracts settled in cash or shares.* If a contract can be settled in either ordinary shares or cash, assume that it will be settled in ordinary shares if the effect is dilutive.
- ○ *Conversion effect.* Convert potential ordinary shares to ordinary shares for the purposes of the dilutive earnings per share calculation only if doing so will

either decrease the earnings per share or increase the loss per share from continuing operations. Conduct this conversion review separately for each issue or series of potential ordinary shares, rather than in aggregate.

○ *Convertible instruments.* Include the effect of convertible instruments in diluted earnings per share when it is dilutive. Convertible preference shares are anti-dilutive when the dividend on the converted shares exceeds basic earnings per share. Convertible debt is anti-dilutive when the interest expense on the converted shares exceeds basic earnings per share. See the following example for Provence Panache.

○ *Dilutive shares.* Add to the denominator the weighted average number of ordinary shares that the entity would issue if all dilutive potential ordinary shares were converted. In the absence of other information, these additional shares are assumed to have been issued at the beginning of the reporting period.

○ *Forward purchase contracts.* If a contract requires the entity to repurchase its own shares, and the settlement price is higher than the average market price during the period, and the effect is dilutive, then include them in the diluted earnings per share calculation. For this calculation, assume that enough shares are issued at the beginning of the period to raise the proceeds to settle the contract, and that the proceeds are used to buy back the required number of shares, and that the difference between these two amounts is included in the diluted earnings per share calculation.

○ *Intraperiod lapses.* If potential ordinary shares are cancelled or lapse during the reporting period, then include them in the diluted earnings per share only for that portion of the reporting period when they were outstanding.

○ *Multiple conversion rates.* If there are multiple bases of conversion of dilutive potential ordinary shares, then use the most advantageous conversion rate from the perspective of the holder.

○ *Nonvested shares.* Treat nonvested shares with determinable terms as though they have vested. Thus, they become potentially dilutive shares as of their grant date.

○ *Options and warrants.* Assume that all dilutive options and warrants are exercised at their exercise price; then convert the proceeds into the number of shares that would have been purchased at the average fair market value, and subtract this amount from the total amount that could have been exercised. See the following example for Snowdonia Cellular.

Do not alter the earnings per share reported for previous periods to reflect market price changes.

There is a dilutive effect only when the average market price is greater than the exercise price of the options or warrants.

○ *Purchased options.* Include purchased put options in the diluted earnings per share calculation only if the exercise price is higher than the market price, and include the effects of a purchased call option only if the exercise price is lower than the market price. All other scenarios with such options are anti-dilutive, and so should not be included.

You should determine the number of dilutive potential ordinary shares independently for each period presented.

EXAMPLE 4.2

Provence Panache earns a net profit of €1 million, and it has 10 million ordinary shares outstanding. In addition, there is a €2 million convertible loan that has a 6 percent interest rate. The loan potentially converts to 3,000,000 of Provence's ordinary shares. Provence's incremental tax rate is 35 percent.

Provence's basic earnings per share is €1 million ÷ 10 million shares, or €0.10/share. The following shows the calculation of its diluted earnings per share:

Net profit	€ 1,000,000
+ Interest saved on €2,000,000 debt at 6%	120,000
− Reduced tax savings on foregone interest expense	(42,000)
Adjusted net earnings	€ 1,078,000
Ordinary shares outstanding	10,000,000
+ Potential converted shares	3,000,000
Adjusted shares outstanding	13,000,000
Diluted earnings per share	**€0.08/share**

Example 4.3

Snowdonia Cellular earns a net profit of £1 million, and it has 10 million ordinary shares outstanding that had an average fair value of £20 during the past year. In addition, there are 3 million share options outstanding that are convertible to ordinary shares at £12 each.

Snowdonia's basic earnings per share is £1 million ÷ 10 million ordinary shares, or £0.10/share.

To determine Snowdonia's diluted earnings per share, first calculate the number of shares that would have been issued at the average fair value. To do so, multiply the 3 million share options by their exercise price of £12, resulting in a total payment for the options of £36 million. Then divide this amount by the £20 average fair value to arrive at 1,800,000 shares that could have been purchased with the option proceeds. Then subtract the 1,800,000 shares from the 3 million options originally exercised. Then add the difference of 1,200,000 shares to the 10 million ordinary shares already outstanding to arrive at 11.2 million diluted shares.

Snowdonia's diluted earnings per share is £1 million ÷ 11.2 million ordinary shares, or £0.09/share.

When Should I Make Retrospective Adjustments to Earnings per Share?

You should retrospectively adjust the calculation of basic and diluted earnings per share for all periods presented, if the number of shares outstanding changes due to a capitalization, share split, or reverse share split. Also, disclose the fact that the share calculations reflect these changes.

How Do I Present Earnings per Share?

You should present basic and diluted earnings per share information in the statement of comprehensive income for every class of ordinary shares that has a different right to share in the period's profits, and for every period for which you present a statement of comprehensive income. If you present diluted earnings per share for at least one period, then you must report it for all periods presented. If the basic and diluted earnings per share are the same, then you can present them together as a single line item in the statement of comprehensive income.

If you report a discontinued operation, then separately disclose the basic and diluted earnings per share for that operation. You can include this information either in the statement of comprehensive income or in its accompanying notes.

EXAMPLE 4.4

Patra Pistachio Wholesalers presents its earnings per share information using the following layout:

Combined Earnings per Year	20x9	20x8	20x7
	€	€	€
From continuing operations			
Basic earnings per share	2.09	1.89	1.75
Diluted earnings per share	2.04	1.84	1.70
From discontinued operations			
Basic earnings per share	0.53	0.29	0.10
Diluted earnings per share	0.49	0.25	0.08
From total operations			
Basic earnings per share	2.62	2.18	1.85
Diluted earnings per share	2.53	2.09	1.78

 ## What Earnings per Share Information Should I Disclose?

You should disclose the following information regarding an entity's earnings per share:

- *Anti-dilutive items.* Any instruments not included in the diluted earnings per share calculation that could potentially dilute earnings per share in the future.
- *Numerators.* A reconciliation of the numerators used to calculate both basic and diluted earnings per share, noting all differences from the profit or loss attributable to the parent entity.

○ *Shares.* A reconciliation of the weighted average number of ordinary shares used in the denominators of both basic and diluted earnings per share.

○ *Subsequent transactions.* Any subsequent share-related transactions occurring after the reporting period that would have significantly changed the number of ordinary or potential ordinary shares outstanding at the end of the period if they had occurred within the period. Examples are shares issued for cash, options issued, convertible instruments converted to shares, and conditions arising that would result in the triggering of convertible instruments. Do not adjust earnings per share calculations for these items.

CHAPTER 5

INTERIM FINANCIAL REPORTING

 ### What Is an Interim Period?

An interim period is a financial reporting period that is shorter than a full fiscal year.

 ### Which Entities Must Issue Interim Financial Reports?

Interim financial reports are generally quarterly financial reports that are required for any entities whose debt or equity securities are publicly traded. Depending on which securities regulator or stock exchange is involved, an entity will be required at least to issue interim financial reports at the end of the first half of its fiscal year, and to do so no later than 60 days after the end of each interim period.

 ### What Is Included in an Interim Financial Report?

An interim financial report includes, for the reporting period in question, the following:

- ◯ Statement of financial position
- ◯ Statement of comprehensive income
- ◯ Statement of changes in equity
- ◯ Statement of cash flows

These reports can be in a condensed format. The statement of comprehensive income can be either a condensed single statement, or a condensed separate income statement and a condensed statement of comprehensive income. If you issue the reports in a condensed format, then the statements must include each of the headings and subtotals used in the most recent annual financial statements.

If the entity normally is required to present basic and diluted earnings per share in its annual financial statements, then it also includes this information in its interim financial report.

The interim financial report includes a statement of financial position as of the beginning of the earliest comparative period when an entity applied a retrospective restatement, reclassification, or accounting policy.

Finally, prepare the interim financial report on a consolidated basis if the entity's most recent annual financial statements were presented in this manner.

What Explanatory Notes Should I Include with the Interim Financial Report?

The interim financial report includes a summary of significant accounting policies and other explanatory information. This may be less information than is provided in the annual financial statements; it is acceptable to provide only an update to the more complete information provided in the annual financial report, thereby avoiding duplication. Do not provide relatively insignificant updates to the information in the annual report. In general, include notes if their omission would make the condensed statements misleading.

Include the following explanatory notes in the interim financial report if they are material, and report the items on a fiscal year-to-date basis:

- ○ *Contingencies.* Any changes in contingent assets or liabilities since the last annual reporting period
- ○ *Dividends.* The amount of dividends paid, either in aggregate or per share, for ordinary shares and for other shares
- ○ *Entity composition.* The effect of changes in the entity's structure during the interim period, from such events as restructurings, discontinued operations, and business combinations
- ○ *Changes in estimates.* The nature and amount of changes in any estimates from prior periods, if there is a material effect on the current period
- ○ *Item impact.* An explanation of the nature and amount of items having an unusual size, nature, or incidence that impact any part of the financial statements
- ○ *Policies.* A statement that the same accounting policies and computation methods used in the

annual financial statements are being used in the interim statements, or, if not, a description of any changes

- ○ *Seasonality.* An explanation of any seasonality or cyclicality that impacts interim results
- ○ *Securities.* Any issuances, repurchases, or repayments of securities
- ○ *Segments.* If segment reporting is required, disclosure, for each segment, of revenue from external customers, intersegment revenue, profit or loss, total assets for which there has been a material change from the annual financial statements, differences in the basis of segmentation from the last annual financial statements, and a reconciliation of segment profit or loss to entity profit or loss (see the Operating Segments chapter for more information about segment reporting)
- ○ *Subsequent events.* Material events occurring subsequent to the end of the interim period

Examples of these disclosable items are asset acquisitions, disposals, and impairments; error corrections; inventory write-downs; litigation settlements; loan defaults; and related party transactions.

For Which Periods Must I Present Interim Financial Statements?

You must include interim financial statements for the following periods:

- ○ Statement of financial position for the current interim period and a comparative statement of financial position for the immediately preceding fiscal year
- ○ Statements of comprehensive income for the current interim period and for the fiscal year-to-date, as well as comparative statements for the current and year-to-date periods of the immediately preceding fiscal year
- ○ Statement of changes in equity for the current fiscal year-to-date and a comparative statement for the year-to-date period of the immediately preceding fiscal year
- ○ Statement of cash flows for the current fiscal year-to-date, with a comparative statement for the year-to-date period of the immediately preceding fiscal year

What Information Should I Provide for a Highly Seasonal Business?

If your business results are highly seasonable, you may present financial information for the 12 months up to the end of the interim period and comparative information for the prior 12-month period. This is not required, but enhances a reader's comprehension of the entity's business.

How Do I Assess Materiality in Interim Periods?

You should assess the materiality of an item in relation to the financial data of the interim period. An item is material if its omission or misstatement could influence the economic decisions of users of the financial statements. The goal is to produce an interim financial report that includes all information relevant to understanding the entity's performance and financial position during and at the end of the interim period.

EXAMPLE 5.1

The Chemical Detection Consortium has revenue of €12,000,000 in its first quarter and eventually will generate revenue of €50,000,000 for its entire fiscal year. Chemical's controller traditionally has considered materiality to be 2 percent of revenue. In the first quarter, Chemical's Arabian Knights Security subsidiary, which is designated as discontinued, earns a profit of €360,000. This is 3 percent of Chemical's revenue in that quarter, and so is material enough to be segregated for reporting purposes in the third quarter. However, it is less than 1 percent of Chemical's full-year results, so there is no need to segregate this information in Chemical's annual financial report.

How Consistently Should I Apply Accounting Policies to Interim Periods?

You should apply the same accounting policies to the interim financial statements as to the annual financial statements. The exception is when you change an accounting policy after the most recent annual report and expect to apply the new policy to the next annual report; in this case, apply the new accounting policy to the interim financial statements.

The consistency of accounting policies between interim periods means that accounting transactions are recognized based on the expected results for the entire year, not just for a single interim period. This is known as the *integral view*. For example, an entity should recognize its income tax expense in an interim period based on its best estimate of the weighted average income tax rate that it expects to incur for the entire year. Also, you should accrue an expense provision within an interim period if an event has created a legal or constructive obligation for which the entity has no realistic alternative other than to make a payment. If there is only an intention or necessity to incur expenses later in the fiscal year, this is not sufficient grounds to accrue an expense in the current interim period.

EXAMPLE 5.2

Tidal Energy Company creates electrical generators that are triggered by wave action. Tidal incurs the following costs as part of its quarterly reporting:

○ It pays €15,000 of trade show fees in the first quarter for a green technology trade show that will occur in the fourth quarter.
○ It pays €32,000 in the first quarter for a block of advertisements that will run throughout the year in *Energy Alternatives* magazine.
○ The board of directors approves a profit-sharing plan in the first quarter that will pay employees 20 percent of net annual profits. At the time of plan approval, full-year profits are estimated to be €100,000. By the end of the third quarter, this estimate has dropped to €80,000, and by the end of the fourth quarter, to €70,000.

Tidal uses the following calculations to record these scenarios:

	Quarter 1	Quarter 2	Quarter 3	Quarter 4	Full Year
Trade show (1)				€15,000	€15,000
Advertising (2)	€8,000	€8,000	€8,000	8,000	32,000
Profit sharing (3)	5,000	5,000	3,000	1,000	14,000

(Continued)

(Continued)

1. The trade show expense is deferred until the show occurs in the fourth quarter.
2. The advertising is proportionally recognized in all quarters as it is used.
3. A profit-sharing accrual begins in the first quarter, when the plan is approved. At that time, one-quarter of the estimated full-year, profit-sharing expense is recognized. In the third quarter, the total estimated profit-sharing expense has declined to €16,000, of which €10,000 has already been recognized. When the profit-sharing expense estimate declines again in the fourth quarter, to €14,000, only €1,000 remains to be recognized.

This heightened level of accrual usage likely will result in numerous accrual corrections in subsequent interim periods to adjust for any earlier estimation errors.

If an asset no longer has any future economic benefits as of the end of an interim period, then charge it to expense at that time; do not wait for the end of the fiscal year to do so. Similarly, a recorded liability must still represent an existing obligation at the end of an interim period.

EXAMPLE 5.3

Bonifacio Bakeries writes down the value of its chestnut-flour inventory by €40,000 during the second quarter of its fiscal year and reports the change in its interim financial report for that period. During the third quarter, the market price of chestnut-flour increases somewhat, so Bonifacio justifiably can reverse a portion of the original write-down; accordingly, it records a reversal of €28,000 in the third quarter and reports the change in its interim report for that period.

 ## What Controls Should I Use for Interim Reporting?

The key problem with interim reporting is the propensity of the accounting staff to diverge from the integral view, and not accrue expenses if an event has created a legal or constructive obligation where there is no realistic alternative other than to make a payment. To mitigate this problem, authorize a recurring internal audit program that investigates how expenses are accrued during interim periods. This certainly should include an ongoing review of the income tax rate used in interim periods, since it is a large expense and will vary considerably over the fiscal year as an entity's increasing year-to-date profits move it into higher tax brackets.

The internal auditors also should verify the presence and use of an interim-period closing procedure, in which the accounting staff reviews a checklist of potential expense accruals and calculates them based on a predetermined set of criteria.

 ## Do I Retrospectively Adjust Interim Financial Statements?

No. If you issue six-month or more frequent interim financial statements, you do not retrospectively adjust the information in the interim statements.

EXAMPLE 5.4

Tidal Energy Company is sued over its alleged violation of a patent in the hydraulic ram used in its wave generators. Under the settlement terms, which Tidal agrees to during the fourth quarter of its fiscal year, it must retroactively pay a 4 percent royalty on all sales of the product to which the patent applies. Sales of the hydraulic ram were €20,000 in the first quarter, €35,000 in the second quarter, €10,000 in the third quarter, and €35,000 in the fourth quarter. In addition, the cumulative total of all ram sales in prior years was €400,000. Tidal cannot restate its previously issued quarterly financial results to include the royalty expense; instead, it reports the entire royalty expense, including the amount applicable to prior years, in the fourth quarter of the current fiscal year. The calculation follows:

	Quarter 1	Quarter 2	Quarter 3	Quarter 4	Full Year
Sales subject to royalty	€20,000	€35,000	€10,000	€35,000	€100,000
Royalty expense	0	0	0	4,000	4,000
Royalty related to prior year sales	0	—	—	16,000	16,000

Do I Restate Interim Financial Statements?

Yes. If you implement a change in accounting policy, then restate the financial statements of prior interim periods of the current fiscal year, as well as the comparable interim periods of prior fiscal years that will be included in the annual financial statements. If it is impractical to do so, then apply the new accounting policy prospectively from the earliest practicable date.

 ## Can I Anticipate or Defer Seasonal or Cyclical Revenue?

No. It is not acceptable to accrue for revenue expected to arise in a later interim period, nor is it allowable to defer the recognition of revenue that has already occurred. Instead, recognize revenues as they occur.

Revenue deferral or accrual is allowable only if it also would be appropriate at the end of an entity's fiscal year.

 ## Can I Anticipate or Defer Expenses Having Uneven Timing?

If it is appropriate to anticipate or defer a cost at the end of the fiscal year, then it is acceptable to also do so for expenses that are incurred unevenly during the fiscal year.

 ## Is it Acceptable to Use More Estimates When Preparing Interim Financial Statements?

Yes. Some amount of estimation is required for both annual and interim financial reports, but you likely will need to rely on estimates to a greater degree when preparing interim financial information.

EXAMPLE 5.5

Spiffy Soap Company conducts a physical inventory count of its thousands of bath products only at the end of its fiscal year. For its quarterly interim reports, Spiffy instead uses the 62 percent gross margin that it recorded in the preceding fiscal year. In the current year's third quarter, Spiffy's controller believes that a fraud situation has resulted in an exceptional amount of inventory loss, and mandates an extra physical inventory count. The result is a year-to-date actual gross margin of only 51 percent. Spiffy then conducts its normal physical count at the end of the fiscal year, resulting in an actual full-year gross margin of 56 percent. As shown in the following table, Spiffy recognizes in the third quarter the entire additional expense that was detected as a result of the extra physical count in that quarter.

	Quarter 1	Quarter 2	Quarter 3	Quarter 4	Full Year
Revenue	€18,000,000	€21,000,000	€23,000,000	€32,000,000	€94,000,000
Standard gross margin percent	62%	62%			
Year-to-date actual gross margin			51%	56%	56%
Cost of goods sold	6,840,000	7,980,000	15,560,000	10,980,000	41,360,000
Gross margin	11,160,000	13,020,000	7,440,000 *	21,020,000	52,640,000

*(€62,000,000 year-to-date revenue x 51% gross margin = €31,620,000) – €11,160,000 Quarter 1 gross margin – €13,020,000 Quarter 2 gross margin

CHAPTER 6

RELATED PARTY DISCLOSURES

 What Is a Related Party?

A party is related to an entity if any of the following situations apply to it:

- *Associate.* The party is an associate of the entity (see the Investments in Associates chapter).
- *Common control.* The party is, directly or indirectly, either under common control with the entity or has significant or joint control over the entity.
- *Family member.* The party is a close family member of a person who is part of key management personnel or who controls the entity. A close family member is an individual's domestic partner and children, children of the domestic partner, and dependents of the individual or the individual's domestic partner.
- *Individual control.* The party is controlled or significantly influenced by a member of key management personnel or by a person who controls the entity.
- *Joint venture.* The party is a joint venture in which the entity is a venture partner (see the Interests in Joint Ventures chapter).
- *Key management.* The party is a member of an entity's or its parent's key management personnel.
- *Post-employment plan.* The party is a post-employment benefit plan for the entity's employees.

The determination of related party status depends on the substance of the relationship, not just its legal form.

The following are not necessarily related parties:

- A business partner with whom the entity transacts a significant volume of business
- Funding providers
- Governments
- Public utilities
- Trade unions

- ○ Two entities that share key management personnel
- ○ Two venturers that share joint control of a joint venture

What Positions Are Considered to Be Key Management Personnel?

The term *key management personnel* includes those people having authority and responsibility for planning, directing, and controlling the activities of an entity, either directly or indirectly. This includes the entity's directors.

What Is a Related Party Transaction?

A related party transaction is a transfer of obligations, resources, or services between related parties. It is possible that a price will not be charged in exchange for these transfers.

What Is Significant Influence?

Significant influence occurs when an individual or entity has the power to participate in the financial and operating policy decisions of an entity, but does not have direct control over those policies.

What Related Party Information Should I Disclose?

You should disclose the following related party information:

- ○ *Compensation.* Total compensation for key management personnel, and separately for these personnel for short-term benefits, post-employment benefits, other long-term benefits, termination benefits, and share-based payments.
- ○ *Relationships.* The relationships between parent and subsidiary entities, even if there have been no transactions between the parties. An entity should disclose the name of its parent, as well as the name of the ultimate controlling party (if different from the parent). If the financial statements of neither the parent nor the ultimate controlling party are available for public use, then also disclose the name of the next most senior parent above the immediate parent

that produces consolidated financial statements that are available for public use.

○ *Transactions.* If there have been related party transactions, the nature of the relationship, a description of the transactions, any outstanding balances (as well as related terms, conditions, and guarantees), the amount of the transactions, provisions for doubtful debts, and the related bad debt recognized during the period. Separately disclose all of these items for related party transactions with the parent, entities with joint or significant control over the entity, subsidiaries, associates, joint ventures, key management personnel, and other related parties.

Examples of possible related party transactions, depending upon the substance of the relationship, are:

○ Financing arrangements
○ Leases
○ Provision of guarantees or collateral
○ Purchase or sale of goods, assets, or property, or services
○ Risk sharing in a defined benefit plan
○ Settlement of liabilities on behalf of the other entity
○ Transfers of research and development, or under license agreements

---

EXAMPLE 6.1

Ajax Machining Company leases storage trailers from an entity owned by the chief executive officer's son. In addition, it is the beneficiary of a low-interest loan from one its directors. Finally, it obtains half of its primary raw materials from the Strasbourg Steel Foundry; there is no ownership arrangement between Ajax and Strasbourg.

Ajax must disclose a related party relationship for the storage trailer lease, since it involves a family member. It also must disclose the low-interest loan, since it involves a member of key management. However, it does not have to disclose the supplier relationship, since there is no indication of a related party relationship.

CHAPTER 7

EVENTS AFTER THE REPORTING PERIOD

 What Is an Event after the Reporting Period?

An event after the reporting period is one that occurs between the end of the reporting period and the date when the financial statements are authorized for issuance. These events provide evidence of conditions existing either at (an *adjusting event*) or after (a *nonadjusting event*) the end of the reporting period. If financial statements are approved by shareholders (such as at an annual meeting) or a supervisory board, then you should consider the statements to be authorized for issuance on the date of issuance; this may be substantially sooner than the meetings of the shareholders or the supervisory board.

An event still qualifies as an event after the reporting period even if it occurs after the public announcement of selected financial information, as long as it occurs before the financial statements are authorized for issuance.

 How Do I Account for Adjusting Events after the Reporting Period?

You should adjust the amounts that an entity recognizes in its financial statements to reflect any adjusting events after the reporting period, but only until the date when the financial statements are authorized for issuance.

EXAMPLE 7.1

The Industrial Donut Company reaches a settlement with a government entity regarding charges that it provided stale donuts for soldiers' combat meals. The
(Continued)

(Continued)

settlement confirms that Industrial had an obligation at the end of its reporting period of £250,000. Industrial previously recognized a provision of £50,000, so it now increases the provision by £200,000.

Industrial Donut receives a report from an independent appraiser, stating that the carrying amount of its donut shrink-wrapping machine was impaired by £25,000 at the end of the reporting period. Accordingly, Industrial writes down the asset value within the reporting period.

Industrial Donut discovers that a major retail chain customer filed for bankruptcy two weeks after the end of the reporting period. Industrial has no reserve for bad debts, and so must write down the entire amount of the related £50,000 account receivable in the preceding reporting period.

Industrial Donut's internal audit staff discovers that the company's warehouse manager has been giving large quantities of donuts to the local police department in exchange for free security, and covered up the inventory shortfall at the end of the reporting period. The amount of the fraud is £10,000, which Industrial records within the reporting period.

In all of the above cases, Industrial Donut should adjust the financial statements of the reporting period only if the events occurred prior to authorization of the financial statements for issuance.

 ## How Do I Account for Nonadjusting Events after the Reporting Period?

You do not adjust the financial statements of a reporting period for nonadjusting events that occur after the reporting period.

EXAMPLE 7.2

The market value of the investments held by Jolt Power Supply Company declines precipitously following the end of a reporting period. This decline in value does not relate to the marketability of the investments at the end of the reporting period, so Jolt does not adjust its financial statements.

How Do I Account for Dividends Declared after the Reporting Period?

If an entity declares dividends after the reporting period, do not recognize the dividends as a liability at the end of the reporting period. This is because there was no obligation at the end of the reporting period.

How Do I Account for a Going Concern Issue That Arises after Period-End?

You should not prepare an entity's financial statements on a going concern basis if management determines after the reporting period that it has no realistic alternative other than to liquidate the entity or cease trading. This applies only if the financial statements have not yet been authorized for issuance.

How Do I Disclose Events Arising after the Reporting Period?

You should disclose the following information related to events arising after the reporting date:

- ○ *Authorization date.* The date when an entity's financial statements were authorized for issuance, and who gave the authorization. If anyone can amend the financial statements after their issuance, disclose this fact.
- ○ *Nonadjusting events.* If there are material nonadjusting events after the reporting period, you should disclose the nature of the events and either estimate their financial effect or state that you cannot make such an estimate.
- ○ *Period-end conditions.* If you receive subsequent information about conditions existing at the end of the reporting period, then update the disclosures to reflect this information.

EXAMPLE 7.3

Following its year-end reporting period, Okeanos Shipping issues several press releases in which it announces the divestiture of its Indonesian subsidiary, the acquisition of a cruise line operating off the

(Continued)

(*Continued*)

coast of Norway, the classification of a group of oil tankers as held for sale, the restructuring of its corporate headquarters staff, a reverse share split, and the issuance of a significant loan guarantee for its African subsidiary.

In all cases, these are nonadjusting events. Okeanos should not adjust its financial statements for the previous period, but it should disclose the events.

CHAPTER 8

FINANCIAL REPORTING IN HYPERINFLATIONARY ECONOMIES

 When Do I Designate an Economy as Hyperinflationary?

There is no fixed standard for determining whether an economy is hyperinflationary. It is indicated by a combination of the following characteristics:

- *Cumulative inflation rate.* The cumulative inflation rate over three years is close to or more than 100 percent.
- *Price indexing.* Interest rates, wages, and prices are commonly linked to and increased based on a price index.
- *Price quotes.* Prices are quoted in a foreign currency.
- *Prices increased for credit.* For customers who intend to buy on credit terms, prices are higher to reflect the expected loss of purchasing power during the credit period.
- *Wealth stored elsewhere.* The general population prefers to store its wealth in a stable foreign currency or in nonmonetary assets.

 How Do I Restate Financial Results in a Hyperinflationary Economy?

If an entity's functional currency is the currency of a hyperinflationary economy, the entity should present its financial statements in terms of the measuring unit current at the end of the reporting period. The entity also should restate the results of any presented financial information from earlier periods in terms of the measuring unit current at the end of the reporting period.

The entity should include any gain or loss on its net monetary position (see next question) in profit or loss, and disclose this amount separately.

How Do I Restate Financial Statements That Use Historical Costs?

You should follow these rules when restating financial statements that used historical costs:

○ *General.* Apply a general price index to amounts in the statement of financial position that are not already expressed in the measuring unit current at the end of the reporting period.

○ *Cash.* Do not restate cash.

○ *Deferred payment items.* If an entity has delayed payment terms on an asset purchase, it may not be practical to impute the amount of related interest expense. Instead, restate the assets from the payment date, rather than the purchase date.

○ *Equity method investments.* If an investor accounts for an investment in an investee under the equity method, the investee should restate its financial results based on a general price index; the investor should use the restated results when calculating its share of the investee's net assets and profit or loss.

○ *Gain or loss on net monetary position.* During a period of hyperinflation, an entity holding more assets than liabilities will lose purchasing power (since its assets are worth less), while the reverse is true for those entities holding more liabilities than assets (since their liabilities are worth less). An entity should record this gain or loss on its net monetary position in profit or loss. Calculate the gain or loss on net monetary position by multiplying the change in the general price index by the weighted average for the period of the difference between the entity's monetary assets and monetary liabilities, and then subtract any changes to index-linked items (see next bullet point).

○ *Index-linked items.* Do not restate items that are already linked to price indexes through contractual agreements. These items will require separate adjustment in accordance with the contractual agreements to which they are linked.

○ *Nonmonetary assets and liabilities.* If an item is already carried at its fair value, then do not restate it. You should restate all other nonmonetary assets and liabilities. If a nonmonetary item is carried at cost (or cost minus depreciation), then apply the change in the general price index from the item's acquisition date to the end of the reporting period. Examples of items carried at cost that require restatement are property, plant, and equipment, inventories, goodwill, and intangible assets. However, the restatement amount of an asset should not exceed its recoverable amount, and the restatement amount of inventory should not exceed its net realizable value.

○ *Owners' equity.* When first restating an entity's financial statements, you should restate owners' equity as of the beginning of the first period, except for retained earnings and any revaluation surplus. Also, eliminate any revaluation surplus from previous periods. At the end of the first period and thereafter, restate all components of owners' equity using a price index from the beginning of the period or the date of contribution (if later).

○ *Statement of comprehensive income.* Restate all items in the statement of comprehensive income, using the change in the general price index from the dates when the income and expense items originally were recorded.

If there is no evidence of the acquisition date of an asset whose cost must be restated, then obtain a professional assessment of its value; this becomes the basis from which future restatements are calculated.

EXAMPLE 8.1

Mashava Minerals has operated several platinum mines within Zimbabwe for one year and purchased all of its assets at the beginning of the year. Its functional currency is the Zimbabwe dollar, which is currently experiencing hyperinflation. Mashava converts its year-end balance sheet based on the following table and a general price index that increased from 100 to 200 in the past year. Mashava has three months' inventory in stock.

(000,000,000s)	Pre-Adjusted Balance Sheet	Calculation	Post-Adjusted Balance Sheet
Cash	250	Monetary item, so no change	250

(Continued)

(Continued)

Inventory	600	600 × (200 ÷ 175)	685
Fixed assets	3,000	3,000 × (200 ÷ 100)	6,000
Assets	3,850		6,935
Loan	1,050	Monetary item, so no change	1,050
Share capital	2,500	2,500 × (200 ÷ 100)	5,000
Retained earnings	300	Remaining balance	885
Liabilities/ Equity	3,850		6,935

How Do I Restate Financial Statements That Use Current Costs?

Do not restate financial statement items that are already stated at their current costs. If any items are not stated at their current costs, then use the restatements already noted for financial statements that use historical costs.

A current cost statement of comprehensive income uses costs as of the date of incurrence or consumption, so use a general price index to restate all of the amounts listed in the statement of comprehensive income into the measuring unit that was current at the end of the reporting period.

How Do I Select a General Price Index?

You should pick a general price index that reflects changes in general purchasing power. Also, for reporting consistency, all entities reporting in the same currency should use the same general price index for restatement purposes.

What If There Is No General Price Index to Use for Restatements?

If there is no general price index available to use for restatements, then you must use an estimated price index. For example, an estimated price index could be based on movements in the functional currency's exchange rate and the exchange rate of a relatively stable foreign currency.

How Do I Consolidate the Results of Subsidiaries Operating in Hyperinflationary Economies?

A subsidiary whose functional currency is within a hyperinflationary economy should restate its financial results using a general price index before they are included in the consolidated results of the parent entity.

If the financial results of a subsidiary are as of a different end date than those of the parent entity, you should restate them into the measuring unit current as of the date of the consolidated financial statements.

What Happens When an Economy Stops Being Hyperinflationary?

When an economy is no longer hyperinflationary, an entity stops using the restatements required for a hyperinflationary economy. Also, it uses the amounts expressed in the measuring unit at the end of the previous reporting period as the carrying amounts in its subsequent financial statements.

What Information Should I Disclose About Hyperinflation?

An entity whose functional currency is the currency of a hyperinflationary economy should disclose the following information:

- ○ *Basis.* Whether its financial statements are based on a historical or current cost approach
- ○ *Price index.* The price index used, and its level at the end of the reporting period, as well as the index's movement during the current period and the previous reporting period
- ○ *Restatement.* The fact that its financial statements have been restated in terms of the measuring unit current at the end of the reporting period

PART II

ASSETS AND LIABILITIES

CHAPTER 9

INVESTMENT PROPERTY

 What Is Investment Property?

Investment property is property that an entity holds to earn rental income and/or capital appreciation. It generates cash flows mostly independently of other assets held by an entity. It is not property that an entity uses to supply goods or services, nor is it used for administrative purposes. Examples of investment property are land held for appreciation and a building held for current or future leases to third parties. Examples of assets that are *not* investment property are property intended for sale in the near term, property being constructed for a third party, owner-occupied property, and property leased to a third party under a finance lease.

If an investment property contains one portion held for either rental income or capital appreciation, and another portion held for other uses, and if the portions could be sold separately, then account for them separately. If it is not possible to do so, then account for the property as an investment only if the portion held for other uses is an insignificant amount of the total asset value.

If an entity provides services to the occupants of a property, it can account for the property as an investment property only if the services it provides are insignificant.

Property held by a lessee under an operating lease may be investment property if it otherwise meets the definition of investment property and the lessee recognizes it under the fair value model. If a lessee classifies such a property as an investment property, then it must account for all of its investment property using the fair value model.

EXAMPLE 9.1

Elbrus Investments owns a number of investments. It classifies them as follows:

○ Its headquarters building. This is an owner-occupied asset, treated as a long-lived asset.
○ A plot of land, for which it has not yet determined a use. This is an investment property.
○ An underutilized office building that it intends to lease. This is an investment property.
○ A hotel, for which a subsidiary provides an insignificant amount of outsourced concierge service. This is an investment property.

 ## What Is Owner-Occupied Property?

Owner-occupied property is property held by its owner for its own productive purposes, such as administration or the production of goods or services.

 ## How Do I Designate Property Leased within a Common Ownership Group?

If an entity leases property to another entity within a common ownership group, the leasing entity can recognize the property as investment property in its own financial statements, but the consolidated entity must treat it as owner-occupied property.

 ## When Can I Recognize Investment Property as an Asset?

You can recognize investment property as an asset only when the entity can reliably measure the cost of the property, and it is probable that the property's future economic benefits will flow to the entity.

 ## What Can I Include in the Cost of an Investment Property?

When initially recognizing an investment property, you can include the cost to acquire the property, transaction costs (such as legal fees and property transfer taxes), as well as subsequent costs to add to, replace parts of, or service the property. If the entity replaces portions of the property, then you should derecognize the portions being replaced. If the property purchase price is deferred, record as cost the cash price equivalent, and record the difference between this amount and the deferred payment as interest expense over the credit period.

If an entity acquires an investment property in exchange for a nonmonetary asset, recognize the cost of this asset at its fair value, unless the exchange lacks commercial substance or the fair value of neither asset is reliably measurable. If fair value is not determinable, then instead use the carrying amount of the asset given up.

Do *not* include the following costs in the cost of an investment property, which instead should be recognized in profit or loss as incurred:

- Daily servicing costs
- Start-up costs (unless needed to bring the property up to the condition intended by management)
- Operating losses before the property achieves the planned occupancy level
- Abnormal construction or development waste

 ## What Is the Fair Value Model?

Under the fair value model, you should initially recognize an investment property at its fair value and remeasure its fair value at reasonable intervals. When there is a gain or loss on a change in the fair value of an investment property, recognize it in profit or loss in the period of the value change.

The fair value of an investment property is the price at which it could be sold at the end of the reporting period to a knowledgeable and willing party in an arm's-length transaction, which does not include any price inflation or deflation caused by atypical terms. Lesser alternatives for determining fair value are to use current prices in an active market for properties of a different nature, recent prices of similar properties in less active markets, and discounted cash flow projections based on reliable and supportable future cash flow projections.

You should include in a property's fair value any equipment integral to the property, such as elevators and air conditioning.

Do not include the following factors when determining fair value:

- Legal rights or restrictions specific to the entity
- Synergies between the entity's properties

- ○ Tax rights or restrictions specific to the entity
- ○ Value gained from having a portfolio of multiloca-
  tion properties

If you replace part of an investment property, it may be necessary to reduce the fair value by the cost of the replaced part. When it is not practical to do so, include the cost of the replacement in the carrying amount of the asset, and then reassess the investment property's fair value.

EXAMPLE 9.2

Kensington Properties constructs an office tower in Edinburgh that has a construction cost of £35 million. Upon completion at the end of Year 1, tenants fully occupy the building. Kensington engages a valuation expert to provide fair value estimates at the end of each successive year. The results of those estimations and Kensington's recognition of gains and losses are noted in the following table:

Year	Cost	Fair Value	Gain/Loss Recognized
1	£35,000,000	£35,000,000	£0
2		37,000,000	2,000,000 Gain
3		42,000,000	5,000,000 Gain
4		41,000,000	1,000,000 Loss
5		32,000,000	9,000,000 Loss

 Should I Include Future Upgrades in a Property's Fair Value?

No. Do not include future capital expenditures in a property's fair value, even if they are projected to enhance the property.

 What If I Cannot Determine an Investment Property's Fair Value?

An entity may judge that it cannot reliably determine a property's fair value on a continuing basis, because comparable market transactions are infrequent and alternative fair value estimation methods are not available. If so, it should use the cost model, as described in the next question, with a residual value of zero. This treatment is allowable only as of the *initial* acquisition of an investment property.

If an entity is already measuring an investment property at fair value and then comparable market transactions become less frequent or market prices less available, the entity must continue to record the property at its fair value.

 What Is the Cost Model?

The cost model is the alternative valuation treatment for investment properties, under which an entity initially recognizes the cost of an investment property at its carrying cost, and then continues to do so over time. In general, the costs to include in an investment property are its purchase cost and any costs incurred to bring the asset to the location and condition needed for it to operate in the manner intended by management. More specifically, include the following costs in an investment property:

- Purchase price of the property and related taxes
- Construction cost of the property, which can include labor and employee benefits
- Site preparation
- Installation and assembly
- Professional fees
- Less: trade discounts and rebates

EXAMPLE 9.3

Ipswich Investments constructs a warehouse in Felixstowe for £15 million. It estimates that the warehouse will have a useful life of 20 years, with no residual value, so it depreciates the property at the rate of £750,000 per year, which will bring the property's carrying cost to zero at the end of 20 years. Since Ipswich is not using the fair value method, there will be no impact on its profit or loss in each successive year if there are any changes in the warehouse's fair value. Instead, the only impact on profit or loss will be an annual charge of £750,000 for depreciation.

If you use the cost model and replace part of an investment property, you must derecognize the carrying amount of the replaced part. However, you cannot include the cost of a replacement part if the replaced part was depreciated separately. If you cannot determine the carrying amount of the replaced part, then the replacement part's cost can indicate what the replaced part cost was when it was originally acquired.

For more information about cost accumulation for assets, see the Property, Plant, and Equipment chapter.

Can I Use Either the Cost Model or the Fair Value Model?

Yes, but once you pick a model, you must apply it to *all* of your investment property. The only exception is when an entity has investment property backing liabilities that pay a return that is linked directly to the returns from, or fair value of, specific assets. In this case, the entity must use the fair value method for that property, and can choose to use either the fair value model or the cost model for all other investment properties.

If an entity sells investment properties between asset pools that use different cost recognition models, then it transfers the property at its fair value, and recognizes the cumulative fair value change in profit or loss.

If you choose the fair value model, it is very unlikely that you subsequently would change to the cost model, since the only valid reason for doing so is that it makes the financial statements more reliable and yields more relevant information—which is difficult to justify.

How Do I Account for Under-Construction Investment Property?

If you plan to use the cost model, then simply recognize the accumulated construction costs of an under-construction investment property. If you plan to use the fair value model and it is not possible to determine the fair value of the investment property, but it should be possible to do so upon its completion, then measure the property at cost until the earlier of construction completion or whenever its fair value becomes reliably determinable. At that time, recognize any difference between the property's fair value and carrying cost in profit or loss.

Is It Necessary to Use an Independent Valuer to Determine Fair Values?

No, although you are encouraged to use an independent valuer who holds a recognized and relevant professional qualification, and who has recent experience with your type of investment property.

 ### When Do I Transfer Properties to and from the Investment Property Classification?

Under certain scenarios, you can transfer a property between the investment property classification, owner-occupied property, and inventory. You should make transfers to or from investment property only when there is a change in use. This condition arises under the following circumstances:

- ○ *Development.* When development of a property begins, with the goal of selling the property, this triggers a transfer from investment property to inventory.
- ○ *Occupation.* When the owner occupies an investment property, this triggers a transfer from investment property to owner-occupied property. Conversely, when the owner stops occupying the property, this triggers a transfer from owner-occupied property to investment property.
- ○ *Operating lease.* When an operating lease is initiated with another party, this triggers a transfer from inventories to investment property.

 ### How Do I Account for the Transfer of Properties to or from the Investment Property Classification?

If you are using the cost model, a transfer does not change the carrying amount of a property. However, if you are using the fair value model, you should reset the carrying amount of a property to its fair value as of the date you transfer it out of the investment property classification and into either owner-occupied property or inventory.

If you transfer owner-occupied property to the investment property classification, then revalue it as of the reclassification date. Then use Exhibit 9.1 to determine the

Exhibit 9.1 CLASSIFICATION OF REVALUED INVESTMENT PROPERTY

Property Value Increases	Recognize in Other Comprehensive Income and as "Revaluation Surplus" in Equity
Property value increases, but reverses a prior revaluation decrease	Recognize as profit to the extent that it reverses a revaluation decrease previously recognized in profit or loss
Property value decreases	Recognize as a loss
Property value decreases, but credit balance exists in the revaluation surplus for the property	Recognize in other comprehensive income to the extent of any revaluation surplus for the property, with any excess recognized as a loss

proper accounting for an investment property that has been revalued.

The treatment of property transferred from inventory to investment property is somewhat different, if you choose to carry it at fair value. In this case, recognize any difference between the carrying amount and fair value on the transfer date in profit or loss.

For more information about revaluations, see the Property, Plant, and Equipment chapter.

How Do I Account for Investment Property Disposals?

You should derecognize an investment property when an entity disposes of it or when it is permanently withdrawn from use and you expect no future economic benefits from its disposal. It is possible to dispose of an investment property either by selling it outright or by entering into a finance lease.

Upon disposal of an investment property, recognize the gain or loss from the transaction in profit or loss. The gain or loss is calculated as the difference between the net proceeds from the disposal and the property's carrying amount.

How Do I Account for Third Party Compensation for Impaired or Damaged Investment Property?

If an entity's investment property is impaired, lost, or damaged, you cannot recognize any compensation from third parties until the compensation is receivable.

EXAMPLE **9.4**

Kensington Properties is constructing an apartment building, which it has designated as an investment property. The building is struck by lightning and burns down. Kensington has fully insured the building against fire damage, but it cannot recognize a gain on the insurance claim until the underwriter formally accepts the claim and acknowledges the amount that it will pay to Kensington.

What Information Do I Disclose about Investment Properties?

An entity should disclose the following general information about its investment properties:

- ○ *Classification criteria.* The criteria it uses to distinguish between investment property, owner-occupied property, and property held for sale
- ○ *Model type.* Whether it uses the cost model or the fair value model to account for its investment properties
- ○ *Obligations.* Any contractual obligations for repairs, maintenance, or enhancements to properties, as well as to purchase or develop properties
- ○ *Profit or loss recognition.* The amounts of rental income, direct operating expenses separately for properties generating and not generating rental income, and the recognized cumulative fair value change on a property sale from a pool using the cost model to a pool using the fair value model
- ○ *Remittance restrictions.* The amount of any restrictions on income remittances and the realizability of investment property

If an entity uses the fair value model, it must disclose the following additional information:

- ○ *Fair value assumptions.* The methods and significant assumptions used to determine investment property fair values, and whether the fair values are supported by market evidence or other factors
- ○ *Independent valuer.* The extent to which valuations are provided by independent valuers having valid qualifications and recent relevant experience, or disclosure of the absence of such valuations

○ *Operating leases.* Under what circumstances it classifies properties held under operating leases as investment properties

○ *Reconciliation.* Reconciliation of the beginning and ending investment property account, showing acquisition additions, subsequent expenditure additions, business combination additions, held-for-sale items, net gains and losses from fair value adjustments, net exchange differences from foreign currency adjustments, transfers between the inventory and owner-occupied property classifications, and other changes; for properties separately using the cost model, description of the properties, why the entity cannot reliably determine fair value, the range of estimates within which the fair value is likely to be located, and (upon disposal) the carrying amount at the sale date and the amount of gain or loss recognized

○ *Valuation adjustments.* Reconciliation of the valuation obtained from adjustments to fair values for financial reporting purposes and the initial fair values of investment properties, with separate disclosure of any add-backs for recognized lease obligations

If an entity uses the cost model, it must disclose the following additional information:

○ *Depreciation calculations.* The depreciation method(s) and lives used

○ *Depreciation reconciliation.* Reconciliation of the gross carrying amount and accumulated depreciation between the beginning and end of the reporting period

○ *Fair values.* The fair value of the entity's investment properties; in cases where fair value cannot be reliably determined, description of the property, why fair value cannot be determined, and the range of estimates within which fair value is likely to be located

○ *Investment reconciliation.* Reconciliation of the acquisition additions, subsequent expenditure additions, business combination additions, held-for-sale items, depreciation, impairment losses and reversals, foreign exchange differences, transfers to and from inventory and owner-occupied property, and other changes between the beginning and end of the reporting period

CHAPTER 10

INTERESTS IN JOINT VENTURES

 What Are the Types of Joint Venture?

There are three types of joint venture:

- *Jointly controlled operations.* There may not be a joint venture legal entity. Instead, the joint venture uses the assets and other resources of the venturers. Each venturer uses its own assets, incurs its own expenses, and raises its own financing. The joint venture agreement states how the revenue and expenses related to the joint venture are to be shared among the venturers.
- *Jointly controlled assets.* Venturers may jointly control or own the assets contributed to or acquired by a joint venture. Each venturer may receive a share of the assets' output and accept a share of the expenses incurred. There may not be a joint venture legal entity.
- *Jointly controlled entities.* This type of joint venture involves a legal entity in which each venturer has an interest. The new legal entity controls the joint venture's assets and liabilities, as well as its revenue and expenses; it can enter into contracts and raise financing. Each venturer is entitled to a share of any output generated by the new entity. A jointly controlled entity maintains its own accounting records and prepares financial statements from those records. If a venturer contributes cash or other assets to a jointly controlled entity, the venturer records this transfer as an investment in the jointly controlled entity.

There also may be a variety of combinations of these concepts, such as when a venturer transfers its assets into a new joint venture entity.

In all three of these types of joint venture, there are two or more venturers that are bound by a contractual agreement that established joint control over the entity.

EXAMPLE 10.1

Plasma Storage Devices enters into a joint venture agreement with Eternal Security Company to offer plasma storage in Eternal's vaults. According to the agreement, Plasma is paid 25 percent of all revenue in exchange for sale of its thermally efficient storage units to customers, while Eternal is paid the remaining 75 percent of revenue as part of an ongoing maintenance contract to store the plasma. Since there are jointly controlled operations to which each venturer contributes assets, this is a joint venture under the concept of jointly controlled operations.

Plasma Storage Devices enters into another joint venture agreement, with Hospital Transport Services, whereby the two entities jointly own a new joint venture entity called Plasma Collection Services, which pays donors to collect their plasma. Both Plasma Storage and Hospital Transport contribute assets to the new entity. This is a jointly controlled entity, and so qualifies as a joint venture.

What Is Significant Influence?

Significant influence is having the power to participate in the financial or operating policy decisions of an economic activity. However, it does not give an entity control or joint control over those policies.

When Does a Venturer Not Have Joint Control?

A venturer may not have control over a venture when the investee is in bankruptcy, since other parties may have taken control during the proceedings. A venturer also may not have control when the investee has severe long-term restrictions on its ability to transfer funds to the venturer.

When Is a Joint Venture Actually a Subsidiary?

A joint venture agreement may identify one venturer as the manager of the joint venture. If this manager can govern the financial and operating policies of the overall venture, then it has control over the venture. In this scenario, the venture is really a subsidiary of the entity acting as its manager.

 Is a Contract Required for Joint Venture Accounting?

Yes. There must be a contractual agreement that distinguishes the interests of the entities having joint control over the investee. The agreement may be a formal contract or the minutes of discussions between the entities. Whatever the form, it is usually in writing and typically addresses the following issues regarding the joint venture:

- Activities of the venture
- Capital contributions by venturers
- Duration of the venture
- Governing body
- Joint control by the venturers over the entity
- Reporting obligations
- Sharing of the financial and operational results of the venture
- Venturer voting rights

 How Do I Account for a Jointly Controlled Operation?

The results of operations, assets, and liabilities of a jointly controlled operation are already included in the financial statements of the venturer, so no other adjustments or consolidation activities are required.

 How Do I Account for Jointly Controlled Assets?

The venturer should record its share of the jointly controlled assets, liabilities it incurred, its share of liabilities jointly incurred with other venturers, and income and expenses generated or incurred by the joint venture. No other adjustments or consolidation activities are required.

The venturer should record assets involved in the joint venture as property, plant, and equipment, not as an investment.

How Do I Use Proportionate Consolidation to Account for a Jointly Controlled Entity?

The venturer normally uses proportionate consolidation to recognize its interest in a jointly controlled entity. *Proportionate consolidation* is when a venturer combines its share of each of the assets, liabilities, income, and expenses of a jointly controlled entity with similar items in its own financial statements, or reports them as separate line items in its own financial statements. The procedures used for proportionate consolidation are similar to those used for consolidating investments in subsidiaries (see the Consolidated and Separate Financial Statements chapter for more information).

There are two proportionate consolidation reporting formats:

- ○ *Combined reporting.* The venturer combines its share of each of the assets, liabilities, income, and expenses of the jointly controlled entity with similar line items in its financial statements.
- ○ *Separate reporting.* The venturer reports its share of each of the assets, liabilities, income, and expenses of the jointly controlled entity as separate line items in its financial statements.

Both approaches result in the same asset and liability totals, as well as net income or loss.

How Do I Use the Equity Method to Account for a Jointly Controlled Entity?

International Financial Reporting Standards recommend using proportionate consolidation over the equity method, but allow use of the equity method. The *equity method* is when a venturer initially records its interest in a jointly controlled entity at cost and later adjusts it for post-acquisition changes in the venturer's share of the jointly controlled entity's net assets. The venturer includes in its profit or loss its share of the profit or loss of the jointly controlled entity. See the Investments in Associates chapter for more information about the equity method.

How Do I Account for the Loss of Control in a Joint Venture?

A venturer should stop using both the proportionate consolidation and equity methods as soon as it stops having joint control over a jointly controlled entity. The accounting then changes to one of the following:

○ *Associate.* If the entity becomes an associate, see the Investments in Associates chapter regarding how to account for the situation.
○ *Subsidiary.* If the entity becomes a subsidiary, then see the Consolidated and Separate Financial Statements chapter regarding how to consolidate the results of the entity with those of the venturer.
○ *Investment.* For the remaining situations, see the Financial Instruments chapter regarding how to account for the entity as an investment.

In all of these cases, on the date of loss of joint control, the venturer measures at fair value its investment in the entity that it formerly jointly controlled. The venturer then recognizes the following calculation in profit or loss:

Fair value of the investment and the proceeds from disposing of any interest in the jointly controlled entity	-	Carrying amount of the investment on the date when the venturer lost control of the jointly controlled entity

If a venturer loses control of a jointly controlled entity, it accounts for any amounts it recognized in other comprehensive income related to that entity as though the jointly controlled entity itself had disposed of the related assets or liabilities. Thus, if a venturer previously recognized a gain or loss in other comprehensive income, it reclassifies the entry to profit or loss when it loses joint control of the entity.

EXAMPLE 10.2

Plasma Collection Services is a jointly controlled entity that has €100,000 of available-for-sale securities. One of its controlling entities, Hospital Transport Services, previously recognized a gain of €10,000 in other comprehensive income on its share of those securities. Hospital Transport loses joint control of Plasma. On the date of its loss of control, Hospital Transport should reclassify the €10,000 gain to profit or loss.

If a venturer's ownership interest in a jointly controlled entity is reduced but the venturer still has joint control, then the venturer reclassifies to profit or loss only a proportionate amount of any gain or loss that it previously recognized in other comprehensive income.

How Do I Account for a Nonmonetary Contribution to a Joint Venture?

When a venturer contributes nonmonetary assets to a joint venture entity in exchange for an equity interest, the accounting varies based on the terms of the transaction:

○ *Full equity payment.* If the venturer receives payment fully in equity, then it recognizes in its profit or loss that portion of the gain or loss on the assets attributable to the equity interests of the other venturers. This does not apply when the venturer has not shifted the significant risks and rewards of ownership of the assets to the joint venture entity, or when it is not possible to reliably measure the gain or loss, or when the contribution lacks commercial substance. If any of these exceptions apply, the gain or loss remains unrealized.

○ *Partial equity payment.* If the joint venture entity also pays the venturer with monetary or nonmonetary assets in addition to some equity, then the venturer recognizes a corresponding portion of the gain or loss on the transaction in profit or loss.

If there are unrealized gains or losses on a nonmonetary contribution, the venturer does not present them as deferred gains or losses. Instead, it eliminates them against the underlying assets when using either the proportionate consolidation or the equity method.

How Do I Account for Transactions between a Venturer and a Joint Venture?

Any gain or loss from a transaction between a venturer and a joint venture should reflect the substance of the transaction. The accounting is different if the transaction flows from the venturer to the joint venture entity, or vice versa:

○ *Transactions from the venturer.* If the venturer has transferred the significant risks and rewards of ownership to the joint venture entity, then the venturer can recognize only that portion of the gain or loss attributable to the ownership interests of the other venturers. However, the venturer recognizes the full amount of any loss when the transfer transaction provides evidence that there was a reduction in the net realizable value of current assets, or that there was an impairment loss.

○ *Transactions to the venturer.* If the venturer buys assets from the joint venture entity, it does not recognize its share of the joint venture's profit on the transaction until the venturer has resold the assets to an independent third party. If the joint venture entity realizes a loss on the resale transaction, the venturer recognizes its share of the joint venture's loss. However, the venturer recognizes losses at once when they are a reduction in the asset's net realizable value, or represent an impairment loss. See the Asset Impairment chapter for more information about impairment losses.

How Does a Joint Venture Manager Account for Fees Billed to the Joint Venture?

If a venturer is the manager of a joint venture, that venturer can recognize any management fees billed to the joint venture as revenue. Correspondingly, the joint venture can account for these fees as an expense.

What Information Should a Venturer Disclose about Jointly Controlled Operations?

A venturer should disclose in its financial statements the amount of any assets it controls or liabilities it incurs that are related to a jointly controlled operation. It also should disclose the expenses it incurs and the share of income it earns from the operations of the joint venture.

What Information Should a Venturer Disclose about Jointly Controlled Assets?

A venturer should disclose in its financial statements its share of jointly controlled assets, liabilities it incurred, and its share of liabilities incurred with other venturers, together with its share of any revenue and expenses generated or incurred by the joint venture.

 ## What Information Should a Venturer Disclose about a Joint Venture?

A venturer should separately disclose the following information regarding any joint ventures in which it is involved:

- ○ *Accounting method.* The method it uses to recognize its interests in jointly controlled entities
- ○ *Commitments.* The aggregate amount of any capital commitments related to its joint ventures, and its share of any jointly incurred commitments; also its share of the capital commitments of a joint venture entity
- ○ *Consolidated results.* If it accounts for a joint venture using proportionate consolidation or the equity method, the aggregate amounts of the current assets, long-term assets, current liabilities, long-term liabilities, revenue, and expenses related to the joint venture
- ○ *Contingent liabilities.* The aggregate amount of any contingent liabilities incurred in relation to its joint ventures, and its share of any jointly incurred contingent liabilities; also its share of any contingent liabilities of the joint venture entity for which it is also liable, and those cases where it is contingently liable for the liabilities of the other venturers in the joint venture (unless the probability of loss is remote)
- ○ *Ownership interests.* Its interests in significant joint ventures, including the proportion of its ownership interests

CHAPTER 11

INVESTMENTS IN ASSOCIATES

 What Is an Associate?

An *associate* is an entity over which an investor has significant influence and that is not a subsidiary or an interest in a joint venture.

 What Is Significant Influence?

Significant influence is the power to participate in the operating and financial policy decisions of an entity; it is not control over those policies. *Control* is the power to govern the operating and financial policy decisions of an entity in order to obtain benefits from the entity.

If an investor holds at least 20 percent of the voting power of an investee, the investor is presumed to have significant influence. Conversely, the investor is presumed not to have significant influence if it holds less than 20 percent of the investee's voting power. In both cases, the assumption of influence can be reversed through a clear demonstration to the contrary.

It is possible for an investor to not have significant influence, even with majority ownership of an investee. It is possible to lose significant influence over an investee even in the absence of a change in ownership. For example, an investee may become subject to the control of a court, regulator, or government, or loss of significant influence may be the result of a contractual agreement.

Any of the following items are considered to be evidence of significant influence:

○ Board of directors representation
○ Management personnel swapping or sharing
○ Material transactions with the investee
○ Policy-making participation
○ Technical information exchanges

When determining the level of influence, you should consider the presence of any share warrants, share call options, or convertible instruments that can increase an entity's voting power. However, also assess the ability of the entity to currently exercise or convert these instruments, which may reduce the probability of increases in the entity's level of influence. You *should not* consider in this assessment the intentions of management or the investor's financial ability to exercise or convert the financial instruments.

What If a Controlled Group Has an Aggregate Share in an Associate?

A parent entity and its subsidiaries may individually have holdings in an associate. If so, aggregate the holdings to determine the level of the group's influence over the associate. When doing so, ignore the holdings of the group's other associates or joint ventures.

How Do I Use the Equity Method?

The equity method is an accounting methodology for initially recognizing an investment at cost and thereafter adjusting it for post-acquisition changes in the investor's share of the investee's net assets. The investor also recognizes a proportionate share of the profit or loss of the investee, and does so in its own profit or loss. If an investee issues a distribution to the investor, this is a reduction of the investor's carrying amount of the investment. An investor accounting for an investment in an associate records the investment as a noncurrent asset.

EXAMPLE 11.1

Gaelic Fire Candy acquires 30 percent of the voting shares of Red Hot Chili Balls, Inc. for £5 million. Gaelic has significant influence over Red Hot. Red Hot's retained earnings were £2 million on the purchase date. At the end of Year 1, Red Hot's retained earnings were £4 million.

The carrying value of Gaelic's investment in Red Hot at the end of Year 1 is calculated as follows:

Investment cost	£5,000,000
Share of post-investment reserves*	600,000
	£5,600,000

*£2 million net change in retained earnings x 30% ownership interest

If the associate itself has subsidiaries, associates, or joint ventures, the investor should account for just those profits or losses and net assets recognized in the associate's financial statements; this will include the associate's share of any profits or losses and net assets of the entities just described.

The investor also may have to alter the carrying amount of its investment to reflect changes in the investee's other comprehensive income. These changes typically are caused by the revaluation of property, plant, and equipment, as well as by foreign exchange translation differences. The investor recognizes its share of these changes in its own other comprehensive income.

If there are potential additional voting rights that the investor can use to increase its voting control over the associate, such as through the presence of convertible financial instruments, do not use them when calculating the investor's share of the investee's profit or loss.

See the Consolidated and Separate Financial Statements chapter for more information about consolidation procedures, which are generally applicable to the equity method.

What If the Investor's Share of an Associate's Losses Exceeds Its Investment?

An associate may incur such substantial losses that an investor's share of them equals or exceeds its investment in the associate. If so, the investor immediately stops recognizing its share of any further losses. If the associate subsequently reports profits, then the investor resumes its recognition of the associate's profits, but only after its share of the profits equals the share of losses that it previously did not recognize.

Once the investor's interest reaches zero, it may still provide for additional losses if it has incurred a legal or constructive obligation or made payments on behalf of the associate.

What If the Associate's Reporting Period Differs from That of the Investor?

If the associate uses a different reporting period from the one use by the investor, then the associate should prepare financial statements for the investor as of the date of the investor's financial statements. The investor then uses these revised financial statements when applying the equity method. This approach is not required if it is impractical for the associate to provide such statements.

If it is necessary to use the financial statements of an associate that have a different end date, then the investor must adjust for the effects of significant transactions or events occurring between the dates of the associate's and the investor's financial statements.

It is never allowable for the difference between the end of the associate's and the investor's financial statements to be more than three months.

What If the Associate's Accounting Policies Differ from Those of the Investor?

If the associate uses different accounting policies than the investor to create its financial statements, then the investor should adjust the associate's financial statements so that they incorporate the accounting policies used by the investor. The investor should then use these adjusted financial statements when applying the equity method.

How Do I Incorporate Preference Shares into the Equity Method?

If parties other than the investor have cumulative preference shares in an associate, and they are classified as equity, then the investor calculates its share of profit or loss after adjusting for the dividends on these shares, even if the dividends have not been declared.

When Can I *Not* Use the Equity Method?

You should *not* use the equity method to account for an investment in an associate in the following cases:

○ *Held for sale.* The investor has classified the investment as held for sale.
○ *Subsidiary reporting.* The investor is itself a subsidiary and its owners do not object to the nonapplication of the equity method; the investor's debt or equity is not publicly traded; the investor is not filing with a regulatory organization to issue any financial instruments in a public market; and the investor's parent entity produces consolidated financial statements

complying with International Financial Reporting Standards.

If an investor has classified its investment in an associate as held for sale and then changes this classification, it should start accounting for the investment under the equity method as of the change date, and also amend its financial statements for the periods since it classified the investment as held for sale.

What Happens When I Stop Using the Equity Method?

You should stop using the equity method when the investor no longer has significant influence over the investee. At that time, measure the investor's remaining investment in the investee at its fair value and recognize in profit or loss the following amount:

Fair value of any retained investment in the associate, plus any proceeds from the disposal of a part interest in the associate	-	Carrying amount of the investor's investment on the date when it loses significant influence over the investee

If an investor loses significant influence over an associate, it accounts for any amounts it recognized in other comprehensive income related to that entity as though the associate itself had disposed of the related assets or liabilities. Thus, if an investor previously recognized a gain or loss in other comprehensive income, it reclassifies the entry to profit or loss when it loses significant influence over the associate.

EXAMPLE 11.2

Hospital Transport Services is an investor in and has significant influence over Plasma Collection Services. Plasma Collection has €100,000 of available-for-sale securities, for which Hospital Transport previously recognized in other comprehensive income a gain of €10,000 on its share of those securities. Hospital Transport loses significant influence over Plasma. On the date of its loss of significant influence, Hospital Transport should reclassify the €10,000 gain to profit or loss.

If an investor's ownership interest in an associate is reduced but the investment continues to be an associate, then the investor reclassifies to profit or loss only a proportionate amount of any gain or loss that it previously recognized in other comprehensive income.

How Do I Account for an Impaired Investment in an Associate?

An investor should test its investment in an associate using the impairment testing requirements outlined in the Financial Instruments chapter. This will determine whether the investor should recognize an impairment loss on its investment in the associate.

The investor also tests the entire carrying amount of the investment for impairment using the testing criteria noted in the Asset Impairment chapter. The general testing decision is to recognize an impairment loss if the recoverable amount of the investment is less than its carrying amount. The recoverable amount is the higher of the fair value less costs to sell, or its value in use (which is either the investor's share of the present value of the associate's future cash flows or the present value of future dividends from the associate and from its eventual disposal).

How Do I Account for Upstream and Downstream Transactions?

An *upstream transaction* involves the movement of assets from the associate to the investor, such as a sale made by the associate to the investor. A *downstream transaction* involves the movement of assets from the investor to the associate, such as a sale made by the investor to the associate.

An investor recognizes in its financial statements the results of either transaction only to the extent of the proportional interests of unrelated investors in the associate. Thus, the investor does not recognize its own share in the associate's profit or loss resulting from upstream and downstream transactions.

EXAMPLE 11.3

Medic First Response Corporation sells €100,000 of first aid supplies to its 25 percent owned associate, Retail First Response. The cost to Medic of the inventory is €60,000.

Medic initially records a profit of €40,000 on the sale to Retail, but it also must reduce the profit by its 25 percent ownership of Retail, resulting in a €30,000 profit. Medic must defer recognition of the remaining profit until Retail sells the inventory to an independent third party.

How Do I Disclose Investments in Associates?

The investor should make the following disclosures regarding its investments in associates:

- ○ *Contingent liabilities.* The investor's share of the contingent liabilities of an associate that it has jointly incurred with other investors, as well as contingent liabilities caused by the investor being severally liable for liabilities
- ○ *Equity method.* Whether or not the investor accounts for an associate using the equity method
- ○ *Fair values.* The fair value of investments in associates if there are published price quotations
- ○ *Financial information – nonequity method.* The amounts of total assets, total liabilities, revenue, and profit or loss for those associates not accounted for using the equity method
- ○ *Financial information.* Aggregated amounts of the assets, liabilities, revenue, and profit or loss of associates
- ○ *Reporting date.* The end of the reporting period of the associate's financial statements that are used in applying the equity method, if that date varies from the date used by the investor, and the reason for the difference in dates
- ○ *Share of associate results.* The investor's share of the profit or loss of its associates, as well as the carrying amount of those investments, and its share of any discontinued operations
- ○ *Significant influence presumption.* The reasons why the investor has significant influence over the associate despite having less than 20 percent voting power over it
- ○ *Transfer restrictions.* The nature and extent of any significant restrictions on the ability of any associates to transfer funds to the investor

○ *Unrecognized losses.* The investor's unrecognized share of losses in any associates, both for the current period and cumulatively (applies only if the investor has stopped recognizing its share of the losses of associates)

CHAPTER 12

INVENTORY

 What Is the Definition of Inventory?

Inventory is an asset held for sale in the ordinary course of business, or that is in the process of being produced for sale, or the materials or supplies intended for consumption in the production process. This can include items purchased and held for resale. In the case of services, inventory can be the costs of a service for which related revenue has not yet been recognized.

 What Is Net Realizable Value?

Net realizable value is the estimated selling price of inventory, minus its estimated cost of completion and any estimated cost to complete its sale. Thus, it is the net amount realized from the sale of inventory. Net realizable value may not equal fair value.

 How Is Fair Value Used in Relation to Inventory?

Fair value is the amount for which inventory could be exchanged between knowledgeable and willing parties in a marketplace transaction. Fair value may not equal net realizable value.

 What Costs Can I Include in Inventory?

Include in the cost of inventory all costs to purchase inventory and convert it to its final form, and any other costs incurred to bring the inventory to its present location and condition. Thus, the following costs can be included in the cost of inventory:

- Direct labor
- Freight

○ Handling
○ Import duties and related taxes
○ Overhead for fixed and variable production costs
○ Purchase price

It is acceptable to include in inventory the cost of designing a product for a specific customer, but the cost allocation must be to the inventory designed for that customer.

Fixed production overhead costs include those costs that remain stable regardless of production volume, such as equipment and building maintenance, depreciation, and factory administration and management. *Variable production overhead costs* include those costs that vary approximately with production volume.

Deduct from the cost of inventory any import duties or other taxes that subsequently are recovered. Also, deduct any trade discounts or rebates related to the inventory.

Do not include in inventory any of the following items:

○ Abnormal waste related to materials, labor, or other production costs
○ Administrative costs
○ Foreign exchange differences arising from the purchase of inventory
○ Interest costs associated with deferred payment terms
○ Selling costs
○ Storage costs, unless they are incurred as part of the production process

EXAMPLE 12.1

Branxholm Industries produces Scottish plaid garments for export throughout Europe. Branxholm has incurred the following expenses, which are itemized in the table as being included in the cost of inventory or charged to expense in the current period:

Category	Amount Incurred	Include in Inventory	Charge to Expense
Accounting department costs	£58,000		£58,000
Dye purchases	229,000	£229,000	
Equipment maintenance	142,000	142,000	

Equipment depreciation	93,000	93,000	
Fleece purchases	1,580,000	1,580,000	
Freight on purchases	42,000	42,000	
Import broker commission	10,000	10,000	
Import duties	19,000	19,000	
Insurance on purchases	12,000	12,000	
Longshoreman handling fees	11,000	11,000	
Sales commission	28,000		28,000
Trade discounts on purchases	−30,000	−30,000	
Warranty costs	21,000		21,000
Totals	£2,215,000	£2,108,000	£107,000

Example 12.2

Provence Panache, maker of stylish women's clothes, installs a FIFO inventory system. The following table shows the FIFO cost calculations for a single inventory item, product number BK0043. The first row indicates the origination of the first layer of inventory, resulting in 50 units of inventory at a per-unit cost of €10.00. In the second row, the monthly inventory usage is 350 units. Under the FIFO system, Provence uses the entire stock of 50 inventory units that were left over at the end of the preceding month, as well as 300 units that were purchased in the current month. This wipes out the first layer of inventory, leaving Provence with a single new layer that is composed of 700 units at a cost of €9.58 per unit. In the third row, there are 400 units of usage, which again come from the first inventory layer, shrinking it down to just 300 units. However, since extra stock was purchased in the same period, Provence now has an extra inventory layer that comprises 250 units, at a cost of €10.65 per unit. The rest of the exhibit proceeds using the same FIFO layering assumptions.

(*Continued*)

EXAMPLE 12.2 (CONTINUED)

FIFO
Costing
Part Number BK0043

Column 1 Date Purchased	Column 2 Quantity Purchased	Column 3 Cost per Unit	Column 4 Monthly Usage	Column 5 Net Inventory Remaining	Column 6 Cost of 1st Inventory Layer	Column 7 Cost of 2nd Inventory Layer	Column 8 Extended Inventory Cost
05/03/10	500	€ 10.00	450	50	(50 × €10.00)	—	€ 500
06/04/10	1,000	€ 9.58	350	700	(700 × €9.58)	—	€ 6,706
07/11/10	250	€10.65	400	550	(300 × €9.58)	(250 × €10.65)	€ 5,537
08/01/10	475	€10.25	350	675	(200 × €10.65)	(475 × €10.25)	€ 6,999
08/30/10	375	€10.40	400	650	(275 × €10.25)	(375 × €10.40)	€ 6,719
09/09/10	850	€ 9.50	700	800	(800 × €9.50)	—	€ 7,600
12/12/10	700	€ 9.75	900	600	(600 × €9.75)	—	€ 5,850
05/07/11	200	€10.80	0	800	(600 × €9.75)	(200 × €10.80)	€ 8,010

What Costs Can I Include in Service Inventory?

Any unbilled services can be charged to inventory at their labor cost. Usually, these costs comprise the labor and related costs of those personnel engaged in providing a billable service. This can include the cost of supervisory personnel and overhead, as long as these costs are eventually to be billed. The cost of nonbillable personnel must be charged to expense in the period incurred.

What Costs Can I Assign to Agricultural Inventory?

Agricultural produce is measured when it is harvested at its fair value minus the estimated cost to sell it.

What Methods Are Acceptable for Measuring Inventory?

The default cost assignment methodology is either the *first-in, first-out* (FIFO) or *weighted average* method. The FIFO method assumes that those items purchased first are consumed first, thereby leaving the most recently purchased items still in stock at the end of the reporting period.

The weighted average method assigns costs based on the weighted average of the cost of similar items in stock at the beginning of or acquired during the reporting period.

EXAMPLE 12.3
Provence Panache considers switching to a weighted average inventory system. Provence's controller elects to model the results of the system using the same transactions just noted for its FIFO costing system. The results appear in the following table. The first row shows that Provence had a remainder of 50 units in stock, at a cost of €10.00. Since there has been only one purchase so far, the controller easily can calculate that the total inventory valuation is €500 by multiplying the unit cost of €10.00 in column 3 by the number of units remaining in stock, as shown in column 6.
In the second row, Provence has purchased another 1,000 units at a cost of €9.58 per unit. After monthly usage, there are 700 units in stock, of which *(Continued)*

> (*Continued*)
> 650 were added from the most recent purchase.
> To determine the new weighted average cost of the in-
> ventory, the controller first determines the extended
> cost of this newest inventory addition. As shown in col-
> umn 7, he arrives at a cost of €6,227 by multiplying the
> value in column 3 by the value in column 6. The con-
> troller then adds this amount to the existing
> total inventory valuation (€6,227 + €500) to arrive at
> the new extended inventory cost of €6,727, as shown
> in column 8. Finally, the controller divides the new
> extended cost in column 8 by the total number of units
> now in stock, as shown in column 5, to arrive at the
> new per-unit cost of €9.61 The rest of the exhibit pro-
> ceeds using the same weighted average calculations.
> (*Continued*)

It is acceptable to use the *standard cost* method to measure the cost of inventory, as long as the results approximate actual cost. Under this method, a standard cost is
assigned to each inventory item for costing purposes; the
standard cost is compared with actual costs periodically
and adjusted to match the actual cost; it is a simplified
way to track costs with reduced effort. The standard costs
assigned to an inventory item should assume normal usage levels for materials, supplies, labor, and facility
utilization.

It is also acceptable to use the *retail method*, which is
used in the retail industry for measuring large volumes of
items having similar margins. Under this approach, reduce the sales value of the inventory by a percentage
gross margin that is based on actual results to arrive at
the estimated inventory cost. If the gross margin varies
substantially by retail department, it is allowable to make
a separate calculation for each department, using the
gross margin that pertains to each one.

The assignment of specific costs to individual inventory items is required when goods are produced for specific projects. However, *specific identification* of costs is not
appropriate when there are many interchangeable inventory items.

The *last-in, first-out* (LIFO) method is specifically
excluded from use in all situations.

A company should use the same cost assignment
method for all inventories of a similar nature and having
a similar use to the company. If inventory does not have

EXAMPLE 12.3 (CONTINUED)

Weighted Average Costing
Part Number BK0043

Column 1 Date Purchased	Column 2 Quantity Purchased	Column 3 Cost per Unit	Column 4 Monthly Usage	Column 5 Net Inventory Remaining	Column 6 Net Change in Inventory During Period	Column 7 Extended Cost of New Inventory Layer	Column 8 Extended Inventory Cost	Column 9 Average Inventory Cost/ Unit
05/03/10	500	€ 10.00	450	50	50	€ 500.00	€ 500.00	€ 10.00
06/04/10	1,000	€ 9.58	350	700	650	€ 6,227.00	€ 6,727.00	€ 9.61
07/11/10	250	€ 10.65	400	550	−150	€ 0.00	€ 5,285.50	€ 9.61
08/01/10	475	€ 10.25	350	675	125	€ 1,281.25	€ 6,566.75	€ 9.73
08/30/10	375	€ 10.40	400	650	−25	€ 0.00	€ 6,323.54	€ 9.73
09/09/10	850	€ 9.50	700	800	150	€ 1,425.00	€ 7,748.54	€ 9.69
12/12/10	700	€ 9.75	900	600	−200	€ 0.00	€ 5,811.40	€ 9.69
05/07/11	200	€ 10.80	0	800	200	€ 2,160.00	€ 7,971.40	€ 9.96

the same nature or use, then it is allowable to use different cost assignment methods. For example, different methods may be allowable for inventory located in different divisions, but not allowable merely because the inventory is located in different geographical regions.

What Controls Do I Use for Inventory Valuation?

The following controls over inventory valuation are useful, irrespective of the specific method of inventory valuation used:

- ○ *Compare unextended product costs with those for prior periods.* Product costs of all types can change for a variety of reasons. An easy way to spot these changes is to create and regularly review a report that compares the unextended cost of each product with its cost in a prior period.
- ○ *Review sorted list of extended product costs in declining cost order.* This report lists the extended cost of all inventory on hand for each inventory item, sorted in declining order of cost. Scanning the report readily reveals those items that have unusually large or small valuations.
- ○ *Investigate entries made to the inventory or cost of goods sold accounts.* Because the inventory and cost of goods sold accounts are so large, it is more common for employees attempting to hide fraudulent transactions to dump them into these accounts. Accordingly, part of the standard month-end closing procedure should include the printing and analysis of a report listing only the manual journal entries made to these two accounts.

If standard costing is used, then consider the following controls to guard against unauthorized costing changes:

- ○ *Review the bill of materials and labor routing change log.* Alterations to the bill of materials or labor routing files can have a significant impact on the inventory valuation. To guard against unauthorized changes to these records, enable the transaction change log of the software (if such a feature exists) and incorporate a review of the change log into the month-end valuation calculation procedure.
- ○ *Control updates to bill of materials and labor routing costs.* The key sources of standard costing information are the bill of materials and labor routing records. One easily can make a few modifications to

these records in order to substantially alter inventory costs. To prevent such changes from occurring, always impose strict security access over these records, and review a usage log to review record changes.

○ *Review variances from standard cost.* When the materials management department creates a standard cost for an item, it is usually intended to be a very close approximation of the current market price for that item. Consequently, consider running a monthly report comparing the standard cost and most recent price paid for all items, with only those items appearing on the report for which a significant variance has occurred.

How Do I Allocate Overhead Costs to Inventory?

Allocate fixed overhead costs to inventory based on the *normal capacity* of the production facilities. Normal capacity is the average level of production expected over multiple time periods and under normal circumstances, incorporating a normal amount of planned maintenance. It is acceptable to use the actual production level as the basis for this calculation, as long as actual production approximates normal production.

It is not acceptable to alter the amount of the fixed overhead allocation if actual production activity is unusually low. This holds true even if the plant is idle; the normal amount of fixed overhead costs should still be charged to expense during that time. However, an unusually high production period calls for a reduction of the fixed overhead allocation in order to avoid allocating more cost to inventory than actually exists in the cost pool. Without making this adjustment, inventory would be recorded above cost.

The formula for allocating variable overhead costs is much simpler—just allocate these costs to each unit of production based on actual production volumes.

If overhead costs cannot be allocated, then charge them to expense in the period incurred.

What Controls Do I Use for Overhead Allocation?

If there is a significant amount of overhead allocated to inventory, use the following controls to ensure that the allocation is performed correctly:

○ *Verify the calculation and allocation of overhead cost pools.* Clearly define which costs to include in the overhead cost pools and precisely how they are to be allocated. In addition, review the types of costs included in the calculations, verify that the correct proportions of these costs are included, and ensure that the costs are being correctly allocated to inventory. A further control is to track the total amount of overhead accumulated in each reporting period — any sudden change in the amount may indicate an error in the overhead cost summarization.

○ *Audit production setup cost calculations.* If the overhead related to production runs is allocated based on the presumed length of the production runs, there is a possibility of substantial costing errors if the assumed number of units produced in a production run is incorrect. For example, if the cost of a production setup is €1,000 and the production run is 1,000 units, then the setup cost should be €1 per unit. To artificially increase the inventory valuation in order to increase profits, the assumed production run size could be reduced to 100 units; the cost per unit would increase tenfold to €10, and this amount could be stored in inventory. A reasonable control is to regularly review setup cost calculations. As an early warning indicator of this problem, you can run and review a report comparing setup costs over time for each product to see if there are any sudden changes in costs.

 ## How Do I Write Down the Value of Inventory?

Always measure inventory at the *lower* of its cost or its net realizable value. *Net realizable value* is the estimated selling price of the inventory, minus its estimated cost of completion and any estimated cost to complete the sale. A write-down to net realizable value may be necessary in the following situations:

○ Inventory is damaged
○ Inventory is obsolete
○ The cost of completion has increased
○ The selling price has declined
○ The cost to complete the sale has increased

Do not write down the value of raw materials if the finished goods into which they are incorporated are expected to sell at or above cost. However, if a subsequent raw materials price decline indicates that the cost of those finished goods exceeds their net realizable value, then write down the raw materials to their net realizable value (which is likely to be their replacement cost).

The write-down to net realizable value is normally on an individual item basis, but can apply to a group of related items that cannot practicably be evaluated individually. However, it is not appropriate to write down the value of an entire class of inventory, such as work-in-process or finished goods.

EXAMPLE 12.4

Bergschrund Designs is a German manufacturer of climbing equipment. It has five major product lines, which are noted in the following table. At its fiscal year-end, Bergschrund calculates the lower of its cost or net realizable value (NRV) as follows:

Product Line	Quantity on Hand	Unit Cost	Inventory at Cost	NRV per Unit	Lower of Cost or NRV
Footwear	2,000	€190	€380,000	€230	€380,000
Ice tools	500	140	70,000	170	70,000
Outerwear	950	135	128,250	120	114,000
Ropes	1,250	180	225,000	140	175,000
Tents	780	270	210,600	350	210,600

Based on the table, the net realizable value is lower than cost on the outerwear and rope product lines. Accordingly, Bergschrund should recognize a loss on the outerwear product line of €14,250 (€128,250 − €114,000) and a loss on the rope product line of €50,000 (€225,000 − €175,000).

When Do I Write Down the Value of Inventory?

Conduct the assessment when circumstances arise that indicate that the net realizable value has declined below the product cost, and charge any write-down to expense at that time. Continue to assess the situation in each subsequent period until circumstances causing the write-down have abated.

Can I Reverse an Inventory Write-Down?

Yes. You can reverse a write-down to the extent of the original write-down. Record it as a reduction in the amount of inventories recognized as an expense in the period when the valuation reversal occurs.

 What Controls Do I Use for Inventory Write-Downs?

The following controls are sufficient for ensuring that inventory is written down to the lower of cost or net realizable value on a regular basis:

- ○ *Follow a schedule of net realizable value reviews.* The primary difficulty with NRV reviews is that they are not done at all. Adding them to the financial closing procedure, at least on a quarterly basis, will ensure that they are completed regularly.
- ○ *Follow a standard procedure for net realizable value reviews.* It is not uncommon for an NRV review to be very informal — perhaps a brief discussion with the purchasing staff once a year regarding pricing levels for a few major items. This approach does not ensure that all valuation problems will be uncovered. A better approach is to formulate a standard NRV procedure and follow it rigorously.

 When Do I Charge Inventory Costs to Expense?

Charge inventory costs to expense when you recognize the revenue related to the sale of the inventory.

 How Do I Allocate Production Costs to By-Products?

If a production process produces multiple products and the cost of producing each one are not separately identifiable, then allocate production costs to each one on a rational and consistent basis. This means that a variety of systems may be used, as long as they are defensible and are used consistently over time. For example, the allocation can be based on the sales value of each of the produced items. Alternatively, if there is a main product and a by-product, measure the net realizable value of the by-product and deduct it from the cost of the main product.

EXAMPLE 12.5

Patra Pistachio is a pistachio nut processor that is based in Greece. Its staff hand-picks pistachio nuts, peels the shells, and processes the nuts for shipment. It sells the shells as a by-product. Patra incurred €80,000 to pick and process a recent batch of pistachio nuts. Of this amount, it incurred €60,000 through the point when the shells were peeled from the nuts. Patra assigns this cost to the nut and shell products based on their relative sales value at the split-off point.

At the split-off point, Patra can sell the nuts for €130,000 and the shells for €5,000, for a total sales value of €135,000. Thus, Patra assigns €57,778 of the cost to the nuts and €2,222 of the cost to the shells based on the following formula:

Item	Calculation		Result
Nuts	(€130,000 sales value ÷ €135,000 total sales value) × €60,000	=	€57,778
Shells	(€5,000 sales value ÷ €135,000 total sales value) × €60,000	=	€ 2,222
	Total		€60,000

In addition, Patra assigns the remaining €20,000 of subsequent processing costs solely to the pistachio nuts, since this processing no longer involves the shells. Thus, the total cost assigned to the nuts is €77,778 and to the shells, €2,222.

What Happens to Inventory Included in Fixed Assets?

If an inventory item is incorporated into the construction of a fixed asset, then include its costs in the accumulated cost of the fixed asset. Then charge the cost of the fixed asset to expense over the useful life of the fixed asset through a systematic method of depreciation.

What Inventory Information Do I Disclose?

Disclose the following information related to inventory:

○ The accounting policies used when measuring inventory

○ The total carrying amount of inventory, by classification (sample classifications are raw materials, work-in-progress, finished goods, supplies, and merchandise; a service provider can categorize its services inventory as work-in-progress)

○ The total carrying amount of inventory at its fair value, less costs to sell

○ The amount of inventory charged to expense during the period

○ The amount of any inventory write-down during the period

○ The amount of any write-down reversal during the period

○ The reason for the write-down reversal

○ The carrying amount of inventory pledged as collateral

CHAPTER 13

PROPERTY, PLANT, AND EQUIPMENT

 What Is Property, Plant, and Equipment?

Property, plant, and equipment (PP&E) are tangible items that are expected to be used in more than one period and that are used in production, for rental, or for administration. This can include items acquired for safety or environmental reasons, since they may be necessary for deriving future economic benefits from other assets.

 What Is a Class of PP&E?

A PP&E class is a group of assets having a similar nature and use. Most PP&E items should belong to a single class, which impacts the type of depreciation used and whether the items are to be periodically revalued. Sample classes are:

Aircraft	Machinery
Buildings	Motor vehicles
Furniture and fixtures	Office equipment
Land	Ships

 What Costs Do I Include in PP&E?

In general, the costs to include in PP&E are an item's purchase cost and any costs incurred to bring the asset to the location and condition needed for it to operate in the manner intended by management. More specifically, include the following costs in PP&E:

- ○ Purchase price of the item and related taxes
- ○ Construction cost of the item, which can include labor and employee benefits

- Import duties
- Inbound freight and handling
- Site preparation
- Installation and assembly
- Asset start-up testing
- Professional fees
- Estimated cost to subsequently dismantle and re-move the item, if this is an obligation
- Less: trade discounts and rebates
- Less: net proceeds from the sale of any items pro-duced during initial testing

EXAMPLE 13.1

Patra Pistachio is building a new pistachio nut proc-essing facility in Preveza, Greece. The following table shows the costs it incurs for the Preveza facility, and whether they can be capitalized or should be charged to expense as incurred:

Cost Type	Expenditure	Capitalized	Expensed
Accounting charges	€65,000		€65,000
Architect's fees	280,000	€280,000	
Borrowing costs	185,000	185,000	
Construction cost	4,095,000	4,095,000	
Estimated dismantling cost	320,000	320,000	
Operating losses	150,000		150,000
Sale of tested items	−25,000	−25,000	
Shipping and handling	410,000	410,000	
Site preparation	500,000	500,000	
Start-up testing	100,000	100,000	
Totals	€6,080,000	€5,865,000	€215,000

Also, include in PP&E the cost of major periodic re-placements. For example, an aircraft requires new engines and a building requires a new roof after a certain usage interval or time period. Upon replacement, the new items are recorded in PP&E, and the carrying amounts of any replaced items are derecognized.

EXAMPLE 13.2

Afjord Defense & Aerospace, operator of the Andoya Rocket Range in northern Norway, uses a €175,000 tractor to haul sounding rockets to its launch towers. Seven years after it purchased the tractor, the tractor engine fails and must be replaced. A new engine costs €75,000. A new engine provides economic benefits and its cost can be measured, so Afjord should recognize it as an asset.

The original invoice for the tractor did not separately specify the cost of the engine, so Afjord can use the cost of the replacement engine as the basis for determining the cost of the original engine. To do so, it uses its 6 percent cost of capital to discount the €75,000 engine for seven years, yielding a discounted cost of €49,880 (€75,000 × 0.66506).

Afjord then eliminates the €49,880 cost of the original engine from the asset record and adds the new engine, resulting in a total new tractor cost of €200,120 (€175,000 − €49,880 + €75,000).

It may be necessary to perform periodic major inspections of an asset for faults, even if parts will not require replacement. This is a common requirement for airplanes, boilers, and elevators. The cost of each such inspection is included in the cost of the PP&E item, and any remaining carrying amount of the preceding inspection is derecognized.

 ## What Costs Do I *Not* Include in PP&E?

Do *not* include the following costs in PP&E:

- Administration and general overhead costs
- Costs incurred after an asset is ready for use, but has not yet been used or is not yet operating at full capacity
- Costs incurred that are not necessary to bring the asset to the location and condition necessary for it to operate
- Initial operating losses
- New customer acquisition costs
- New facility opening costs
- New product or service introduction costs
- Relocation or reorganization costs

Do not recognize in PP&E the ongoing costs of servicing a PP&E item, which typically includes maintenance labor, consumables, and minor maintenance parts; these costs instead should be charged to expense as incurred.

If a PP&E item is self-constructed, the cost of any abnormal waste related to materials, labor, or other resources cannot be included in the asset cost.

When Do I Stop Accumulating Costs in PP&E?

Recognize costs in the carrying amount of PP&E only until the item is in the location and condition for it to be *capable of* operating in the manner intended by management. Thus, no further costs should be added to PP&E once the asset achieves this status, even if it actually is not yet used in the manner intended by management.

When Can I Include Borrowing Costs in PP&E?

You can include borrowing costs only for those assets that take a substantial period of time to prepare for use. This does not include assets that are ready for their intended use when acquired. Within this restriction, you can capitalize borrowing costs that are directly attributable to a PP&E item as part of its cost, if the borrowing costs can be reliably measured and will result in future economic benefits.

How Do I Calculate Borrowing Costs to Include in PP&E?

Generally, borrowing costs attributable to a PP&E item are those that otherwise would have been avoided if the asset had not been acquired. There are two ways to determine the borrowing costs to include in PP&E:

○ *Directly attributable borrowing costs.* If borrowings were incurred specifically to obtain the asset, then the borrowing cost to be capitalized is the actual borrowing cost incurred, minus any investment income earned from the interim investment of those borrowings.

○ *Borrowing costs from a general fund.* Borrowings may be handled centrally for general corporate needs and may be obtained through a variety of debt instruments. In this case, derive an interest rate from the weighted average of the entity's borrowing costs during the period applicable to the asset. The amount of allowable borrowing costs using this method is capped at the entity's total borrowing costs during the applicable period.

Example 13.3

The Arabian Knights security company is building a new world headquarters in Westminster, near New Scotland Yard. Arabian made payments of £25,000,000 on January 1 and £40,000,000 on July 1; the building was completed on December 31.

For the construction period, Arabian can capitalize the full £25,000,000 of the first payment and half of the second payment, as noted in the following table:

Date	Payment	Capitalization Period*	Average Payment
1/1	£25,000,000	12/12	£25,000,000
7/1	40,000,000	6/12	20,000,000
			£45,000,000

*The number of months between the payment date and the date when interest capitalization ends

During this time, Arabian has a loan outstanding on which it pays 7.5 percent interest. The amount of interest cost it can capitalize as part of the construction project is £3,375,000 (£45,000,000 × 7.5% interest).

You can begin capitalizing the borrowing costs associated with an asset when the entity begins incurring expenditures and borrowing costs for the asset, and begins preparing the asset for its intended use. This does not include the period when an asset is being held without any activities that change the asset's condition.

Example 13.4

Florentine Flatware is constructing a new corporate headquarters. It has acquired land in Scandicci, on the outskirts of Florence, for this purpose and is engaged
(*Continued*)

(*Continued*)
in obtaining a variety of building permits. In the meantime, there is no activity to alter the land. Florentine cannot capitalize any borrowing costs until it begins to develop the property.

Also, if you suspend active development of an asset for an extended period, you cannot capitalize borrowing costs during that time. This restriction does not apply if the entity continues to engage in substantial technical and administrative work related to the asset, or if a temporary delay is a necessary part of the asset preparation process.

EXAMPLE 13.5

Bergschrund Designs is constructing a new facility in Niedernach, Germany, near the Austrian border. The facility is located in the middle of a roe deer migration path, so the town council requires Bergschrund to shut down construction activities during the April through May migration period. Since this delay is a necessary part of construction, Bergschrund can continue to capitalize borrowing costs during the shutdown period.

Capitalization of borrowing costs terminates when the entity has substantially completed all activities needed to prepare the asset for its intended use. Substantial completion is assumed to have occurred when physical construction is complete; work on minor modifications will not extend the capitalization period. If the entity is constructing multiple parts of a project and it can use some parts while construction continues on other parts, then it should stop capitalization of borrowing costs on parts as they are completed.

EXAMPLE 13.6

Danish Energy is constructing a wind farm off the coast of Hanstholm, in Denmark. It can begin using each of the wind turbines as they are completed, so it stops capitalizing the borrowing costs related to each one as soon as it becomes usable.

Calculate the borrowing costs in any period by multiplying the interest rate by the average carrying amount of the asset during the period.

 ## When Do I Recognize Spare Parts as PP&E?

Major spare parts can qualify as PP&E if there is an expectation of using them for more than one period. Also, if spare parts and servicing equipment are used only with PP&E, then account for them as PP&E.

 ## What Is the Residual Value of an Asset?

An asset's residual value is the estimated amount that the owner currently would obtain by disposing of the asset, less any disposal cost, assuming that the asset is of the expected age and condition at the end of its useful life.

Review the residual value of an asset at least at the end of each fiscal year. If the estimate changes, then account for it as a change in accounting estimate (see the Changes in Accounting Policies, Estimates, and Errors chapter).

 ## Should I Aggregate Assets into a Single PP&E Asset?

It is acceptable to account for multiple items as a single PP&E asset if the items are individually insignificant. Examples of such items are molds, tools, and dies.

 ## How Do I Account for an Exchange of Assets?

When a PP&E item is acquired in exchange for another nonmonetary asset, measure the acquired asset at its fair value. However, do not measure it at fair value if the exchange lacks commercial substance or it is not possible to reliably measure the asset received or the asset given up. If it is not possible to measure at fair value, then measure the acquired asset at the carrying amount of the asset given up. If the fair values of both the acquired asset and the asset given up are available, then use the fair value of the asset given up to measure the cost of the acquired asset.

An asset exchange has commercial substance if:

○ The risk, timing, and amount of the post-tax cash flows of the acquired asset vary from those of the transferred asset, and the difference is significant relative to the fair value of the asset exchanged; or
○ The acquiring entity's value is affected by the exchange, and the difference is significant relative to the fair value of the asset exchanged.

It is possible to reliably measure the fair value of an acquired asset if there is not a significant variability in the range of fair value estimates, or it is possible to assess the probabilities associated with each estimate.

 ## How Do I Subsequently Measure PP&E?

You can either carry an asset at its cost or periodically revalue it to its fair value. In either case, subsequent measurement must include reductions for any accumulated depreciation and impairment losses. If you choose to revalue a single asset, then you also must revalue the entire class of PP&E to which it belongs, in order to avoid selective revaluation. It is acceptable to revalue a class of assets on a rolling basis, as long as the revaluation is completed within a short period of time.

If you choose periodic revaluation, then conduct revaluations with sufficient regularity to ensure that the carrying amount does not vary significantly from its fair value. For those PP&E items having significant and volatile changes in fair value, it may be necessary to revalue annually. When there are insignificant changes in fair value, a revaluation once every three to five years is sufficient.

Revaluations normally are conducted by the following means:

Asset Type	Source
Buildings	Professionally qualified valuers
Equipment	Market value determined by appraisal
Land	Professionally qualified valuers

In all of the above cases, if there is no market-based evidence of fair value, it is allowable to estimate fair value using either the income or depreciated replacement cost methods.

How Do I Account for Revaluations?

Use the following table to determine the proper accounting for an asset that has been revalued:

Asset value increases	Recognize in other comprehensive income and as "revaluation surplus" in equity
Asset value increases, but reverses a prior revaluation decrease	Recognize as profit to the extent that it reverses a revaluation decrease previously recognized in profit or loss
Asset value decreases	Recognize as a loss
Asset value decreases, but credit balance exists in the revaluation surplus for the asset	Recognize in other comprehensive income to the extent of any revaluation surplus for the asset, with any excess recognized as a loss

EXAMPLE 13.7

Gothic Designs creates elaborate church pews. It owns a three-dimensional CNC router that automatically carves six pews at once. Gothic bought the router for £600,000. It elects to revalue the router at three-year intervals. At the first revaluation, the router has accumulated £150,000 of depreciation, and an appraiser assigns a fair value of £475,000 to the router. Gothic's controller creates the following entry to eliminate the existing accumulated depreciation:

	Debit	Credit
Accumulated depreciation	150,000	
Equipment		150,000

In addition, Gothic's controller creates the following entry to increase the net asset value of the router to its fair value:

	Debit	Credit
Equipment	25,000	
Other comprehensive income—gain on revaluation		25,000

(Continued)

(*Continued*)

Three years later, the next revaluation reveals a fair value decline of £30,000. The following entry records the transaction:

	Debit	Credit
Other comprehensive income—gain on revaluation	25,000	
Loss on revaluation—equipment	5,000	
Equipment		30,000

When an asset is retired or disposed of, transfer any revaluation surplus for that item to retained earnings. You also can transfer that portion of a revaluation surplus to retained earnings that is the difference between the depreciation on the original and revalued asset costs.

 ## What Controls Do I Use for Asset Valuation?

The compilation of costs to be assigned to a fixed asset can be a complex process that resists automation, so use the following controls to mitigate the risk of an incorrect capitalized cost:

- ○ *Procedure*. A procedure should detail capitalization limits, costs to include and exclude, the contents of a project binder, and a summary of the applicable accounting standards.
- ○ *Project Binder*. A project binder contains a summary of the costs included in the capitalized cost of an asset and also may include copies of the invoices for larger asset components. It also includes descriptions of subsequent asset revaluations and related appraisal documents, additions, and deletions.
- ○ *Audit*. The internal audit staff should review a selection of the project binders to ensure compliance with the asset capitalization procedure, and make note of exceptions that can be addressed through subsequent retraining and procedure changes.

 ## Which Assets Are Not Depreciated?

Land is not depreciated, since it has an unlimited useful life. If land has a limited useful life, as is the case with a quarry, then it is acceptable to depreciate it over its useful life. If the cost of land includes any costs incurred for site dismantlement and/or restoration, then depreciate these costs over the period in which any resulting benefits are obtained.

If an entity acquires a parcel of land that includes a building, then separate the two assets and depreciate the building.

 ## How Do I Aggregate and Disaggregate Items for Depreciation?

In general, separately depreciate each part of a PP&E item having a proportionally significant cost. For example, it may be necessary to separately depreciate the airframe, engines, and seating of an airplane. Also, if some parts of a PP&E item are separately depreciated, then aggregate the remaining less significant parts for depreciation.

Conversely, it is allowable to group together multiple parts of a PP&E item for depreciation calculations if their useful lives and depreciation methods are similar.

 ## Over What Time Periods Do I Allocate Depreciation Expense?

Begin depreciating an asset when it is available for use, even if it is not actually in use at that time. Spread the depreciation on a systematic basis over the asset's useful life. Consider the following factors when determining an asset's useful life:

- ○ *Expected usage.* Refers to the expected volume of production output.
- ○ *Expected wear.* Can be impacted by such factors as the level of maintenance and the number of shifts over which the asset is used.
- ○ *Legal limits.* Can be caused by government-mandated usage levels or lease expiration dates, for example.
- ○ *Obsolescence.* Can be caused by changes in technology or market demand, for example.

Review the useful life of each asset at least at the end of every fiscal year. If the estimate changes, then account for it as a change in accounting estimate (see the Changes in Accounting Policies, Estimates, and Errors chapter).

EXAMPLE 13.8

Hadrian's Brewery, maker of the famous Hadrian's Premium Bitter, built a brewery in the village of Once Brewed, near Hadrian's Wall. Part of its brewing equipment is a large mash tun (for mashing), which has an original cost of £250,000. At the time of acquisition, management estimated that the mash tun would have a useful life of 10 years, with a residual value of £50,000. Thus, the depreciable asset value was £200,000 (£250,000 − £50,000).

At the end of year seven, management reviews both the useful life and residual value of the mash tun; it concludes that the useful life can be extended to 13 years, due to its use of a spray ball for periodic deep cleaning. Given the longer useful life and greater usage, however, the mash tun's residual value will likely decline to £25,000.

At the end of year seven, Hadrian's had accumulated £140,000 of depreciation on the mash tun. The original depreciable asset value of £200,000 has declined to £60,000 because of the ongoing depreciation, but is now increased by the £25,000 reduction in the mash tun's residual value, for a remaining depreciable asset value of £85,000. With the change in useful life, the mash tun can now be depreciated for six more years. Consequently, the future annual depreciation rate should be £14,167 (£85,000 ÷ 6 years).

Stop depreciating the asset at the earliest of the date when it is classified as being held for sale, when it is derecognized, or when it is fully depreciated. Thus, do not stop depreciating an asset simply because it is currently idle or retired from active use. However, if the asset is being depreciated based on some method of asset usage, then there may be no depreciation while the asset is not being used.

Charge all periodic depreciation to the accounting period in which it is incurred, except when the asset is used to produce other assets. In that case, charge the depreciation to the other assets. For example, depreciation on production equipment can be included in an overhead cost pool that then is allocated to the cost of inventory.

What Amount of an Asset Do I Depreciate?

The depreciable portion of an asset is its entire cost, less any residual value. In most cases, the residual value is so small as to be immaterial to the depreciation calculation.

Continue charging depreciation expense until such time as the asset's residual value matches its carrying value, and then stop.

 ## What Depreciation Method Should I Use?

Select a depreciation method that reflects the pattern in which the entity expects to consume the asset's future economic benefits.

Review the depreciation method applied to an asset at least at the end of each fiscal year, and revise the method if there has been a significant change in the pattern of consumption. This is a change in accounting estimate (see the Changes in Accounting Policies, Estimates, and Errors chapter).

The following depreciation methods are acceptable:

○ *Diminishing balance method.* Charges depreciation at a decreasing rate over the useful life of the asset.
○ *Straight-line method.* Charges depreciation at a constant rate over the useful life of the asset.
○ *Units of production method.* Charges depreciation based on expected usage.

EXAMPLE 13.9

Kittila Forest Products Company harvests timber in northern Finland and maintains a sawmill on the outskirts of Kittila.

Straight-line method. Kittila separately depreciates the building that houses its sawmill equipment. This structure cost €3,000,000 to construct and should be usable for 30 years, with no residual value. Given the steady usage pattern likely to occur, Kittila uses the straight-line depreciation method to depreciate it. The annual depreciation is €100,000 (€3,000,000 cost ÷ 30 years).

Diminishing balance method. Kittila finds that the band saws it uses in the sawmill wear out fast, and so
(Continued)

(Continued)
uses double-declining balance depreciation to reflect their rapid decline in value. Each band saw cost €40,000 and should be fully depreciated, with no residual value, after four years. The diminishing balance method requires use of twice the straight-line rate, multiplied by the book value at the beginning of the year. Any remaining asset value is fully depreciated in the final year. The calculation appears in the following table:

Beginning Balance		Straight-Line Rate		Rate Doubler		Annual Depreciation	Remaining Balance
€40,000	×	25%	×	2	=	€20,000	€20,000
€20,000	×	25%	×	2	=	€10,000	€10,000
€10,000	×	25%	×	2	=	€ 5,000	€ 5,000
€5,000	×	Remaining value			=	€ 5,000	€ 0

Units of production method. Kittila owns a grapple-skidder, for collecting downed timber. Its wear pattern is closely tied to the number of trees that it collects, so the units of production method is the most appropriate form of depreciation. The grapple-skidder cost €120,000 and has an estimated residual value of €20,000. Management estimates it can lift 200,000 trees during its estimated useful life, which results in per-unit depreciation of €0.5 (€100,000 depreciable value ÷ 200,000 units of production). In June, the grapple-skidder lifts 2,500 trees, so depreciation during that month is €1,250 (2,500 trees × €0.5/unit).

How Do I Handle Depreciation for Revalued Items?

When a PP&E item is revalued to its fair value, you have two available means for dealing with any accumulated depreciation:

1. Eliminate the accumulated depreciation against the gross carrying amount of the item, and restate its net amount to the revalued amount.
2. Make the carrying amount of the asset equal the revalued amount by restating the accumulated

depreciation proportionately with the change in the gross carrying amount.

 ## When Do I Derecognize an Asset?

An asset is derecognized upon its disposal, or when no future economic benefits can be expected from its use or disposal. Derecognition can arise from a variety of events, such as an asset's sale, scrapping, or donation.

 ## What Is the Accounting for Asset Derecognition?

You can recognize a gain or loss from an asset's derecognition, although a gain on derecognition cannot be recorded as revenue. The gain or loss on derecognition is calculated as the net disposal proceeds, minus the asset's carrying value.

If an entity replaces part of an asset, then that part is derecognized, even if the replaced part was not depreciated separately. If the entity cannot determine the carrying amount of the part that has been replaced, it can use the cost of the replacement part as a reasonable estimate of the cost of the part when the asset was acquired or built.

However, an entity may be in the business of routinely selling assets that it previously held for rental. If so, it transfers the assets to inventory, which then become held for sale; it can then recognize revenue upon their sale to a third party.

 ## What Property, Plant, and Equipment Information Do I Disclose?

Disclose the following information related to PP&E:

> *PP&E summary.* The following information for each class of PP&E:

- Carrying amount reconciliation during the period, showing additions, assets held for sale, acquisitions from business combinations, revaluation changes, impairment losses, depreciation, and net exchange differences caused by currency translation
- Depreciation methods used
- Gross carrying amount and accumulated depreciation at the beginning and end of the period

- Measurement bases used
- Useful lives used

○ *Borrowing costs.* The amount of any borrowing costs capitalized during the period, and the capitalization rate used

○ *Change in estimate.* Any changes in accounting estimate for residual values, useful lives, depreciation methods, or estimated costs to dismantle, remove, or restore PP&E items

○ *Commitments.* The amount of any contractual commitments to acquire PP&E

○ *Construction-in-progress.* The carrying amount of any PP&E items while under construction

○ *Dispositions.* The amount received from asset dispositions

○ *Restrictions.* Any restrictions on title to PP&E items, or PP&E pledged as collateral

○ *Revalued items.* For any revalued items, the date of the revaluation, whether an independent appraiser was used, the methods applied to estimate fair values, and the extent to which fair values were derived from market transactions; also, for each class of revalued items, the carrying amount that would have been recognized without a revaluation; finally, the revaluation surplus, any changes in it, and shareholder distribution restrictions for the surplus

○ *Other.* The following items are recommended for disclosure, but not required:

- Carrying amount of temporary PP&E
- Gross carrying amount of any fully depreciated PP&E still in use
- Carrying amount of any retired PP&E that is not held for sale
- When recording PP&E at cost, any asset fair values that are materially different from the carrying amounts

CHAPTER 14

INTANGIBLE ASSETS

 What Is an Intangible Item?

There are many types of intangible items, which generally fall into the following categories:

- ⊃ Intellectual property
- ⊃ Licenses
- ⊃ Market knowledge
- ⊃ Process or system implementation
- ⊃ Scientific or technical knowledge
- ⊃ Trademarks

All of the following are examples of intangible items:

Copyrights	Franchises	Mortgage servicing rights
Customer lists	Import quotas	Motion pictures
Customer loyalty	Market share	Patents
Customer relationships	Marketing rights	Software
Fishing licenses		

If an intangible item meets the criteria of identifiability, control over the resource, and the existence of future economic benefits (see the next question), then you can record it as an asset. If it does not meet all of these criteria, then recognize any expenses incurred to acquire or generate an intangible item when incurred. However, if you acquire the item in a business combination, then you may include it in the goodwill asset.

 What Are the Criteria an Item Must Meet to Be an Intangible Asset?

An intangible item must meet all of the following criteria in order to be recorded as an asset:

○ *Control.* The entity has the power to obtain the future economic benefits generated by the item, and can restrict the access of other entities to those benefits. This normally is demonstrated by having legal rights to the item, such as a copyright, patent, or restraint of trade agreement.

○ *Future economic benefits.* The item creates revenue, cost savings, or other benefits. For example, an entity has intellectual property that allows it to double the efficiency of a production line, thereby generating cost savings.

○ *Identifiability.* The item must be capable of being separated from the entity and exchanged, licensed, rented, sold, or transferred. Alternatively, the item must arise from contractual or other legal rights, even if those rights are not transferable.

How Do I Recognize an Intangible Asset?

If an item meets the definition of an intangible item and meets the criteria for an intangible asset, then you can record the expenditures associated with the item as an asset. These expenditures can include the costs incurred to acquire or create the item. Expenditures incurred to subsequently add to, replace part of, or maintain an intangible asset are almost always charged to expense in the period incurred, on the grounds that they cannot be distinguished from expenditures to develop the entire business.

EXAMPLE 14.1

Jackrabbit Ltd., purveyor of the Jackrabbit energy drink, expends 20 percent of its revenue on brand enhancement through such methods as triathlon and adventure athlete sponsorships and advertising at extreme sports events. These expenditures clearly support Jackrabbit's brand, but cannot be recorded as an intangible asset, because they cannot be distinguished from general business development expenditures.

Expenditures that cannot be included in the cost of an intangible asset are the costs of introducing a new product or service, or adding a new location or class of customer, and general overhead costs.

You can recognize an intangible asset only when you can reliably measure the cost of the asset, and it is probable that expected future economic benefits attributable to the asset will flow to the entity. You should assess the probability of expected future economic benefits using reasonable and supportable assumptions.

EXAMPLE 14.2

Grasp & Sons Door Handle Corporation has created a unique door handle design. It spends £25,000 in legal fees and £15,000 of in-house labor costs to register the patent. Later, it spends £50,000 in legal fees to defend the patent.

Grasp can record the initial £40,000 registration cost as an intangible asset, as long as it can identify future economic benefits associated with the patent. It must charge the defense costs to expense. Further, if it loses the lawsuit, this calls into question the viability of the asset, which may require Grasp to write down the asset's carrying value.

How Do I Recognize Acquired Intangible Assets?

If the entity acquires an intangible asset, then all of the previously noted recognition criteria are assumed to be satisfied. The following costs are included in the total cost of an acquired intangible asset:

- Purchase price
- Import duties
- Nonrefundable purchase taxes
- Directly attributable cost of preparing the asset for use, such as professional fees, labor, and testing (this does not include the cost of incidental operations not necessary to prepare the asset for use)
- Less: trade discounts and rebates

You must stop accumulating costs to be recorded as part of the intangible asset once it is capable of operating in the manner intended by management, nor can you include the cost of initial operating losses. Also, do not include the cost of redeploying an intangible asset.

If you defer payment for an intangible asset beyond normal credit terms, then record its purchase price as the cash price equivalent; record any cost above this amount as interest expense over the credit period.

 ## How Do I Recognize Intangible Assets Acquired through a Business Combination?

If you acquire an intangible asset in a business combination, then record its fair value at the acquisition date as its cost. Use the following four valuation methods, which are presented in declining order of preference:

1. *Bid price.* Use the asset's bid price in an active market.
2. *Most recent transaction.* If there are no current bid prices but there is an active market, then use the price of the most recent similar transaction, unless there has been a significant change in economic circumstances since the transaction date.
3. *Arm's-length transaction.* If there is no active market, then use the amount that the entity would pay for the asset in an arm's-length transaction between knowledgeable parties. You should consider the outcome of recent similar transactions when deriving this amount.
4. *Multiples or cash flows.* Apply a multiple, such as a revenue or profit multiple, to the asset's cash flows that reflects current market transactions. Alternatively, calculate its discounted estimated future cash flows.

The recognition of an intangible asset is separate from any goodwill recognized as part of a business combination.

If the intangible asset arises from contractual or other legal rights, there is enough information to measure its fair value.

EXAMPLE 14.3

Jolt Power Supply Company acquires Sodium Solutions, which manufactures sodium-sulphur batteries to store the electricity generated by wind farms. Sodium Solutions has a major in-process research and development project to create lower cost sodium-sulphur batteries. It is conducting the work under a €20,000,000 contract with Danish Energy, from which it expects discounted cash flows of €4,500,000. Jolt can use the discounted cash flows as the fair value of the research work and records €4,500,000 as the cost of the intangible asset.

If an acquired intangible asset may not be separated from another asset, then recognize the group of assets as a single asset separately from goodwill.

EXAMPLE 14.4

Düsseldorf Engineers acquires the well-known Arthur Bates Compton (ABC) consulting firm. Düsseldorf cannot separately value the ABC name, since it may not be sold separately from the customer list. Instead, Düsseldorf values the two intangible assets together as an asset group.

What Is a Class of Intangible Assets?

A class of intangible assets is a group of assets having a similar nature and use in an entity's operations. Examples of intangible asset classes are brand names, copyrights, franchises, licenses, models, patents, recipes, and software.

Are Web Site Development Costs an Intangible Asset?

Yes. You can record the development expenditures associated with the development stages of a web site as an intangible asset, but only if they meet the preceding control, future economic benefits, and identifiability criteria. If the web site only promotes the entity's own products and so cannot clearly show a stream of future economic benefits, then charge all expenditures related to its development to the period in which they are incurred.

Charge web site development costs to either an intangible asset or to expense based on the following categories of expenditure:

- ○ *Planning stage.* Charge to expense. This stage includes feasibility studies, defining specifications, evaluating alternatives, and selecting preferences.
- ○ *Application, infrastructure, and graphical design development stages.* Charge to the intangible asset if the expenditures meet the control, future economic

Exhibit 14.1   Cost Allocation Table

Expenditure Type	Charged to Expense	Capitalized
Feasibility study	√	
Define specifications	√	
Evaluate alternatives	√	
Final system selection	√	
Domain name procurement		√
Computer hardware		√
Software development		√
Application installation		√
Web page design		√
Stress testing		√
Overhead allocations	√	
System backups	√	
System maintenance	√	
General and administrative	√	

benefits, and identifiability criteria noted earlier. This stage includes obtaining a domain name, purchasing hardware, developing software, installing applications, designing web pages, and stress testing.

○ *Content development stage.* Charge to expense. This stage includes the creation, purchase, and uploading of information to the web site prior to completion of the web site.

○ *Operating stage.* Charge to expense. This stage includes maintenance and ongoing enhancements to the web site after initial development has been completed.

Exhibit 14.1 shows the proper accounting treatment of the various expenditures incurred to develop a web site.

Expenditures related to the advertising and promotion of an entity's own products and services should always be charged to expense.

The best estimate of a web site's useful life should be short, so the amortization of its carrying amount will be compressed.

How Do I Recognize Research and Development Expenditures?

If an entity incurs expenditures on a research and development project, then recognize them as an expense if they are research-related expenditures. You can record a development-related expenditure as an intangible asset only if it meets all of the following criteria:

- ○ *Completion intent.* The entity intends to complete the asset, and to either use or sell it.
- ○ *Feasibility.* It is technically feasible to make the asset available for use or sale.
- ○ *Future benefits.* There is a demonstrated ability to generate future economic benefits, such as the existence of a market for the asset or its output.
- ○ *Measurement.* The entity can reliably measure development-related expenditures for the asset.
- ○ *Resources.* There are adequate resources to complete the development process and use or sell the asset, which can be detailed in a business plan and supported by the entity's demonstrated ability to procure the necessary resources.
- ○ *Use intent.* The entity is able to use or sell the asset.

If an entity does not meet all of these requirements for a development project, then charge the expenditures to expense in the period incurred.

Examples of research activities include obtaining new knowledge, searching for research results, and searching for and selecting alternatives to current materials, products, and systems. Examples of development activities include the design, construction, and testing of prototypes, tools, molds, dies, pilot plants, and alternatives to existing materials, products, and systems.

EXAMPLE 14.5

Sodium Solutions is developing a new, lighter version of its sodium-sulphur battery that is to be used to store electricity from residential wind turbines. During Year 1, it expends €290,000 on basic research to create greater storage capacity. During Year 2, it incurs €200,000 per fiscal quarter to incorporate the new battery into its existing production process. At the beginning of the fourth quarter of Year 2, Sodium Solutions demonstrates that the improved production process meets the criteria for recognition as an intangible asset. Sodium also incurs €450,000 of expenditures in Year 3 to complete the development process.

Sodium Solutions can recognize €650,000 as an intangible asset. This is the expenditure it incurred since

(Continued)

> (*Continued*)
> the date when it met the recognition criteria. Sodium
> charges all of the expenditures it incurred prior to this
> date to expense.

Can I Recognize Past Expenses as Part of an Asset?

No. Once you record an expenditure as an expense, it is
not allowable to later recognize it as part of the cost of an
intangible asset.

How Do I Recognize an Intangible Asset Acquired through a Government Grant?

When a government transfers intangible assets to an
entity (such as fishing rights or airport landing rights), the
entity can record both the intangible asset and the grant
either at fair value or at a nominal amount plus any additional expenditures attributable to preparing the asset for
its intended use.

How Do I Recognize an Intangible Asset Acquired through a Nonmonetary Exchange?

If an entity acquires an intangible asset through a nonmonetary exchange, record the cost of the intangible asset
at its fair value. If the entity can determine the fair value of
either the asset received or the asset given up, then use the
fair value of the asset given up to measure the cost of the
asset received.

However, if the exchange lacks commercial substance
or if the fair values of either asset are not reliably measurable, then measure the cost of the asset received at the carrying amount of the asset given up. An exchange has
commercial substance if:

- The risk and timing of the cash flows of the asset received differ from the cash flows of the asset transferred, or
- The value of that portion of the entity's operations
  affected by the exchange changes because of the
  exchange; and

○ The difference in either of the preceding two items is significant in proportion to the fair value of the exchanged assets.

How Do I Measure Intangible Assets after Initial Recognition?

You can measure an intangible asset after its initial recognition using one of the following methods:

○ *Cost model.* Carry the asset at its cost, minus any accumulated amortization and impairment losses.

○ *Revaluation model.* Carry the asset at its periodically revalued fair value, minus any subsequent accumulated amortization and subsequent impairment losses. Revaluations should be sufficiently frequent to ensure that the asset's carrying amount does not differ materially from its fair value, with frequency being dictated by the volatility of fair values. This method can be used to revalue an intangible asset that was received as part of a government grant and initially recorded at a nominal amount.

   If you use this method for an asset, then you also must measure all other intangible assets in its class simultaneously and using the same model, unless there is no active market for those assets. A class of intangible assets is a group of assets having a similar nature and use.

It can be difficult to obtain a fair value for an intangible asset, since many assets, such as trademarks and patents, are by their nature unique. However, there is an active market for many types of licenses and quotas, and it can provide fair market information for a periodic revaluation.

If it is impossible to revalue an intangible asset, then carry it at its cost, minus any accumulated amortization and impairment losses.

If you revalue an intangible asset, there are two ways to treat any accumulated amortization outstanding as of the revaluation date:

1. *Proportional restatement.* Restate the accumulated depreciation so that it remains in the same proportion to the gross carrying amount, such that the carrying amount after revaluation matches its revalued amount.

2. *Elimination.* Eliminate the accumulated depreciation, so that the carrying amount of the asset matches its revalued amount.

EXAMPLE 14.6

Harlequin Taxi owns a taxi operator's license, which it acquired for €30,000. The license term is five years, after which the city government will auction it again to the highest bidder. Harlequin also can sell its rights to the license at any time, and there is an active market for doing so.

Harlequin has been amortizing the cost of the license using the straight-line method for the past year, so that €6,000 of the acquisition price has now been amortized. At the end of the year, the city government reduces 20 percent of the outstanding taxi operator licenses by retiring them upon their renewal dates. This immediately increases the price of the remaining taxi operator's licenses to €40,000, as evidenced by multiple license resales on the open market.

Harlequin revalues the license based on these new prices by using the elimination method to eliminate the accumulated amortization and increase the net book value of the license asset. The entries are:

Accumulated amortization	€6,000	
Intangible assets		€6,000
Intangible assets	€16,000	
Revaluation reserve		€16,000

Harlequin now has four years in which to amortize the €40,000 carrying amount of the license, so it will amortize €10,000 in each of the next four years.

How Do I Recognize Changes in Intangible Asset Revaluations?

If you use the revaluation model to adjust the carrying amount of an intangible asset, use the following table to record changes in value:

Result	Treatment
Increased valuation and there was no prior valuation decrease	Increase in other comprehensive income and in equity as a revaluation surplus
Increased valuation and there was a prior valuation decrease	Increase in profit or loss to offset any earlier revaluation decrease of the same asset. Any remainder is an increase in comprehensive income.
Decreased valuation and there was no prior valuation increase	Decrease in profit or loss
Decreased valuation and there was a prior valuation decrease	Decrease in other comprehensive income to offset any earlier revaluation increase of the same asset; also decrease in the revaluation surplus in equity. Any remainder is a decrease in profit or loss.

When the revaluation surplus is realized, as upon the retirement or disposal of an asset, transfer the surplus to the retained earnings account.

How Do I Account for Internally Generated Goodwill?

Do not record internally generated goodwill as an asset. Instead, charge it to expense in the period incurred.

How Do I Determine the Useful Life of an Intangible Asset?

An intangible asset can have either a finite or an indefinite life. You assign an asset an indefinite life when there is no foreseeable limit to the period over which the asset is expected to generate net cash flows for the entity. Consider the following factors when determining the useful life of an intangible asset:

- ○ *Competition.* Projected actions by current and potential competitors
- ○ *Control period.* The time period over which the entity has control of the asset
- ○ *Dependencies.* Whether the asset's useful life is dependent upon the useful life of other assets
- ○ *Life cycle.* The typical product life cycle of this type of asset, including public information about similar products

○ *Maintenance.* The amount of maintenance expenditures needed to obtain future economic benefits, and the entity's willingness to make those expenditures
○ *Market stability.* Changes in market demand for the asset, and the stability of the industry in which the asset is used
○ *Obsolescence.* Any type of obsolescence that may impact the asset
○ *Usage.* The expected usage of the asset

An indefinite useful life is not necessarily an infinite useful life. If the useful life span is uncertain, then estimate it on a prudent basis, giving full consideration to the impact of obsolescence caused by rapid changes in technology.

Limit an intangible asset's useful life to the period of any contractual or other legal rights associated with it.

EXAMPLE 14.7

The Better Back Chair Company acquires the mailing list of the *Chiropractor Today* magazine, with the intent of sending direct mail pieces to everyone on the list. Better Back's marketing manager believes the mailing list will have a useful life of between 6 and 18 months, and so adopts a useful life of 12 months for the purpose of amortizing the acquisition cost of the mailing list.

If these rights are renewable, then extend the useful life into the renewal periods only if there is evidence that the entity can renew without significant cost. This evidence should indicate that the renewal will occur, that required renewal conditions will be satisfied, and that the renewal cost is not significant in relation to the future economic benefits arising from renewal.

EXAMPLE 14.8

EuroNews Network buys the radio stations of Lichtenstein Holdings for €5 million. These stations all hold broadcast licenses that have just been renewed and are renewable every five years, subject to minimum service levels and the broadcasting of occasional public service messages. Lichtenstein has renewed all of the licenses at least once before, and can do so again at minimal cost. EuroNews intends to continue renewing the licenses indefinitely, and there are no technological reasons why the broadcast licenses will not continue to provide a predictable future stream of cash flows. Based on this information, EuroNews is justified in assigning an indefinite useful life to the broadcast licenses.

After two years, the Belgian government decides to auction all broadcast licenses when they come up for renewal. Given the uncertainty of renewal, EuroNews splits the broadcast licenses into two classes, one for Belgian licenses and one for all other radio stations. It assigns a useful life of three years to the class of intangible assets comprising Belgian broadcast licenses, and amortizes them over that period.

If the entity acquires through a business combination an intangible asset that is a reacquired right, then set its useful life at the remaining period of the contract in which the right was granted. Do not extend the right for any contractual renewal periods.

When Do I Review Intangible Assets with Indefinite Useful Lives?

You should review an intangible asset with an indefinite useful life once a year, and whenever there is an indication that the asset may be impaired. This review will assess whether there is any asset impairment and whether the indefinite useful life is still warranted. If the useful life is no longer indefinite, then determine a useful life and begin amortization over that period. See the Asset Impairment chapter for more information about impairment.

EXAMPLE 14.9

Gaelic Fire Candy acquires the Red Hot Chili Balls candy line from a competitor, along with the trademark for the Red Hot Chili Balls name. Gaelic initially considered the Red Hot Chili Balls name to have an indefinite useful life, along with continuing cash flows at the current level. However, management estimates that recent competition from the Atomic Jalapenos candy line will reduce future cash inflows by 25 percent.

(Continued)

(*Continued*)

Based on this information, there is no need for Gaelic to assign a useful life to the Red Hot Chili Balls trademark, but it should determine whether the estimated recoverable amount is now less than its carrying amount. If so, Gaelic should record an impairment charge to reduce the carrying amount to the recoverable amount.

How Do I Calculate Amortization for an Intangible Asset?

Amortization of an intangible asset having a finite useful life begins when the asset is available for use, and stops on the earlier of being classified as held for sale or when it is derecognized. The most appropriate amortization method is the one that most closely matches the expected pattern of consumption of the asset's expected future economic benefits. If there is no way to determine the pattern of consumption, then use the straight-line method for amortization. Alternative methods to consider are the diminishing balance method and the units of production method. Do not change the amortization method unless there is a change in the expected pattern of consumption of future economic benefits.

Where Do I Record the Amortization Expense?

You normally recognize amortization expense in profit or loss. However, there are situations where the future economic benefits of an intangible asset are used in the production of other assets. If so, include the amortization expense in the cost of the other assets. Any amortization expense treated in this fashion will then be charged to expense when the economic benefits of the other assets are realized.

EXAMPLE 14.10

Iberian Tile Company buys the rights to a patented production process that allows it to fuse custom-designed images to tile substrate in high temperature kilns. Iberian pays €100,000 to use the process, and elects to amortize it under the units of production method, whereby it amortizes €1 for every tile produced. It then includes the €1/unit amortization in the bill of materials for each tile. When Iberian completes a tile, it transfers the standard cost of the tile (including the amortization charge) to inventory. It charges the inventoried cost of the tile to the cost of goods sold every time it sells a tile.

What Is the Residual Value of an Intangible Asset?

The residual value of an intangible asset with an indefinite life is zero. There are two circumstances where residual value *can* be used. The first is when a third party commits to purchase the asset at the end of its useful life. The second is if there is an active market for the asset, it is possible to determine the residual value through that market, and it is probable that the market will still exist at the end of the asset's useful life. In the latter case, the appropriate residual value to use is the amount recoverable from disposal using prices prevailing on the estimated date of sale for a similar asset.

You must review the residual value at least at the end of each fiscal year. If the residual value increases to an amount equal to or greater than the asset's carrying amount, then there is no further amortization charge until such time as the residual value declines below the asset's carrying value.

EXAMPLE 14.11

Hadrian's Brewery acquires, for £150,000, the rights to a patent for a hops separation process, which it believes it can use to increase the efficiency of its brewing operation at Once Brewed, near Hadrian's Wall. Hadrian's believes it can achieve net cash inflows from the patent for at least the next 10 years. Hadrian's also has a signed commitment letter from Great Wall Breweries to buy the patent in three years for £100,000.

Based on this information, Hadrian's amortizes the patent asset over the three-year period before it intends to sell the patent to Great Wall. The residual value of the patent is the present value of the £100,000 price at which Great Wall intends to buy it in three years.

How Frequently Should I Review the Amortization Period and Method?

Review the amortization period and amortization method at least at the end of each fiscal year for all intangible assets having finite lives. If the expected useful life of the asset is different from the period you currently use, then change the amortization period to the new estimate. If there has been a change in the pattern of consumption of the asset's future economic benefits, then change the amortization method to reflect the new pattern. These are changes in accounting estimates, and so require no retrospective application.

How Do I Account for the Derecognition of an Intangible Asset?

Derecognize an asset at the time of its disposal, or when you expect no future economic benefits from its further use or its disposal. If there is a difference between the net disposal proceeds and the carrying amount of the asset, then recognize it in profit or loss when you derecognize the asset. Do not classify a gain on derecognition as revenue.

If the proceeds from disposal are other than cash, record the proceeds at their fair value. If the payment is deferred, then recognize the consideration received at its cash price equivalent, and record the difference between the total payment and the cash price equivalent as interest revenue.

What Controls Should I Install for Intangible Assets?

There are two procedures that can improve an entity's ability to properly value intangible assets. The first is to maintain and follow a schedule of intangible asset reviews, not only to assess impairment, but also to ensure that the useful lives and residual values of the assets are periodically assessed. The second procedure is to schedule the services of outside appraisers to conduct at least some of these assessments. It may be more cost-effective to use internal staff to assess these issues, but an independent entity also should be involved from time to time, to ensure that there is no manipulation of carrying amounts.

Another control problem is the tendency of an entity to assess acquired assets at reduced carrying amounts. Entities do this in order to shift more of the acquisition cost into goodwill, thereby avoiding the amortization expense that they must charge to any intangible assets having finite lives. This is a difficult problem to control, since valuation involves some degree of judgment for those assets not sold in an active market. Accordingly, it is best to have an outside appraiser conduct all valuations for intangible assets obtained through an acquisition.

What Information Do I Disclose Regarding Intangible Assets?

Disclose the following information for each class of intangible assets:

- ○ *Amortization methods.* The amortization methods used for those assets having finite useful lives
- ○ *Carrying amounts.* The gross carrying amounts, accumulated amortization, and accumulated impairment losses at the beginning and end of the period
- ○ *Line items.* The line items in the statement of comprehensive income where amortization is included
- ○ *Reconciliation.* A reconciliation of the carrying amounts at the beginning and end of the period, including additions, assets classified as held for sale, revaluation changes and impairment changes impacting other comprehensive income, impairment losses and reversals impacting profit or loss, amortization, net foreign exchange differences resulting from translation into the presentation currency, and any other changes in the carrying amount
- ○ *Useful lives.* Whether the useful lives are indefinite or finite; if finite, either the useful lives or the amortization rates being used

When disclosing the preceding information, distinguish between internally generated and other intangible assets.

It also may be necessary to disclose the following information:

- ○ *Accounting estimate.* Any changes in accounting estimate, such as modifications of an asset's useful life, amortization method, or residual value, that either has a material effect on the current period or is expected to have a material effect in subsequent periods

○ *Commitments.* The amounts of any contractual commitments to acquire intangible assets

○ *Government grants.* If intangible assets were acquired through government grants and initially recognized at their fair value, the fair value initially recognized, the carrying amount, and whether the assets are measured under the cost or revaluation models

○ *Indefinite useful life.* If an intangible asset has an indefinite useful life, its carrying amount and the reasons why it is assessed as having an indefinite useful life

○ *Material assets.* A description of any individual intangible asset that is material to the entity's financial statements, as well as its carrying amount and remaining amortization period

○ *Research and development.* The aggregate amount of research and development expenditures recognized as expense during the period

○ *Restricted assets.* The carrying amounts of any intangible assets whose title is restricted or that are pledged as security for other liabilities

○ *Revaluation.* If intangible assets have been revalued, disclosure (for each class of assets) of the date of the revaluation, the revalued carrying amounts, and the carrying amount that would have been recognized under the cost model; the amount of the revaluation surplus relating to intangible assets at the beginning and end of the period, changes during the period, and any restrictions on distributing the surplus to shareholders; and the methods and assumptions used in estimating the assets' fair values

Do not aggregate asset classes if this would result in classes containing assets measured under both the cost and revaluation models.

It is not mandatory, but is useful, to also disclose descriptions of any fully amortized intangible assets that are still in use, and descriptions of any significant intangible assets controlled by the entity but not recognized as assets.

CHAPTER 15

ASSET IMPAIRMENT

 Why Test Assets for Impairment?

You should not carry assets at more than their recoverable amount. Asset impairment happens when the carrying amount is greater than the amount recoverable through either using or selling an asset. In that case, the asset is impaired, and you must recognize an impairment loss to reduce the carrying amount.

 What Is an Asset's Recoverable Amount?

An asset's recoverable amount is the greater of its fair value less costs to sell, and its value in use.

 What Is an Asset's Value in Use?

An asset's value in use is the present value of future cash flows expected to be derived from it.

 What Is the Carrying Amount of an Asset?

An asset's carrying amount is the recorded amount of the asset, net of any accumulated depreciation or accumulated impairment losses.

 To What Assets Should Impairment Testing Be Applied?

Impairment testing applies to all assets *other than* the following:

Agricultural assets measured at fair value	Financial instruments
Assets arising from construction contracts	Held-for-sale assets
Assets arising from employee benefits	Inventory
Deferred acquisition costs of insurance contracts	Investment property measured at fair value
Deferred tax assets	

How Frequently Should I Conduct Impairment Testing?

In general, an entity must assess at the end of every reporting period whether there is any indication of asset impairment. If so, it must estimate the recoverable amount of the asset as of the end of that period. Use Exhibit 15.1 to determine the frequency of impairment testing.

How Do I Determine Fair Value Less Costs to Sell?

There are a variety of information sources for determining the fair value of an asset, less costs to sell. Here are three sources, presented in declining order of information quality:

1. *Sales agreement.* The price noted in a binding arm's-length sales agreement.
2. *Price in an active market.* The asset's price in an active market, which is usually the current bid price, less disposal costs. In the absence of a current bid, the

Exhibit 15.1   Impairment Test Frequency

Asset Type	Impairment Test Frequency*
Intangible, with indefinite useful life	Annual
Intangible, not yet available for use	Annual
Goodwill acquired in business combination	Annual

*To be conducted even if there is no indication of impairment, and to be completed for each item at the same time every year. It is acceptable to measure different intangible assets at different times of the year.

next best information is the price of the most recent transaction.

3. *Disposal cost.* The asset's price in an arm's-length disposal transaction between knowledgeable, willing parties. This can be based on recent transactions involving similar assets in the same industry, but should not be a forced sale, unless management must sell immediately.

The costs to sell noted in these transactions include taxes and the costs of legal services, asset removal, and preparation of the asset for sale.

 ## What Factors Do I Use in an Impairment Assessment?

At a minimum, consider the following factors when assessing asset impairment:

- *Asset use.* The asset is or will become idle or discontinued.
- *Damage.* The asset is damaged.
- *Dividend.* The dividend from a subsidiary or jointly controlled entity exceeds the total comprehensive income of that entity when the dividend was declared.
- *Environmental changes.* There have been or will be significant negative changes to the entity related to the legal, economic, technological, or market environment.
- *Interest rate changes.* The market interest rate has increased, affecting the entity's discount rate used for calculating asset valuations. This does not apply for changes in short-term interest rates that do not impact the discount rate for assets having a long remaining life.
- *Life.* The asset is reclassified from having an indefinite life to having a finite life.
- *Market value.* The asset's market value has significantly declined more than expected through normal use or the passage of time.
- *Obsolescence.* The asset is obsolete.
- *Performance.* The economic performance of the asset either is or will be worse than expected. This may include increased usage costs.

If a previous analysis showed that an asset's recoverable amount was not sensitive to some of the above items, then those factors do not need to be considered again.

If the preceding calculation of an asset's valuation re-veals a recoverable amount much greater than its carrying amount, and there have been no events that would alter the difference, then there is no need to re-estimate the re-coverable amount.

How Do I Measure an Asset's Recoverable Amount?

If either an asset's fair value less costs to sell, or its value in use (present value of future cash flows) is greater than the asset's carrying amount, then it is not impaired. If it is not possible to measure fair value less costs to sell, then use the value in use.

If an asset is being held for disposal, then its value in use can be ignored (since future cash flows will be negligi-ble) in favor of its fair value less costs to sell.

The recoverable amount normally is determined by in-dividual asset. However, if a single asset generates cash flows only as part of a group of assets, then conduct the assessment for the group of assets.

EXAMPLE 15.1

Danish Energy owns a wind farm off the coast of Hanstholm, Denmark. The gross cost of the facility is €80,000,000, less €15,000,000 of accumulated depreci-ation. The company has received a signed letter of in-tent to buy the facility for €68,000,000; the offer includes a requirement that Danish Energy complete €1,000,000 worth of maintenance prior to the sale. Danish Energy also has determined that the facility's value in use is €52,000,000. Is the wind farm's value impaired?

No. The carrying amount of the facility (gross cost less depreciation) is €65,000,000, and the fair value less costs to sell is €67,000,000, so the recover-able value exceeds the carrying amount. The value in use is not relevant, as long as the fair value less costs to sell exceeds the carrying amount.

Can I Roll Forward Impairment Assessment Calculations?

If a detailed assessment was performed in a previous pe-riod for an intangible asset then the calculation used for that assessment may be used for the current-period impairment assessment, provided that the last such calculation revealed a substantial excess of recoverable amount over carrying amount, and subsequent events indicate that a decline of the recoverable amount to a level below the carrying amount is remote.

What Other Changes Can Arise from an Impairment Assessment?

An impairment assessment may not require the recognition of an impairment loss. However, the assessment process is a good time to review the remaining useful life, depreciation or amortization method, and residual value of the asset being assessed. The result may be adjustments of these items, even if there is no impairment loss.

What Source Information Do I Use in a Cash Flow Projection?

When calculating an asset's value in use (present value of future cash flows), consider the future cash flows specifically derived from it, as modified by future cash flow variations, the current risk-free interest rate, and other factors influencing cash flows. These other factors can modify either the interest rate or the future cash flows. If there are multiple estimates of cash flows, then compile a weighted average of the various estimates.

Base the cash flow projections on reasonable and supportable assumptions comprising the range of economic conditions most likely to exist over the remaining useful life of the asset. The projections should be founded upon the most recent budget or forecast, but such projections should *not* cover a period of more than five years, unless there is a justifiable reason for using a longer period, you are confident that these projections are reliable, and you have a demonstrated ability to forecast cash flows accurately over a longer period. When extrapolating cash flows beyond the term of a budget or forecast, incorporate a steady or declining growth rate for later years, unless there is a justifiable reason for increasing the growth rate. This growth rate should not exceed the long-term average growth rate for the product, industry, or country, without justification.

Cash flow projections should extend as far as the end of an asset's useful life. Since the useful life may extend well beyond the five-year budget limitation, it is acceptable to extrapolate cash flow projections based on the shorter term budget, usually using a growth rate for subsequent years that is steady or declining.

Do not include in future cash flows any estimated changes arising from future restructurings or the projected enhancement of an asset's performance. Thus, cash flows are based on the asset's remaining in its current condition.

EXAMPLE 15.2

Electro Tram is reviewing its Czech subsidiary for impairment. There is no active market for the sale of this type of business, so no market-based fair value can be obtained. The subsidiary's carrying amount is €42,000,000. Management creates two computations of the subsidiary's value in use. The first computation of €38,000,000 excludes the cost reductions expected from a future employee layoff, while the second computation of €43,000,000 includes them.

Electro Tram should not take into account the benefit of the future layoff when calculating value in use. Consequently, there is an impairment of 4 million because the value in use from the first computation is lower than the carrying amount of €42,000,000.

Do not include in future cash flows any inflows or outflows from financing activities, because the discounting of future cash flows to their present value already incorporates financing costs. Also, do not include any inflows or outflows from income taxes, since the discount rate is determined on a pretax basis.

You also should assess the reasonableness of any differences between historical and projected cash flows, including a review of how the assumptions used for current projections have changed from the past.

How Does a Corporate Restructuring Alter Cash Flow Projections?

When an entity commits to a restructuring, it can revise its estimates of cash flows that are used for determining an asset's value in use (present value of future cash flows).

What Is a Cash-Generating Unit?

A cash-generating unit is the smallest group of assets that independently generates cash flow and whose cash flow is largely independent of the cash flows generated by other assets.

EXAMPLE 15.3
Dusseldorf Airship operates a semirigid blimp for use in advertising at arena sporting events. The blimp comprises two primary assets—the gas bag and the control car. The cash flow specifically traceable to either the gas bag or the control car is essentially zero. Instead, the two assets must be grouped together into a cash-generating unit to evaluate their combined cash flows as an operating vehicle.

 ## How Do I Recognize Impairment Losses for Assets Other Than Goodwill?

Reduce the carrying amount of an asset to its recoverable amount if the recoverable amount is less than the carrying amount. This reduction is an asset impairment loss. Recognize this loss in the current period.

If it is not possible to estimate the recoverable amount for an individual asset, then determine it for the cash-generating unit of which the asset is a part. This situation arises when the cash flow linked to an asset is negligible.

EXAMPLE 15.4
Electro Tram operates an articulated tram system in Budapest. It does so under a contract with the city government to provide a minimum amount of system-wide service. It is possible to identify cash flows by tram line, and one of the tram lines clearly operates at a loss. The service contract is for the entire city area, and Electro Tram is not allowed to modify or terminate any tram line. Consequently, the lowest level of identifiable cash flows is for the entire tram network.

Identify cash-generating units consistently over time for the same asset or group of assets. Do not alter the composition of cash-generating units without justification.

The cash flows from a cash-generating unit should be based on management's best estimate of future prices that could be achieved in an arm's-length transaction, even if most or all of the output from that unit is used internally. These estimated cash flows override any internal transfer pricing used by the entity.

See the Property, Plant, and Equipment chapter for a discussion of losses recognized on revalued assets. In brief, treat an impairment loss on a revalued asset as a revaluation decrease. Recognize this loss in other comprehensive income up to the amount of the revaluation surplus, and recognize any additional impairment as a loss.

Following recognition of an impairment loss, adjust future depreciation charges to allocate an asset's revised carrying amount over its remaining useful life.

 ## What Is Goodwill?

When an entity acquires another entity, goodwill is the difference between the purchase price and the amount of the price not assigned to assets acquired in the acquisition that are specifically identified. Goodwill does not independently generate cash flows, and it may not be possible to allocate goodwill on a nonarbitrary basis to individual cash-generating units.

 ## How Do I Allocate Goodwill to Cash-Generating Units?

Allocate goodwill acquired in a business combination to each of the acquirer's cash-generating units that will benefit from the acquisition synergies. Each cash-generating unit receiving a goodwill allocation cannot be larger than an operating segment, and it must be the lowest level at which management conducts monitoring.

If you do not allocate goodwill before the end of the fiscal year in which the acquisition took place, then complete it before the end of the following fiscal year.

 ## How Do I Allocate Corporate Assets to Cash-Generating Units?

If there are corporate assets that can be reasonably and consistently associated with a specific cash-generating unit, then allocate those assets to the cash-generating unit.

What Happens to Allocated Goodwill If a Cash-Generating Unit Is Disposed of?

If a portion of a cash-generating unit to which goodwill has been allocated is disposed of, include an allocation of the amount of goodwill in the carrying amount of the unit when calculating any gain or loss on the disposal. The allocation is based on the relative values of the disposed asset and the remainder of the cash-generating unit.

EXAMPLE 15.5

Gaelic Fire Candy, maker of very hot, cinnamon-laced hard candy, has allocated £80,000 of goodwill from a recent acquisition to a hard candy production line (a cash-generating unit). Gaelic disposes of a large-batch sugar boiler that was included in the production line. The relative values of the sugar boiler and the remainder of the production line are £75,000 and £2,000,000, which is a proportion of 3.75 percent. Gaelic therefore allocates 3.75 percent of the goodwill, or £3,000, to the sugar boiler, which leaves the cash-generating unit with a goodwill allocation of £77,000.

If the composition of a cash-generating unit is changed, and goodwill has been assigned to it, then reallocate the goodwill to the units affected based on relative value.

EXAMPLE 15.6

Gaelic Fire Candy decides to terminate production of hard candy with the production line noted in the preceding example. It allocates the equipment in that production line to three other production lines. The remaining £77,000 of goodwill is apportioned to the other production lines based on the relative values of the equipment being sent to them, as noted in the following table:

Equipment Moving to:	Value	Percentage	Allocable Goodwill	Allocated Goodwill
Production line A	£300,000	15%	× £77,000	= £11,550

(Continued)

(*Continued*)					
Production line B	700,000	35%	× 77,000	=	26,950
Production line C	1,000,000	50%	× 77,000	=	38,500
	£2,000,000	100%			£77,000

How Frequently Do I Test for Goodwill Impairment?

If goodwill has been allocated to a cash-generating unit, test it for impairment annually. In addition, test it whenever there is an indication of impairment. The annual test can be performed at any time of the year, as long as you test it at the same time every year. There is no requirement to test all cash-generating units at the same time; each unit may be scheduled for a test at a different time of the year. If goodwill is allocated to a unit in the current fiscal year, then conduct an impairment test before the end of the current fiscal year.

How Do I Calculate Impairment Losses for Goodwill?

To test for impairment, compare the recoverable amount of a cash-generating unit to its carrying amount (including any allocated goodwill). If the carrying amount exceeds the recoverable amount, then recognize the difference between the two values as an impairment loss.

If there is an indication of impairment of an asset within a cash-generating unit to which goodwill has been allocated, follow these two impairment assessment steps:

1. Test the specific asset for impairment, and recognize any impairment loss on the asset.
2. Then test the cash-generating unit of which the asset is a part, and recognize any impairment loss on the unit.

Corporate assets should be allocated to a cash-generating unit before conducting an impairment test. If is not possible to allocate corporate assets on a reasonable and consistent basis, then follow these two steps:

1. Test for and recognize any impairment without an allocation of corporate assets.

2. Move up from the cash-generating unit under examination to the next-largest cash generating unit to which corporate assets can be allocated on a reasonable and consistent basis; test for and recognize any impairment at that level.

 ## How Do I Recognize Impairment Losses for Goodwill?

If an impairment assessment reveals an impairment loss, then allocate the loss to reduce the assets in the cash-generating unit as follows:

1. Reduce the carrying amount of goodwill allocated to the unit; and then
2. Allocate the loss to the other assets in the unit. Do this based on the carrying amount of each asset in the unit.

EXAMPLE 15.7

Luminescence Corporation has conducted an asset impairment test for its LED light cash-generating unit. Prior to the assessment, it had assets with the following carrying amounts:

Production facility	€28,000,000
Property	16,000,000
Goodwill	12,000,000
	€56,000,000

Luminescence now determines that the recoverable amount of the cash-generating unit is €40,000,000. The following table shows its allocation of the impairment loss to the net assets of the unit:

	Production Facility	Property	Goodwill	Total
Carrying amount	€28,000,000	€16,000,000	€12,000,000	€56,000,000
Proportion of carrying amount *	64%	36%	–	100%

(Continued)

(Continued)				
Impairment loss	(2,560,000)	(1,440,000)	(12,000,000)	(16,000,000)
Carrying amount after impairment	€25,440,000	€14,560,000	€0	€40,000,000

*Not including the goodwill asset

It is not allowable to reduce the carrying amount of an asset below the highest of the asset's value in use (present value of future cash flows), fair value less costs to sell, or zero. If this means that the amount of an impairment loss allocated to an asset cannot be fully charged against that asset, then allocate it to the other assets in the unit on a pro rata basis.

If it is not practicable to estimate the recoverable amount of each asset in a unit, then it is allowable to arbitrarily allocate an impairment loss among the assets of a unit.

EXAMPLE 15.8

A large-batch sugar boiler on one of Gaelic Fire Candy's production lines sustains permanent damage that reduces its safe production volume by 25 percent. There are several other sugar boilers in the production line, so management shifts work to the other boilers, resulting in no net change in the production line's total output. The smallest cash-generating unit is the entire production line, since no smaller aggregation of assets produces cash flow.

Management does not intend to replace the damaged boiler, but rather will continue to use it. Since the boiler is generating cash flow as part of the greater cash-generating unit, the recoverable amount can be estimated only as part of the unit, so it is not possible to recognize impairment for the boiler.

The boiler's condition deteriorates further. Management now commits to sell it and removes it from the production line. It now has no discernible cash flows, so its recoverable value is based solely on its fair value less costs to sell of £15,000. This value is less than the boiler's carrying amount of £25,000, so Gaelic recognizes an impairment loss on the boiler of £10,000.

Can I Reuse Prior-Period Impairment Calculations?

It is allowable to use the detailed impairment calculations from a preceding period to determine the recoverable amount of a cash-generating unit to which goodwill has been allocated only if:

○ The most recent impairment test revealed that the recoverable amount substantially exceeded the carrying amount
○ The assets and liabilities constituting the unit have not changed significantly since the last test
○ The circumstances since the last test have not changed sufficiently to indicate the presence of impairment.

When and How Do I Reverse an Impairment Loss?

At the end of each reporting period, assess whether there is any indication that a previously recognized impairment loss (not including goodwill) either may have declined or no longer exists. Use the following indicators to make the determination:

○ *Favorable effects.* There are or will be favorable effects involving the entity's business environment.
○ *Interest rates.* Market interest rates have declined and will affect the discount rate used to determine the present value of cash flows associated with the asset.
○ *Internal improvements.* The asset's usage or expectations for its use have changed, such as through efficiency improvements.
○ *Market value.* The asset's market value has increased.
○ *Usage period.* The entity expects a longer performance period for the asset.

Estimate the recoverable amount of the asset if one or more of these indicators have changed. It is allowable to reverse an impairment loss *only* if there is a change in the estimates used to determine the asset's recoverable amount. If so, increase the carrying amount of the asset to its recoverable amount. The amount of the reversal cannot exceed what the asset's carrying amount (net of depreciation) would have been had no impairment originally been recognized.

At the time of the impairment loss reversal, recognize the change in the current-period income statement. If the reversal is for a revalued asset, the treatment is different. See the Property, Plant, and Equipment chapter for more information.

Once the impairment reversal is complete, adjust the asset's depreciation or amortization charge in future periods to allocate the newly revised carrying amount, less any residual value, over the remainder of its estimated useful life.

Regardless of whether this review reveals a change in the impairment loss, the entity should consider whether any of the indicators warrant alterations to the asset's useful life, depreciation method, or residual value.

How Do I Account for an Impairment Loss Reversal for a Cash-Generating Unit?

The immediately preceding discussion applies equally to an individual asset or a cash-generating unit. In addition, allocate the reversed impairment loss to the assets within a cash-generating unit in proportion to the carrying values of those assets. When allocating the reversed impairment loss, do not increase the carrying amount of an asset above the lower of:

1. Its recoverable amount; or
2. The asset's carrying amount (net of depreciation) had no impairment originally been recognized.

If the allocation of the reversed impairment loss is capped by this requirement, then allocate the remaining reversed impairment amount pro rata to the other assets constituting the unit.

Can I Reverse a Goodwill Impairment Loss?

No. If an impairment loss has already been recognized for goodwill, you cannot reverse it in a subsequent period. You also cannot reverse an impairment loss recognized in a previous interim period. This would constitute the recognition of internally generated goodwill, which is not allowed.

EXAMPLE 15.9

Luminescence Corporation previously recognized a €16,000,000 impairment loss on its LED light cash-generating unit. The original loss calculation follows:

	Production Facility	Property	Goodwill	Total
Carrying amount	€28,000,000	€16,000,000	€12,000,000	€56,000,000
Proportion of carrying amount*	64%	36%	–	100%
Impairment loss	(2,560,000)	(1,440,000)	(12,000,000)	(16,000,000)
Carrying amount after impairment	€25,440,000	€14,560,000	€0	€40,000,000

*Not including the goodwill asset

After a three-year interval, Luminescence conducts another impairment assessment, which reveals that the value in use of the cash-generating unit has increased by €10,000,000. Since the last assessment, Luminescence has incurred depreciation of €2,000,000 on its production facility and €500,000 on its property. It allocates the valuation increase based on the current carrying amount of the production facility and property, but does not allocate it to the goodwill asset. The result appears in the following table:

	Production Facility	Property	Goodwill	Total
Prior carrying amount	€25,440,000	€14,560,000	€0	€40,000,000
Less: subsequent depreciation	(2,000,000)	(500,000)	0	(2,500,000)
Current carrying amount	23,440,000	14,060,000	0	37,500,000
Proportion of carrying amount	63%	37%	–	100%
Impairment loss reversal	6,300,000	3,700,000	–	10,000,000
Carrying amount after impairment	€29,740,000	€17,760,000	€0	€47,500,000

What Controls Should I Install for Asset Impairment?

There are two control problems with asset impairment analysis. First, it is not a frequent accounting event, so it quite possibly will not take place simply due to inattention. When an assessment does happen, the lengthy periods between analyses increases the likelihood that each assessment will be performed inconsistently from the previous assessment. Second, an impairment assessment involves the use of external fair value information that can be selectively gathered to improperly alter the outcome, presumably in favor of smaller impairments or larger impairment reversals.

You can mitigate the frequency issue by building impairment assessments into an annual calendar of accounting events. Also, create a detailed impairment assessment procedure with an attached checklist, which makes it easier to perform each assessment in the same way, every time.

The best way to mitigate the risk of assessment modifications is to involve the internal audit department in a selective review of the documentation that was created for each assessment. This group should pay particular attention to any impairment reversals and cases where an impairment was avoided by a narrow margin, since these areas are indicators of improper assessment modifications.

What Impairment Information Do I Disclose for Asset Classes?

For each class of assets, disclose the following information:

- ○ *Impairment losses.* The amount of impairment losses recognized during the period and the line items where they are located
- ○ *Impairment reversals.* The amount of impairment reversals recognized during the period and the line items where they are located
- ○ *Revalued asset impairments.* The amount of impairment losses on revalued assets during the period
- ○ *Revalued asset reversals.* The amount of impairment reversals on revalued assets recognized during the period

What Impairment Information Do I Disclose for Reportable Segments?

If an entity is required to report segment information (see the Operating Segments chapter), disclose the following information by segment:

- ○ *Impairment losses.* The amount of impairment losses recognized during the period
- ○ *Impairment reversals.* The amount of impairment reversals recognized during the period.

What Information Do I Disclose for Impairment Losses Recognized or Reversed?

If you recognize a material impairment loss or loss reversal for an asset or a cash-generating unit, then disclose the following information for that reporting period:

- ○ *Asset classes.* The main asset classes affected by the impairment losses and reversals, and the events and circumstances leading to those losses and reversals.
- ○ *Asset information.* For an individual asset, the nature of the asset.
- ○ *Circumstances.* The events and circumstances causing the impairment or reversal.
- ○ *Quantification.* The impairment or reversal amount.
- ○ *Type of valuation.* Whether the recoverable amount of the asset or cash-generating unit was derived from its fair value less costs to sell, or its value in use (present value of cash flows). If the former, state how the fair value was derived; if the latter, state the discount rate used in the current and previous derivations of value in use.
- ○ *Unallocated goodwill.* If any goodwill acquired in a business combination has not been allocated to a cash-generating unit by the end of the reporting period, the unallocated amount and the reason for nonallocation.
- ○ *Unit information.* For a cash-generating unit, a description of the unit, the amount of loss or reversal by class of assets, any changes in the composition of the unit, and the reason for altering the composition.

What Information Do I Disclose for Estimations of Recoverable Amounts?

Disclose the following information for each cash-generating unit where there is a significant amount of allocated goodwill or intangible assets with indefinite useful lives:

- *Goodwill allocation.* The carrying amount of allocated goodwill.
- *Intangible assets.* The carrying amount of intangible assets with indefinite useful lives.
- *Basis.* Whether the recoverable amount of the unit is based on fair value less costs to sell, or value in use (present value of cash flows).
- *Value in use information.* If the recoverable amount is based on the unit's value in use, describe the key assumptions used to create the cash flow projections, whether those assumptions are consistent with past experience or external information (or why they differ from such information), the duration of projections (and why any duration longer than five years is justified), the discount rates used for the projections, and the growth rate used to extrapolate cash flow projections (and the reason for using a growth rate above the norm).
- *Fair value information.* If the recoverable amount is based on the unit's fair value less costs to sell, then state the valuation methodology; if this does not involve an observable market price, describe the key assumptions used to derive the fair value and whether those assumptions are consistent with past experience or external information (or why they differ from such information). If the fair value is based on discounted cash flow projections, describe the period of the projections, the growth rate used to extrapolate projections, and the discount rate applied to them.
- *Sensitivity analysis.* If a reasonable possible change in a key assumption would cause a cash-generating unit's recoverable amount to drop below its carrying amount, then describe the amount by which the unit's recoverable amount currently exceeds its carrying amount, the value assigned to this key assumption, and the amount by which this value must change for the recoverable amount to equal its carrying amount.

What Information Do I Disclose for Allocated Goodwill or Intangible Assets?

If any portion of the carrying amount of goodwill or intangible assets with indefinite lives is allocated among more than one cash-generating unit, and the amount allocated to each unit is *not* significant, then disclose the following information:

○ *Significance.* State that the allocation amount is not significant.
○ *Carrying amount.* State the aggregate carrying amount of goodwill or intangible assets with indefinite useful lives allocated to the units.

If the recoverable amounts of the cash-generating units are derived from the same key assumptions and the aggregate carrying amount of goodwill or intangible assets with indefinite useful lives allocated to them *is* significant, then disclose that fact, along with the following:

○ *Carrying amount.* The aggregate carrying amount of goodwill and/or intangible assets with indefinite useful lives allocated to the units.
○ *Assumptions.* A description of the key assumptions.
○ *Value determination.* A description of how management determines the values assigned to key assumptions, whether those values either reflect past experience or external information sources, and, if not, why they differ.
○ *Sensitivity analysis.* If a reasonably possible assumption change causes the unit's carrying amounts to exceed the recoverable amounts, then describe the values assigned to the key assumptions, the amount by which the recoverable amounts exceed carrying amounts, and the amount by which the assumption values must change for the recoverable amounts to equal the carrying amounts.

CHAPTER 16

PROVISIONS AND CONTINGENCIES

 What Is the Difference Between Provisions, Payables, and Accruals?

A provision is a liability that has an uncertain timing or amount. A trade payable is a liability to pay for goods or services received and either invoiced or agreed to. An accrual is similar to a trade payable, except that the amount has not yet been invoiced or formally agreed to, but there is little uncertainty regarding the amount or timing. Accruals frequently are reported as part of trade payables, whereas provisions are reported separately.

 What Is a Contingent Liability?

A contingent liability is either a possible obligation arising from past events and depending on future events not under the entity's control, or a present obligation not recognized because either the entity cannot measure the obligation or settlement is not probable. Do not recognize a contingent liability. Instead, disclose the existence of the contingent liability, unless the possibility of payment is remote.

Assess contingent liabilities continually to determine whether payment has become probable. If a payment becomes probable for an item previously disclosed as a contingent liability, then create a provision in the period in which the change in probability occurs (unless you cannot create a reliable estimate of the amount of the payment).

 When Do I Recognize a Provision?

You can recognize a provision when there is a *present obligation* resulting from a *past event*, there is a *probable payment* required to settle the obligation, and you can *reliably*

estimate the amount of the obligation. If the provision does not meet these conditions, then do not recognize the provision. The conditions creating a provision are discussed further as follows:

- ○ *Present obligation.* If it is not clear whether there is a present obligation, then assume there is an obligation if it is more likely than not that a present obligation exists at the end of the reporting period, taking into account all available evidence. This assessment can include any additional evidence arising after the reporting period has ended. If an obligation does exist, then recognize a provision. If it is more likely that no obligation exists at the end of the reporting period, then disclose a contingent liability, unless there is a remote possibility of payment.
- ○ *Past event.* A past event creates an obligation for payment if there is no reasonable alternative to settling

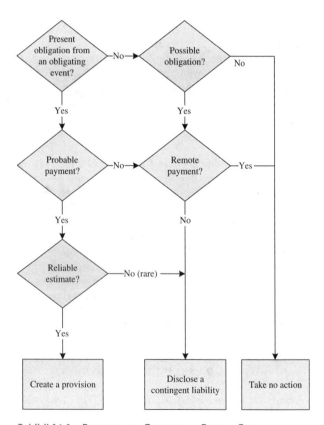

Exhibit 16.1 PROVISION AND CONTINGENCY DECISION TREE

the obligation. This is the case only when the settlement can be enforced by law or if there is a constructive obligation. A constructive obligation is an obligation derived from an entity's prior indications that it will accept certain responsibilities, which creates an expectation that it will fulfill those obligations. Do not recognize a provision for costs to be incurred in the future.

○ *Probable payment.* There must be a probability of payment to settle the obligation. Probability of payment arises when the event is more likely than not to occur. When payment is not probable, then disclose a contingent liability, unless the probability of payment is remote.

○ *Reliable estimate.* You should be able to determine a range of possible outcomes, thereby allowing you to make an estimate of the obligation amount that is reliable enough for you to recognize a provision. If it is not possible to create a reliable estimate, then disclose the liability as a contingent liability.

A decision tree based on the preceding conditions shows when to create a provision, disclose a contingent liability, or do nothing.

EXAMPLE 16.1

Silesian Gravel operates a gravel pit on the shore of the Oder River. Environmentalists have protested that Silesian Gravel is destroying the soil on its property. There is no local legislation requiring Silesian to restore the site once its operations have been completed, but the president of Silesian has stated in numerous televised interviews that the company is very conscious of its environmental responsibilities; it also has a history of restoring its other properties.

The company's actions and statements create a constructive obligation. Silesian also knows how much it cost to restore other properties, so it knows there will be a quantifiable outflow of resources. Therefore, it should create a provision related to the site restoration.

It is not necessary to know to whom an obligation is owed at the time of recognizing a provision. The obligation may even be to the public at large, as would be the case with a prospective penalty to be paid to the government.

Do not recognize a provision for prospective repair and maintenance expenditures, since there is no obligation to incur these costs independently of an entity's future actions; an entity instead could sell the assets prior to their repair.

 ## How Do I Measure a Provision?

The amount that you recognize as a provision is your best estimate of the expenditure required to settle the present obligation at the end of the reporting period. This is the amount that the entity would rationally pay to settle the obligation or transfer it to a third party. This may require the input of management and outside experts, supplemented by experience with similar transactions, and may include information obtained from events occurring after the reporting period.

If there are a number of possible outcomes of a provision, then estimate the obligation by weighting all possible outcomes by their associated probabilities to derive an expected value. If there is an equal probability of multiple outcomes occurring, then use the mid-point of the range.

EXAMPLE 16.2

Lullaby Swing Company makes the Baby Care Swing product, for which it provides a one-year full warranty for all manufacturing defects. Lullaby sells 100,000 Baby Care Swings in the current year. If consumers find minor repair issues in all 100,000 swings, Lullaby will incur a cost of €2,000,000 for repairs. If consumers detect major problems, then Lullaby will incur a cost of €50,000,000 to replace all of the swings.

The swing product has been in the marketplace for three years, so there is a history of having 5 percent of the swings returned for minor repairs, and 0.5 percent for major repairs. Management believes that the same proportions can be expected in the future. Based on this information, Lullaby creates a warranty provision in the following amount:

$$€350,000 = (€2,000,000 \times 5\%) + (€50,000,000 \times 0.5\%)$$

Even if a single outcome to an obligation appears to be the most likely estimate of a liability, you should consider other possible outcomes. If other outcomes are mostly higher or mostly lower than the most likely outcome, then you should record either a higher or lower amount, respectively.

EXAMPLE 16.3

Jolt Power has sold a wind turbine to Danish Energy for its wind farm off the coast of Hanstholm in Denmark. Danish calls in Jolt to fix the turbine, which is malfunctioning. Jolt is liable for any repairs during the first year of operation. Jolt believes the most likely problem is worn bearings, which is a simple replacement costing €500. However, all other potential problems with the turbine are more expensive to repair, costing anywhere from €10,000 to €80,000. Jolt should record a provision for a higher amount than €500 until it has more complete information about the exact nature of the required repair.

If there is a significant amount of risk or uncertainty regarding a provision, this likely increases the amount of the provision. This does not justify creating a deliberate overstatement of a liability; you should create prudent estimates when factoring high risk levels into your estimates.

 ### How Do I Factor Future Events into a Provision?

You should factor into a provision any future events affecting the amount needed to settle an obligation. This is necessary only if there is sufficient objective evidence that the future events will occur. For example, a future event can be possible new legislation that is virtually certain to be enacted, or expected cost reductions associated with increased experience in applying existing technology.

EXAMPLE 16.4

Luxembourg Petrochemicals has operated a small refinery at Junglinster for more than 30 years. There has been increasing evidence that leaks from the Junglinster facility have penetrated the water table, causing problems with the local drinking water. Consequently, it is virtually certain that the Luxembourg Chamber of Deputies will pass legislation shortly after year-end requiring that all refineries implement
(*Continued*)

(Continued)
groundwater remediation activities. The company has already engaged a consulting firm to determine the monetary impact of the new legislation, and accordingly creates a €35 million provision, based on the most likely estimates in the consulting report.

Can I Include a Gain from an Expected Asset Disposal in a Provision?

No. You cannot include in a provision the gain you expect from the future disposal of assets. This is not allowable even if the disposal is closely linked with the event causing the provision.

Do I Create a Provision for a Future Operating Loss?

No. You cannot recognize a provision for a future operating loss, since it is not a current liability. However, an expectation of a future loss may indicate the presence of an asset impairment. See the Asset Impairment chapter for more information.

Do I Create a Provision for an Onerous Contract?

Yes. An onerous contract is a contract requiring expenditures or net exit costs that exceed any economic benefits to be expected from it. You should recognize the present obligation under such a contract as a provision.

EXAMPLE 16.5

Genomics Software operates its software development group from a facility in Edinburgh under a lease having a five-year term. At the end of Year 1, Genomics buys a company in nearby Queensferry and shifts its Edinburgh staff into the Queensferry location. Genomics is still required to make monthly lease payments on the old facility for the next four years, it cannot cancel the lease, and the landlord refuses to allow subtenants.

There are no economic benefits that Genomics can realize from the Edinburgh facility, and all lease payments
are probable, so Genomics should recognize a provision
for the present value of the remaining lease payments.

 **Do I Create a Provision for
a Restructuring?**

It is acceptable to create a provision for a restructuring
only when it meets the general criteria for a provision. In
addition, there is an obligation to restructure only when
an entity has a formal restructuring plan that identifies
the business, location, and employees to be terminated;
the expenditures to be undertaken; and when this will
happen, and has created a valid expectation of implementation (such as through a detailed public announcement).
If there is a long delay prior to the restructuring, or if the
restructuring will take a long time, then this does not create a valid expectation of implementation, and a provision
is not needed. If the board of directors has approved a
restructuring, this is not sufficient grounds to recognize
a provision; the approval must be accompanied by
actual implementation or the announcement of a detailed
restructuring plan. If a restructuring is based on the sale of
an operation, do not record a provision until there is a
binding sale agreement.

Include in a restructuring provision only those expenditures necessarily entailed by the event and not associated with any ongoing activities of the entity. Thus, you
cannot include in the provision expenditures for retraining or relocating continuing staff, marketing, or investments in new systems and distribution networks; future
operating losses; or gains on future asset disposals.

Examples of restructuring events are the sale or termination of a business, the closure or relocation of business
locations, changes in the management structure, or other
events having a material effect on operations.

EXAMPLE 16.6

Plasma Storage Devices maintains low-temperature
storage facilities for fresh frozen plasma, with multiple power redundancies to avoid temperature increases. Plasma's board of directors concludes that its
Italian facility is unprofitable and approves a detailed
(Continued)

(*Continued*)

plan to close it. In addition, the company sends letters to its Italian hospital customers, notifying them of the shutdown and advising them regarding alternative storage facilities. It also notifies the staff of the Italian facility that they will be terminated. The cost associated with the restructuring is €15 million. Since the company has created a valid expectation of closure and payments are probable, Plasma should record a €15 million restructuring provision.

Do I Record the Present Value of a Provision?

Yes. If the effect of the time value of money is material, then record a provision at the present value of the expenditure you expect will be needed to settle the obligation. Thus, recording the present value of an obligation that likely will be settled in a few months is not necessary.

Use a discount rate for the present value calculation that reflects current market assessments of the time value of money and the risks specific to the liability.

EXAMPLE 16.7

The management of the Dampierre Nuclear Power Plant expects to decommission it in 20 years. Management has already identified €55 million of environmental damage caused by the plant, which must be rectified during decommissioning. Management uses a discount rate of 5 percent, which results in a present value of the provision of €20,729,000 (€55,000,000 × 0.376889). Accordingly, Dampierre records a provision of €20,729,000, which it gradually increases over the succeeding 20 years, until it reaches a total provision of €55,000,000.

When Do I Adjust Provisions?

Review all provisions at the end of each reporting period and adjust them to reflect the current best estimate. As time passes, increase the amount of any provisions for which discounting has been used, to reflect the passage of time. This incremental increase is a borrowing cost.

How Do I Record an Obligation That Is Jointly and Severally Liable?

If the entity is jointly and severally liable for an obligation, disclose as a contingent liability the part of the obligation expected to be met by other parties. Recognize a provision for any part of the obligation for which payment by the entity is probable, except when it is not possible to make a reliable estimate of the amount.

How Do I Record a Provision That Will Be Reimbursed?

If you expect the entity to be reimbursed for any expenditure under a provision, then recognize the reimbursement when it is virtually certain that the entity will receive reimbursement. Treat it as a separate asset. Do not record a reimbursement asset that exceeds the amount of the provision. It is allowable to present the provision net of the projected reimbursement.

EXAMPLE 16.8

Okeanos Shipping loses an entire shipload of cargo to a rogue wave off the coast of Patagonia. The value of the cargo is €15 million. The cargo was insured, less a 20 percent deductible, and the insurer has stated in writing that it will not contest Okeanos's claim.

Okeanos can recognize a contingent reimbursement (asset) of €12 million, which is the net amount its insurance company has committed to pay it.

What Is a Contingent Asset?

A contingent asset is a possible asset arising from past events and that will be confirmed only by future events not under the entity's control. Do not recognize a contingent asset; only disclose it when an incoming payment is probable. However, if the realization of income is virtually certain, then the related asset is no longer a contingent asset and you can recognize it in the period when the change occurs.

You should continually assess contingent assets to ensure that they are properly disclosed in the financial statements.

EXAMPLE 16.9

Amundsen Salvage rescues the passengers and crew of the *Southern Seas* passenger ship after it hits an iceberg in the Weddell Sea, and also refloats the ship. Amundsen files suit against the owner of the *Southern Seas*, claiming that the *Southern Seas'* captain agreed to a "no cure, no pay" contract, under which Amundsen is entitled to 20 percent of the hull value only if it can salvage the ship. The *Southern Seas'* owner claims that the contract was actually for time and materials only, which would result in a much smaller settlement.

In Year 1, the outcome of the lawsuit is uncertain throughout the legal proceedings, so Amundsen cannot recognize a contingent asset. At the beginning of Year 2, a court ruling requires that the *Southern Seas'* owner must pay Amundsen the full amount of its claim within 90 days. During that 90-day period, Amundsen can record a contingent asset for the payment amount.

What Provision and Contingency Information Should I Disclose?

For each class of provision, you should disclose the following:

- ○ *Balances and activity.* The carrying amount at the beginning and end of the period, changes during the period, unused amounts reversed during the period, and any increases caused by discounted amounts arising from either the passage of time or changes in the discount rate
- ○ *Description.* A description of the nature of the obligation, payment timing, any uncertainties about payment timing, expected reimbursements, and major assumptions made regarding future events

For each class of contingent liability, you should disclose the following unless there is only a remote possibility of payment:

- ○ *Description.* The nature of the contingent liability
- ○ *Quantification.* Its estimated financial effect
- ○ *Reimbursements.* The possibility of any reimbursement
- ○ *Uncertainties.* Uncertainties relating to the amount or timing of payments

If there is a probable inflow of economic benefits, describe the nature of the contingent asset and estimate its financial effect.

Examples of classes of provisions or contingencies are warranties and amounts subject to legal proceedings, which you should aggregate into separate classes.

If the same set of circumstances create both a provision and a contingent liability, disclose the link between the provision and the contingent liability.

If any of the preceding disclosures may seriously prejudice an entity's position in a dispute with another party, then do not disclose the information. Instead, disclose the general nature of the dispute, as well as the reason why additional information has not been disclosed.

PART III

REVENUE AND EXPENSES

CHAPTER 17

REVENUE RECOGNITION

 How Do I Measure Revenue for Goods Sold?

Revenue is measured at the fair value of the consideration received, taking into account the amount of any trade discounts and volume rebates accepted by the entity. When paid in cash, the amount of revenue recognized is the amount of cash received or receivable.

 How Do I Measure Revenue When There Are Deferred Payments?

In the event of a deferred cash payment, the fair value of the consideration received may be reduced. When a delayed payment effectively constitutes a financing transaction, revenue should be recognized as the discounted cash flow of the transaction, using an imputed interest rate that is the more clearly determinable of either (a) the prevailing interest rate for a similar transaction by an entity with a similar credit rating; or (b) a rate of interest that discounts the transaction to the current cash price of the underlying goods or services.

If a transaction is discounted for revenue recognition purposes, then the difference between the fair value and face value of the consideration paid is recorded as interest revenue.

EXAMPLE 17.1
Somnolent Sofas is offering a year-end deal for its luxury leather sofas, under which customers can either pay €2,000 in cash or a zero down payment with 24 monthly payments of €100 each, totaling €2,400. Since there is a difference of €400 between the cash price and the extended terms, the zero down payment *(Continued)*

(Continued)
deal essentially comprises separate financing and sale transactions. For any sale under the zero down payment plan, Somnolent should record a sale of €2,000, which is the amount of consideration attributable to the sofa. The difference between the cash price and the total payment stream is interest revenue, and Somnolent should record it under the effective interest method over the two-year payment period.

How Do I Recognize Revenue under a Barter Exchange of Goods?

A transaction does not generate revenue if it involves the exchange of goods or services of a similar nature or value. If the exchange is for dissimilar goods or services, the transaction does create revenue; this is measured at the fair value of the goods or services received, as modified by the amount of any cash transferred. If the fair value of received goods or services cannot be reliably measured, then use instead the fair value of the goods or services given up, as modified by the amount of any cash transferred.

What Controls Should I Use for Barter Transactions?

Require the creation of a business case detailing why a barter transaction is required, and what type of accounting should be used for it. The case should be approved by a senior-level manager before any associated entry is made in the general ledger. The case should be attached to the associated journal entry and filed. This approach makes it less likely that sham barter swap transactions will be created.

When Can I Recognize the Sale of Goods?

Revenue from the sale of goods can be recognized when *all* of the following conditions have been recognized:

- *Benefits assured.* The economic benefits associated with the transaction will flow to the entity.
- *Costs measurable.* The costs related to the transaction can be reliably measured.
- *Ownership relinquished.* The entity no longer retains management control over the goods sold.

○ *Revenue measurable.* The amount of revenue to be recognized can be reliably measured.
○ *Risks and rewards transferred.* All significant risks and rewards associated with the goods have been transferred to the buyer. This usually coincides with the transfer of legal title or possession to the buyer.

The economic benefits of a transaction may not be assured until the entity receives the consideration it is due, or an uncertainty is removed. If so, it cannot recognize revenue until these conditions have been met.

EXAMPLE 17.2

Bright Star Corporation has manufactured an advanced telescope that is built to withstand extremely cold temperatures, for use at a South Pole observatory. Bright Star has manufactured the device specifically for the nonprofit organization operating the observatory, and it is unlikely that the device could be used elsewhere in the world. Bright Star has not manufactured a telescope before for this environment, and so expects a number of problems to arise during its first year of operation. Bright Star is contractually obligated to correct any such problems that arise during the first year of use.

Given the high risk of significant extra costs being incurred, and Bright Star's inability to quantify these costs, it should not recognize any revenue until the contract period has expired.

 What If I Retain Ownership Risk in Sold Goods?

If an entity retains significant risks of ownership in ostensibly transferred goods, then it cannot recognize related revenue. Examples of significant retained ownership risks are:

○ *Contingent conditions.* The buyer of the goods in turn must sell the goods before it pays the entity for the sale.
○ *Installation conditions.* Installation is a significant part of the contract, and it has not yet been completed. The seller can recognize revenue immediately after the buyer accepts delivery if the installation process

is simple, or when the inspection is performed only for purposes of final determination of contract prices.

○ *Performance obligations.* The entity retains an obligation for unsatisfactory performance that exceeds normal warranty provisions.

○ *Return rights.* The buyer is entitled to rescind the purchase, and the probability of such return is uncertain. The seller can recognize revenue when the buyer has formally accepted delivery or when the time period allowed for rejection has expired.

EXAMPLE 17.3

Florentine Flatware sells its tableware through the Upper Crust retail chain. Upper Crust purchases tableware from Florentine under a consignment agreement. Florentine should recognize revenue from the sale of its tableware only when the goods are sold by Upper Crust.

If an entity retains an *insignificant* risk of ownership, it can recognize revenue. For example, if an entity has transferred the significant risks and rewards of ownership, except for legal title in order to protect collectibility, then revenue may be recognized. Similarly, a retail establishment can recognize revenue even when customers have a refund right, as long as the retailer can reliably estimate future returns and recognizes a related liability.

What Controls Should I Use for Rights of Return?

Include a sales return allowance calculation in the standard closing procedure. By requiring someone to address the issue of return allowances as part of every period-end close, there is a much greater chance that the allowance amount will be verified against actual returns, resulting in an accurate return allowance. Also, verify the amount of the return allowance against actual experience. One can examine the basis for a specific return allowance amount being recorded, comparing it with actual experience with the same or similar products in the recent past. However, this is an after-the-fact control that must be repeated regularly to ensure that allowance levels are reasonable.

When Can I Recognize Revenue in a Cash on Delivery Transaction?

If a seller is selling goods based on cash on delivery terms, then it should recognize revenue when it delivers the goods and collects the cash from the transaction.

 ## How Do I Recognize Revenue from Subscription Sales?

When the seller makes deliveries of publications and similar items to the buyer under a subscription agreement, it normally recognizes revenue on a straight-line basis over the period when the items are issued. However, if the items vary in value by period, then the seller should recognize revenue based on the sales value of each item in proportion to the total estimated sales value of all items included in the subscription.

 ## When Do I Recognize Advance Payments?

The buyer may send either full or partial payment to the seller in advance of the delivery of goods. The seller may not yet have the items in inventory, they may still be in the production process, or they will be drop shipped by a third party. Under these circumstances, the seller should not recognize revenue until the goods are delivered to the buyer.

 ## How Do I Recognize Installment Sales?

The buyer may send a series of payments to the seller in exchange for the immediate delivery of goods from the seller to the buyer. In this case, the seller can recognize revenue once the goods are delivered; however, the amount recognized is the present value of all payments, which the seller calculates by discounting the payments at the imputed rate of interest. The seller recognizes the interest portion of the payments, which it calculates using the effective interest method, as it earns them.

 ## How Do I Recognize Layaway Sales?

Layaway sales occur when goods are delivered to the buyer only when the buyer has completed the final payment in a series of installment payments. In a layaway sale, the seller recognizes revenue only when it delivers the goods. However, if the seller's historical experience shows that most layaway transactions are converted into sales, then it can recognize revenue when it receives a significant deposit, provided that the goods are on hand, identified, and ready for delivery.

Some features of this transaction are similar to bill and hold transactions, which are discussed next.

When Do I Recognize Bill and Hold Transactions?

In a bill and hold sale, the buyer requests that delivery be delayed, but accepts billing and takes title to the goods. The seller recognizes revenue when the buyer takes title and the following conditions are satisfied:

- Normal payment terms apply to the transaction.
- The buyer acknowledges the delayed delivery instructions.
- It is probable that delivery will be made.
- The goods are identified, on hand, and ready for delivery.

The seller cannot recognize revenue related to a bill and hold transaction if there is only an intention to acquire or produce the goods in time for delivery, as opposed to their actually being on hand.

What Controls Should I Use for Bill and Hold Transactions?

Verify that a signed acknowledgment of bill and hold transaction has been received for every related transaction, which keeps managers from incorrectly inflating revenues with fake bill and hold transactions. Also, confirm the signed documents with customers, to ensure that an authorized person actually approved them.

How Do I Handle Sale and Repurchase Transactions?

A sale and repurchase transaction arises when the seller concurrently agrees to repurchase the same goods at a later date, or when either party has an option to force the seller to repurchase the goods. If the seller has transferred the risks and rewards of ownership to the buyer, then the seller can recognize revenue. Alternatively, if the seller has retained the risks and rewards of ownership, even if legal title has been transferred, then the transaction is treated as a financing arrangement instead, and does not generate revenue.

What General Controls Should I Use for the Sale of Goods?

Compare the shipping log and shipping documents with invoices issued at period-end. This control is designed to spot billings on transactions not completed until after the reporting period has closed. An invoice dated within a reporting period whose associated shipping documentation shows the transaction as having occurred later is clear evidence of improper revenue reporting. Also, issue the financial statements within one day of the period-end. By eliminating the gap between the end of the reporting period and the issuance of the financial statements, you can make it impossible for anyone to create additional invoices for goods shipping subsequent to the period-end, thereby automatically eliminating any cutoff problems.

When Can I Recognize the Sale of Services?

An entity usually is able to make reliable revenue estimates after the parties to the transaction have agreed to the terms of settlement, consideration to be exchanged, and each party's rights regarding services to be provided and received. An entity can recognize the revenue associated with services provided when it satisfies all of the following conditions:

- *Revenue measurable.* The amount of revenue to be recognized can be reliably measured.
- *Benefits assured.* The economic benefits associated with the transaction will flow to the entity.
- *Completion measurable.* The stage of completion at the end of the reporting period can be reliably measured.
- *Costs measurable.* The costs related to the transaction can be reliably measured, as can the costs to complete it.

How Do I Calculate Revenue from the Sale of Services?

The following issues drive the calculation method used to recognize services revenue:

○ *Straight-line recognition.* If the services provided comprise an indeterminate number of acts over a specified period of time, revenue should be recognized on a straight-line basis over the designated time period, unless some other method better represents the provision of services.

○ *Significant activities.* If a specific activity is substantially more significant than other activities, then an entity should defer revenue recognition until that activity has been completed.

○ *Unreliable estimates.* When an entity cannot reliably estimate the outcome of services, it should recognize revenue only to the extent of the expenses recognized that are recoverable. Under this scenario, no profit is recognized. If it is not probable that the costs incurred are recoverable, then the entity does not recognize revenue and recognizes all costs incurred as expenses.

 ## What Controls Do I Use for Service Revenue?

Losses on service contracts must be recognized as expenses immediately, even if the losses are only estimated. Since there is a natural reluctance to recognize losses in advance of the actual event, a good control is to include a standard review of estimated losses on service contracts as part of the monthly closing process.

 ## When Do I Recognize Admission Fees?

The fees generated from artistic performances and other special events are recognized when the event takes place. If the seller is selling subscriptions to a number of events, then it allocates the subscription to each event covered by the subscription, based on the extent to which services are performed at each event.

 ## When Do I Recognize Professional Service Commissions?

Commissions can be earned for a variety of transactions. Here are the recognition criteria for several types of commissions:

○ *Advertising.* An advertising agency can recognize commissions when the related advertisements are released. If it earns commissions for production work, it recognizes revenue based on the stage of completion of the project.

○ *Financial services.* Revenue recognition of fees earned for financial services requires the seller to distinguish between the following:

  • Fees that are really part of the interest rate of a financial instrument, which should be treated as an adjustment to the effective interest rate.
  • Fees earned for services to be rendered, such as a loan servicing fee or an investment management fee.
  • Fees earned upon the completion of a significant act, such as a loan placement fee or a loan syndication fee.

○ *Insurance.* An insurance agent normally is not obligated to render further services once the policy commences. If so, the agent can recognize the commission as revenue on the policy commencement date. If the agent is required to render further services during the policy period, then the agent must recognize the commission over the policy period.

When Do I Recognize Franchise Fees?

Franchise fees are recognized based on the purpose for which they were charged. The following types of fee recognition can be used:

○ *Assets.* The franchisor recognizes fees as revenue either when it delivers assets to franchisees or when it transfers title.

○ *Services.* The franchisor recognizes revenue associated with continuing services over the period during which the services are rendered. If the related fee is not sufficient to cover the franchisor's provisioning costs and a reasonable profit, then it must defer the necessary additional amount from its initial franchise fee and recognize it as revenue over the servicing period. The franchisor can recognize the remainder of any initial fee when it has performed all of its obligations to the franchisee.

○ *Continuing franchise fees.* When the franchisor charges a fee for various continuing rights or services, it recognizes revenue over the applicable period.

○ *Agency transactions.* If the franchisor acts as an agent for a franchisee, such as when it orders supplies on behalf of the franchisee at no profit, related transactions cannot be recognized as revenue.

If franchise fees are collectible over an extended period and there is significant collection uncertainty, then the franchisor recognizes revenue as it collects cash installments.

If the franchisor's obligations under an area franchise agreement depend on the number of outlets established, revenue recognition should be based on the proportion of outlets for which services have been substantially completed.

 ## What Controls Do I Use for Franchise Sales?

To ensure that revenue recognition is not accelerated through the use of an excessively high initial franchise fee in proportion to services generated, a periodic audit could calculate and compare the gross margins earned on initial and ongoing franchise fees. It is also possible that revenue could be recognized on an initial franchise fee before all related services have been completed, thereby falsely accelerating revenue recognition. To detect this problem, a periodic audit could compare the completion of services with the recognition of initial franchise fee revenue for each franchise agreement.

It is possible to incorrectly accelerate the recognition of initial franchise fees when area franchise sales have been made, simply by underestimating the number of franchise locations to be situated within the area franchise. A periodic audit can investigate the number of actual and estimated franchise locations used in the revenue recognition calculation to determine if improperly low estimates have been used.

The franchisor may recognize ongoing franchise fees automatically, without regard to whether related services have been provided at the same time. This is most likely to occur when certain activities, such as advertising campaigns, are conducted only at long intervals, and therefore do not coincide with the receipt of franchisee payments. As a result, revenue is incorrectly recognized prior to the completion of all related services by the franchisor. To detect this issue, a periodic audit should review the calculations used to recognize ongoing franchise revenue, and whether some revenue recognition is withheld pending the completion of such services.

 ## How Do I Recognize Initiation Fees?

If an initiation or membership fee only creates a membership condition, then the seller can recognize revenue when there is no significant uncertainty regarding fee collectibility. However, if the fee entitles the buyer to services or publications or discounted purchases from the seller during the membership period, then the seller recognizes revenue on a basis that reflects the timing, nature, and value of the benefits provided.

When Do I Recognize Installation Fees?

When a seller charges an installation fee associated with delivery of goods, the seller recognizes revenue in accordance with the stage of completion of the installation. However, if the installation fee is incidental to the sale of goods, then the fee is recognized when the goods are sold.

When Do I Recognize Servicing Fees?

A seller of goods may include in the selling price a fee for subsequent servicing or product upgrades. If so, the seller should defer the amount of revenue related to the servicing fee, which should cover the servicing cost and a reasonable profit. It should then recognize the associated revenue over the servicing period.

When Do I Recognize Tuition Fees?

A provider of educational services should recognize revenue from tuition fees over the period of instruction.

When Are Construction Contracts Separated or Aggregated?

When a contract covers a number of assets, treat the construction of each asset as a separate contract when:

- Separate proposals were submitted for each asset.
- Each asset was subject to separate negotiation.
- The revenues and costs associated with each asset can be identified.

When there are a group of construction contracts, treat them as a single contract when:

- The contracts were negotiated as a single package.
- The contracts are, in effect, part of a single project.
- The contracts are performed concurrently or in a continuous sequence.

If a contract provides for construction of additional assets at the customer's option, treat the extra work as a separate contract when the asset differs in design or function from the assets in the original contract and the price of the additional work is negotiated separately from the original contract price.

When Do I Recognize Revenue under a Construction Contract?

The contractor can recognize the revenue and expenses associated with a contract through the stage of completion of the contract at the end of the current reporting period (the *percentage of completion method*), when it can reliably estimate the outcome of the contract.

If the contract is fixed price, the contractor can consider the contract's outcome to be reliably estimated when the following four conditions are satisfied:

- All contract revenue can be reliably measured.
- The benefits of the contract will probably flow to the contractor.
- The remaining contract costs and the stage of completion at the end of the reporting period can be reliably measured.
- Costs attributable to the contract can be identified and reliably measured, so that costs actually incurred can be compared with prior cost estimates.

If the contract is cost plus, the contractor can consider the contract's outcome to be reliably estimated when the following two conditions are satisfied:

- The benefits of the contract will probably flow to the contractor.
- Contract costs, whether or not reimbursable, can be reliably measured.

If the contractor cannot reliably estimate the outcome of a contract, then it can recognize revenue only to the extent of contract costs incurred that it will probably recover, with no profit recognition.

Under the percentage of completion method, the contractor matches revenue with contract costs incurred in reaching a designated stage of completion; this results in the reporting of both revenue and expenses that can be attributed to the proportion of work completed. If the contractor has incurred costs that relate to future contract activity, then it categorizes these costs as an asset (assuming that the costs are recoverable) designated as contract work in progress.

A contractor can use a variety of methods to determine the stage of completion of a contract, including the following:

- Surveys of work performed.
- Completion of a physical proportion of the work.
- The contract costs incurred to date as a percentage of the estimated total contract costs. This calculation should exclude contract costs related to future activity on a contract and payments made to subcontractors in advance of work performed.

EXAMPLE 17.4

Hephaestus Construction, builder of Greek-style homes, is working on a contract for Ms. Hestia, involving a main house and guest house. The first segment of the contract is for the main house. Hephaestus spends €180,000 for building materials that have been delivered to the construction site, but that are designated for the guest house, for which no work has yet begun. Hephaestus also has made an advance payment of €25,000 to Poseidon Concrete for the construction of an Olympic-size swimming pool. In both cases, Hephaestus cannot include the expense in its percentage of completion calculations, since they do not reflect work performed to date.

The percentage of completion method involves making ongoing changes in accounting estimates. These changes in estimate are recognized in the period in which the change is made and in subsequent periods; they do not alter the accounting in prior periods.

EXAMPLE 17.5

Eagle Construction enters into a fixed-price contract with Avignon Prefecture to build a suspension bridge. The amount of revenue listed in the contract is €5,800,000. Eagle's initial estimate of project costs is €5,000,000 over the expected three-year term of the project.

At the end of Year 1, Eagle revises its estimate of project costs upward to €5,100,000.

(Continued)

(*Continued*)

In Year 2, Avignon approves a change in the contract scope to include temperature sensors on the bridge surface that will transmit a warning when the road temperature drops below freezing. The scope change calls for a revenue increase of €300,000, and Eagle estimates additional contract costs of €250,000. At the end of that year, Eagle has spent €150,000 for materials that are stored at the construction site, but that are intended for use in the following year.

Eagle calculates its revenue recognition based on the percentage of completion method. A summary of its calculations follows:

	Year 1	Year 2	Year 3
Initial revenue in contract	€5,800,000	€5,800,000	€5,800,000
Contract scope changes	—	300,000	300,000
Total contract revenue	€5,800,000	€6,100,000	€6,100,000
Costs incurred to date	1,785,000	4,013,000	5,350,000
Estimated costs to completed	3,315,000	1,337,000	—
Total estimated contract costs	5,100,000	5,350,000	5,350,000
Estimated profit	€700,000	€750,000	€750,000
Stage of completion	40%	80%	100%

Eagle calculates the 80 percent stage of completion at the end of Year 2 without the €150,000 of contract costs related to materials stored for use in Year 3.

Based on the preceding information, Eagle recognizes revenue and expenses by year in the following amounts:

	Project to Date	Prior-Years Recognition	Current-Year Recognition
Year 1			
Revenue (€5,800,000 × 40%)	€2,320,000	—	€2,320,000
Expenses (€5,100,000 × 40%)	2,040,000	—	2,040,000
Profit	280,000	—	280,000

Year 2			
Revenue (€6,100,000 × 80%)	4,880,000	€2,320,000	2,560,000
Expenses (€5,350,000 × 80%)	4,280,000	2,040,000	2,240,000
Profit	600,000	280,000	320,000
Year 3			
Revenue (€6,100,000 × 100%)	6,100,000	4,880,000	1,220,000
Expenses (€5,350,000 × 100%)	5,350,000	4,280,000	1,070,000
Profit	750,000	600,000	150,000

When Do I Recognize Losses under a Construction Contract?

The contractor should recognize an expected loss immediately when it is probable that total contract costs will exceed total contract revenue. The amount of the loss recognized is not impacted by the stage of project completion or the amount of profits that the contractor may earn from contracts that are not treated as part of the same contract. Examples of situations where contract recoverability is in doubt are:

- Contracts that are not enforceable
- Contracts that are subject to litigation or legislation
- Contracts for property that is likely to be condemned or expropriated
- Contracts where the customer is unlikely to meet its obligations
- Contracts where the contractor cannot meet its obligations

When an uncertainty arises about the collectibility of an amount already recognized in revenue, the contractor records the uncollectible amount as an expense, rather than a downward adjustment of contract revenue.

What Controls Do I Use for Construction Contracts?

Consider using all of the following controls for construction contracts in order to mitigate the risk of revenue recognition problems:

○ *Compare declared percentage of completion to estimated work required to complete projects.* A common way to record excessive revenue on a construction project is to falsely state that the percentage of completion is greater than the actual figure, thereby allowing the company to record a greater proportion of revenue in the current period. To detect it, match the declared percentage of completion to a percentage of the actual hours worked divided by the total estimated number of hours worked. The two percentages should match.

○ *Ensure that project expenses are charged to the correct account.* A common problem with revenue recognition under the percentage of completion method is that extra expenses may be erroneously or falsely loaded into a project's general ledger account, which can then be used as justification for the recognition of additional revenue related to that project. Auditing expenses in active project accounts can spot these problems.

○ *Promptly close project accounts once projects are completed.* It is not a difficult matter to incorrectly store project-related expenses in the wrong accounts, and this may be done fraudulently in order to avoid recognizing losses related to excessive amounts of expenses being incurred on specific projects. This problem can be resolved by promptly closing general ledger project accounts once the related projects are complete.

○ *Control access to general ledger accounts.* Employees are less likely to shift expenses between general ledger construction accounts if they are unable to access the accounts, or if they have no way of reopening closed accounts. This can be achieved by tightly restricting account access, and especially access to the closed or open status flag for each account.

○ *Consistently aggregate expenses into overhead accounts and charge them to individual projects.* One could charge different overhead expenses to various projects, thereby effectively shifting expenses to those projects that would result in the greatest revenue increase under the percentage of completion method. To avoid this problem, periodically verify that the same expenses are being charged consistently to overhead cost pools over time, and that the same allocation method is used to shift these expenses from overhead cost pools to project accounts.

○ *Watch for expense loading on cost-plus contracts.* When a company is guaranteed that a customer will pay for all expenses incurred, there is a temptation to charge extra expenses to that customer's project. These expense additions can be spotted by looking for charges from suppliers whose costs normally are not charged to a specific type of contract, as well as by looking for expense types that increase significantly over expenses incurred in previous periods, and by investigating any journal entries that increase expense levels.

When Do I Recognize Royalty Revenue?

Recognition is in accordance with the terms of the relevant agreement, unless the substance of the agreement calls for a different method. From a practical perspective, recognition may be on a straight-line basis over the term of the agreement. If the agreement is an assignment of rights in exchange for a fixed fee or nonrefundable guarantee where the licensor has no remaining performance obligations, the licensor can recognize revenue at the time of sale. If payment under the agreement is contingent upon the occurrence of a future event, revenue should be recognized when it is probable that the fee or royalty will be received.

How Do I Value Agricultural Assets?

An entity should recognize a biological asset or agricultural produce when it controls the asset, future benefits associated with the asset will probably flow to the entity, and the asset's fair value or cost can be reliably measured.

An entity should measure its biological assets at the end of each reporting period at its fair value minus costs to sell. If fair value cannot be reliably measured, then the entity should measure biological assets at their cost, less accumulated depreciation and impairment losses. If a biological asset becomes reliably measurable, the entity should value it at its fair value minus costs to sell. Agricultural produce that has been harvested should be measured at its fair value, less costs to sell, as of the harvesting date.

If an entity enters into a contract to sell its biological assets or agricultural produce at a future date, it should not use the prices in the contract to value the assets, since these terms may be onerous. Instead, it should use the quoted prices in an active market for its assets. If there are prices available from multiple active markets, the entity should use prices existing in the market that it expects to use.

If there is no active market, then the entity should use one of the following methods to determine fair value:

- The most recent market transaction price, provided that there have not been significant changes in economic circumstance since the date of the last price
- Market prices for similar assets, adjusted to reflect any differences between them and the entity's assets
- Sector benchmarks expressed as a standard unit of measure

If no fair value information is available, then the entity may use the present value of expected net cash flows to determine the value of its assets, using the current market interest rate as the discount rate. These expected net cash flows should incorporate the entity's expectations for variations in cash flows.

 ## When Do I Recognize a Gain or Loss on Agricultural Assets?

An entity should recognize a gain or loss arising from the difference between the fair values of its biological assets, less costs to sell, in the current reporting period versus the preceding reporting period. A gain or loss also may arise upon the initial recognition of a biological asset. The entity should recognize these gains or losses in the period in which they arise.

An entity should measure the fair value of agricultural produce, less costs to sell, at the point of harvest. Once harvested, no further fair value adjustment for agricultural produce should be made.

 ## When Do I Recognize an Agriculture-Related Government Grant?

An entity should recognize the fair value of a government grant, less costs to sell, only when the grant becomes receivable. If the grant is conditional, the entity should recognize the grant only when it has met all of the conditions attached to the grant. If the grant allows for some degree of funds retention due to the passage of time, then the entity can recognize that portion of the grant as the requisite time periods pass.

How Do I Record Barter Transactions for Advertising Services?

A company may enter into a barter transaction to provide advertising services in exchange for receiving advertising services from its customer. This can involve the exchange of no cash at all, or approximately equal amounts of cash or other consideration. Two forms of revenue recognition can arise from this scenario:

1. *Similar services.* If there is an exchange of similar advertising services, then the exchange does not result in revenue recognition by either party.
2. *Dissimilar services.* If there is an exchange of dissimilar advertising services, the seller can recognize revenue. It is not allowable to do so based on the fair value of advertising services received. Instead, the seller can measure revenue based on the fair value of the advertising services it provides, by reference to nonbarter transactions that:

   a. Involve advertising similar to that included in the barter transaction
   b. Occur frequently
   c. Involve a different counterparty than in the barter transaction
   d. Involve cash or other consideration that has a reliably measurable fair value
   e. Represent a predominant number of transactions and amounts as compared with the barter transaction.

EXAMPLE 17.6

Stoked TV enters into an advertising barter transaction with *Dude* magazine, where Stoked advertises *Dude* on its cable network in exchange for similar coverage in *Dude* magazine. Stoked is providing *Dude* with five advertising spots of 30 seconds duration. Stoked normally provides such coverage at a rate of $10,000 per spot, and does so frequently with other parties, who pay cash. The proportion of transactions where Stoked is paid cash for advertising is approximately 90 percent of all of its advertising transactions. Accordingly, Stoked TV can recognize the fair value of its advertising as revenue, which is $10,000 multiplied by five coverage spots, or $50,000.

When Do I Record Revenue for a Customer Loyalty Program?

A customer loyalty program is used by a company to give its customers an incentive to buy its goods or services. Customers earn award credits by buying from the company, which they can then use to obtain free or discounted goods or services.

A company that issues award credits should treat them as a separately identifiable component of the sales transaction in which they are granted. The company must allocate the sale between the award credits and the other components of the sale. The amount of the allocation to the award credits should be based on the fair value of credits, which is the price at which the credits can be sold separately, or the fair value of the awards for which they can be redeemed. In the latter case, the fair value of the awards should be reduced to account for the proportion of award credits that the company does not expect its customers to redeem. If customers can select from a number of awards, then the fair value analysis should reflect an average of the award fair values, weighted for the frequency of expected award selection. If an allocation of consideration to award credits is not possible based on fair values, a company may use alternative methods.

If the company pays out awards itself, then it recognizes revenue for the consideration allocated to the award credits when customers redeem the awards and the company delivers the awards.

EXAMPLE 17.7
Ace Auto Magic has a customer loyalty program. It grants participating customers award points every time they purchase from Ace. Customers can redeem their points for free oil changes at any Ace store. The points are valid for three years from the date of each customer's last purchase, so that points essentially have no termination date as long as customers keep buying from Ace.
During February, Ace issues 80,000 award points. Management expects that 75 percent of these points, or 60,000 points, eventually will be redeemed. Management estimates that the fair value of each award point is 10 cents, and so defers revenue recognition on €6,000.

After one year, customers have redeemed 30,000 of the award points for oil changes, so Ace recognizes revenue of €3,000 (30,000 redeemed points/60,000 estimated total redemptions × €6,000 deferred revenue).

During the second year, management revises its redemption estimate, and now expects that 70,000 of the original 80,000 award points will be redeemed. During that year, 20,000 points are redeemed, so that a total of 50,000 points have now been redeemed. The cumulative revenue that Ace recognizes is €4,286 (50,000 redeemed points/70,000 estimated total redemptions × €6,000 deferred revenue). Since Ace already recognized €3,000 in Year 1, it now recognizes €1,286 in Year 2.

During the third year, customers redeem an additional 20,000 award points, which brings total redemptions to 70,000. Management does not expect additional redemptions. Accordingly, Ace recognizes the remainder of the deferred revenue, which is €1,714.

If a third party pays out the awards, the company essentially is collecting the consideration allocated to the awards on behalf of the third party. In this scenario, the company measures its revenue as the difference between the consideration allocated to the award credits and the amount payable to the third party for supplying the awards. The company can recognize this net difference as revenue as soon as the third party becomes obligated to supply awards and is entitled to be paid for doing so. This recognition may arise as soon as the company grants award credits. However, if customers can claim awards from either the company or the third party, revenue recognition occurs only when customers claim awards.

EXAMPLE 17.8

Organic Delights, a purveyor of organically grown farm produce, participates in the customer loyalty program operated by Dakota Airlines. Organic grants its participating customers one air travel point for every dollar they spend on farm produce. These customers can then redeem the points for air travel with Dakota. Organic pays Dakota €0.008 for each point. During the first year of the program's operation, Organic awards 3 million points.

(Continued)

> (*Continued*)
>
> Organic estimates that the fair value of an award point is €0.01. It therefore allocates to the 3 million issued points €30,000 of the consideration it has received from the sale of its produce. Organic has no further obligation to its customers, since Dakota is now obligated to supply the awards. Accordingly, Organic can recognize the €30,000 of revenue allocated to the award points at once, as well as the €24,000 expense payable to Dakota (€3,000,000 × €0.008).
>
> If Organic had acted as an agent for Dakota and simply collected funds on behalf of Dakota, then it would recognize revenue only as the net amount it retained, which would be €6,000 (€30,000 allocated to the awarded points – €24,000 paid to Dakota).

If the cost of the obligation to supply awards exceeds the consideration received, the company should recognize a liability for the excess amount. This situation can arise, for example, when the cost of supplying awards increases, or when the proportion of award credits redeemed increases.

 ## How Do I Record a Bad Debt?

When an uncertainty arises about the collectibility of an amount that has already been recognized as revenue, the uncollectible amount is recognized as an expense, rather than a reduction of the revenue already recognized. This rule applies to revenue recognized from the sale of goods, the provision of services, and interest, royalties, and dividends.

 ## How Do I Record Revenue Collected for a Third Party?

Revenue can be recognized by an entity only if the related transactions occur on its own account. For example:

- ○ *Agencies.* Amounts collected by an agent are on behalf of the principal and so do not alter the equity of the agent. These amounts are therefore not revenue; the agent instead should record commissions received as revenue.
- ○ *Taxes.* Amounts collected on behalf of government entities, such as sales taxes and value added taxes, do not create economic benefits for the entity and do

not alter its equity; therefore, such transactions are excluded from revenue.

What General Revenue Recognition Controls Should I Use?

Investigate all journal entries increasing the size of revenue. Any time a journal entry is used to increase a sales account, this should be a "red flag" indicating the potential presence of revenue that was not created through a normal sales journal transaction. It is especially important to review all sales transactions where the offsetting debit to the sales credit is *not* accounts receivable or cash. This is a prime indicator of unusual transactions that may not really qualify as sales. For example, a gain on an asset sale or an extraordinary gain may be incorrectly credited to a sales account that may mislead the reader of a company's financial statements into thinking that its operating revenue has increased.

Compare customer-requested delivery dates with actual shipment dates. If customer order information is loaded into the accounting computer system, run a comparison of the dates on which customers have requested delivery to the dates on which orders actually were shipped. If there is an ongoing tendency to make shipments substantially early, there may be a problem with trying to create revenue by making early shipments.

What General Revenue Information Do I Disclose?

An entity should disclose the following items:

- *Policies.* The revenue recognition policies the entity has adopted, including the methods it uses to determine stages of completion for the provision of services
- *Revenue categories.* The amount of revenue associated with each of the following categories:

  - Sale of goods
  - Rendering of services
  - Interest
  - Royalties
  - Dividends

- *Exchanges.* The revenue caused by exchanges of goods or services in each of the preceding categories

What Agricultural Revenue Information Do I Disclose?

The following disclosures related to revenue recognition are required of an entity that engages in agricultural activity:

- ◯ *Assumptions.* The significant assumptions applied in determining the fair value of each group of agricultural produce at the point of harvest and each group of biological assets
- ◯ *Basis of change.* Separate disclosure of the physical changes in the biological asset and price changes in the market that aggregate into the total fair value change (both disclosures are reduced by the costs to sell)
- ◯ *Fair value.* The fair value, less costs to sell, of agricultural produce harvested during the period, as determined at the point of harvest
- ◯ *Gains and losses.* The aggregate gains and losses arising during the current period on the initial recognition of biological assets and agricultural produce, as well as from the change in fair value, less costs to sell, of biological assets
- ◯ *Metrics.* Nonfinancial measures of the physical quantities of each group of biological assets at the end of the period and the output of agricultural produce during the period

If an entity uses cost less accumulated depreciation and impairment losses to measure its biological assets, then it must disclose the following information:

- ◯ Asset description
- ◯ Why fair value cannot be used
- ◯ The range of estimates within which fair value is highly likely to lie
- ◯ The depreciation method and useful lives used
- ◯ The gross carrying amount and accumulated depreciation and impairment losses at the beginning and end of the period

If an entity is able to begin valuing at their fair value biological assets that previously were valued at cost, it should disclose a description of the assets, explain why fair value is now reliably measurable, and the effect of the change.

If an entity has received government grants, then it must disclose the nature and extent of the grants, any unfulfilled conditions of the grants, and any expected decreases in the level of the grants.

What Construction Contract Revenue Information Do I Disclose?

At an aggregate level, a contractor should disclose the amount of contract revenue recognized in the period, the methods used to determine revenue, and the methods used to determine contract stages of completion.

For contracts in progress, a contractor should disclose the aggregate amount of costs incurred and recognized profits to date, the amount of advances received, and the amount of retentions (i.e., the amount of progress billings not paid until conditions in the contract have been satisfied).

The contractor also should report as an asset the gross amount due from customers for contract work. This is the net amount of costs incurred plus recognized profits, minus the sum of recognized losses and progress billings for all contracts in progress where costs incurred plus recognized profits exceed progress billings.

The contractor also should report as a liability the gross amount due to customers for contract work. This is the net amount of costs incurred plus recognized profits, minus the sum of recognized losses and progress billings for all contracts in progress where billings exceed costs incurred plus recognized profits.

CHAPTER 18

EMPLOYEE BENEFITS

 What Types of Employee Benefits Are There?

Short-term employee benefits are those due to be settled within 12 months of the period in which employees render the related service. *Post-employment benefits* are those payable following the completion of employment. *Termination benefits* are payable as a result of either the entity's decision to terminate employment prior to the retirement date, or an employee's voluntary acceptance of redundancy in exchange for those benefits. *Other long-term benefits* are those other than post-employment and termination benefits that will be settled after the 12 months following the period when employees render related services.

 What Are Vested Employee Benefits?

Vested employee benefits are benefits granted to employees that are not conditional on any future employment.

 What Is a Qualifying Insurance Policy?

A qualifying insurance policy is issued by an insurer that is not related to the entity. Also, the proceeds of the policy can be used only to pay or fund employee benefits under a defined benefit plan and are not available to the entity's creditors. The proceeds also cannot be paid to the entity, unless they are surplus assets not needed to meet benefit obligations, or the proceeds are reimbursement to the entity for benefits already paid.

 What Are Actuarial Gains and Losses?

Actuarial gains and losses include adjustments for the differences between previous actuarial assumptions and what actually has occurred, and changes in actuarial assumptions.

 What Is Past Service Cost?

Past service cost is the change in the present value of defined benefit obligations caused by employee service in prior periods. This cost arises from changes in post-employment benefits or other long-term employee benefits. The change in this cost may be either positive or negative.

 What Are Short-Term Employee Benefits?

Short-term employee benefits include:

- ○ *Absences.* Compensated absences where payment is settled within 12 months of when employees render related services, for example, vacation, short-term disability, jury service, and military service
- ○ *Base pay.* Wages and social security contributions
- ○ *Nonmonetary benefits.* Medical care, housing, cars, and various subsidies for other goods or services
- ○ *Performance pay.* Profit sharing and bonuses payable within 12 months of when employees render related services

The entitlement to compensated absences can be accumulating or nonaccumulating. An *accumulating compensated absence* is carried forward and can be used in future periods. An accumulating compensated absence can be vesting, so that employees are entitled to a cash payment for unused entitlement when they leave the entity. If an accumulating compensated absence is nonvesting, then employees do not receive such a cash payment when they leave the entity.

 How Do I Account for Short-Term Employee Benefits?

Recognize the cost of short-term employee benefits in the period incurred. There is no need to incorporate actuarial assumptions in these costs. Also, do not discount these costs with a present value calculation.

Record a short-term employee benefit as an accrued expense, after deducting any amount already paid. If the amount paid exceeds the undiscounted benefit cost, then record the overage as a prepaid asset to the extent that it will reduce the amount of a future payment or yield a cash refund.

How Do I Account for a Short-Term Compensated Absence?

Recognize the expected cost of a short-term compensated absence when employees render service that increases their entitlement to future compensated absences. Conversely, do not recognize a liability or expense for a non-accumulating compensated absence until the absence occurs.

You must recognize the cost of a compensated absence even if it is nonvesting, although it is permissible to incorporate the possibility of employee departures in the cost calculation.

EXAMPLE 18.1

Tango Mural Company has 50 employees, and all are entitled to three days of paid sick leave each year, which they can carry forward for five years. At the end of the first year, the average unused entitlement accruing during that year is one day per employee. Tango's experience is that all carried forward sick days are used before the end of the five-year period. Thus, Tango expects that it will pay an additional 50 days of sick pay in a future period (50 employees × 1 unused sick day each), and it recognizes a liability for this amount.

How Do I Account for a Profit-Sharing or Bonus Plan?

Recognize the expected cost of a profit-sharing or bonus payment only when the entity has a legal obligation to make such a payment based on past events, and if it is possible to reliably estimate the obligation. To have a reliable estimate, there should be a formal plan containing a benefit formula, the amounts to be paid should be determined before the financial statements are authorized for issuance, or the entity's past practices should clearly indicate the amount of the obligation.

EXAMPLE 18.2

Sodium Solutions, the maker of sodium-sulphur batteries, has a profit-sharing plan under which it pays
5 percent of its net profits to those employees who
have worked for the company for all 12 months of the
year. Sodium retains the profit distribution for any
employees who are not still working for the company
at the end of the year. Based on its historical 10 percent employee turnover rate, Sodium estimates that it
will pay out 4.5 percent of its profits, and so it recognizes a liability and expense for that amount.

An entity may not be legally required to pay a bonus,
but has done so in the past, which creates a constructive
obligation to do so in the future. If so, recognize the
expected cost of the profit-sharing or bonus payment,
while also factoring in the possibility of a liability reduction caused by the departure of employees who leave
without their profit-sharing or bonus payments.

What Types of Employee Benefit Plans Are There?

A *post-employment benefit plan* is an arrangement whereby
an entity provides post-employment benefits for its
employees. A *defined contribution plan* is a post-employment
benefit plan under which the entity pays a fixed contribution
into a fund. A *defined benefit plan* is a post-employment benefit plan under which the entity provides specific benefits
to current and former employees. The employee bears all
actuarial risk under a defined contribution plan, while the
entity bears all actuarial risk under a defined benefit plan.

A *multi-employer plan* is a defined contribution or
benefit plan that pools the assets contributed by various
entities and uses the assets to provide benefits to the
employees of multiple entities. A plan is a defined benefit
multi-employer plan if participating entities contribute
just enough to it to pay the benefits due in the same period, employee benefits are determined by the length of
employees' service, and participating entities realistically
cannot withdraw without paying an additional contribution for benefits earned but not yet paid.

A defined benefit plan that shares risks between entities
that are under common control is not a multi-employer
plan.

A *state plan* is one established by legislation and operated by a government, and that covers all entities or a subset thereof. An entity accounts for its participation in a state plan in the same manner it would account for a multi-employer plan. A state plan is usually a defined contribution plan.

 ## What Is a Group Administration Plan?

A group administration plan is an aggregation of individual employer plans that are combined so that participating employers can pool their assets to reduce investment and administration costs. Employee claims within the plan are segregated by employer. From an accounting perspective, a group administration plan is identical to a single employer plan.

 ## How Do I Account for a Multi-Employer Plan?

If a multi-employer plan is a defined benefit plan, then an entity within the plan accounts for its proportionate share of the defined benefit obligations, assets, and costs associated with the plan in the same way as for any other defined benefit plan.

If there is not enough information to account for the entity's share of a defined benefit plan as such, then account for it as a defined contribution plan.

It also may be necessary to disclose a contingent liability for actuarial losses relating to other entities participating in the plan, or if the plan makes participating entities liable for any shortfalls that arise if other entities stop participating.

 ## How Do I Account for a Plan under the Control of a Single Entity?

If the plan is actually under the control of a single entity and there is an agreement or policy for charging the net defined benefit cost to individual group entities, then recognize the net defined benefit cost as stated in the agreement or policy. If there is no such agreement or policy, then the sponsoring employer for the plan should recognize the net defined benefit cost, while the other entities recognize a cost equal to their contribution payable for the period.

How Do I Account for Insured Benefits?

If an entity pays insurance premiums that pay for a post-employment benefit plan, then treat it as a defined contribution plan. However, if the entity has an obligation to directly pay employee benefits or pay additional amounts if the insurer does not pay all benefits, then treat it as a defined benefit plan.

 How Do I Account for a Defined Contribution Plan?

The entity's obligation matches the amount it contributes to the plan in a period, so recognize the contribution amount as an expense. This should be an accrued expense, after deducting any contributions already paid. If the contribution paid exceeds the amount due, then recognize the excess as a prepaid expense, if the prepaid amount reduces future payments or will result in a refund.

Do not use any actuarial assumptions to measure the obligation, since there is no possibility of an actuarial gain or loss. Do not measure obligations on a discounted basis, unless they are due later than 12 months from the period when employees render the related services.

 How Do I Account for a Defined Benefit Plan?

Follow these six steps to account for each separate defined benefit plan:

1. *Benefit estimation.* Use actuarial methods to estimate the amount of employee benefits earned in the current and prior periods. This requires the use of demographic variables, such as employee turnover and mortality, as well as financial variables, such as future changes in salaries and medical costs, that influence benefit costs.
2. *Discounting.* Discount the resulting benefit using the projected unit credit method. This results in the present value of the obligation, as well as the current service cost.
3. *Fair value.* Determine the fair value of any plan assets.
4. *Gains and losses.* Determine total gains and losses, as well as the amount of those actuarial gains and losses that can be recognized.

5. *Past service cost.* If the plan has been introduced or changed, calculate the past service cost.
6. *Settlement cost.* If the plan has been curtailed or settled, calculate the resulting gain or loss.

EXAMPLE 18.3

Mr. Trent Nectar, president of Ambrosia Cuisine, will receive a benefit upon his retirement from Ambrosia of 20 percent of his final annual salary for each of his remaining years of employment. He will retire in three years. Ambrosia expects his salary in each of the three remaining years to be €200,000, €220,000, and €240,000, respectively. The discount rate is 4 percent. The current service cost, pension liability, and interest cost associated with Mr. Nectar's retirement benefit follow:

Year	Salary	Current Service Cost*	Discounted Current Service Cost	Interest Cost**	Year-end Liability***
1	€200,000	€24,000	€22,189	—	€22,189
2	220,000	24,000	23,077	€888	46,154
3	240,000	24,000	24,000	1,846	71,077
		€72,000	€69,266	€2,734	

*20% of the final-year salary
**4% of the year-end liability
***Cumulative discounted current service cost plus cumulative interest cost

---

The amount an entity recognizes as a defined benefit liability at the end of a reporting period is the net total of:

+	Present value of the benefit obligation
+	Any unrecognized actuarial gains
−	Any unrecognized actuarial losses
−	Any unrecognized past service cost
−	Fair value of any plan assets from which obligations are to be directly settled
=	Amount recognized as a defined benefit liability

If this calculation (see preceding comment) results in an asset, then measure it at the lower of the calculated amount or the total of any cumulative unrecognized net actuarial losses and past service cost and the present value of any refunds from or reductions in future contributions to the plan.

An entity has a right to a refund only if it has an unconditional right to it during the life of the plan irrespective of whether the plan liabilities are settled, or on the assumption that the plan will be settled gradually until there are no members left in the plan, or assuming the full settlement of liabilities in a single event. Do not recognize a refund if the right to it depends on a future event. Measure a refund net of any associated costs, such as taxes and professional fees.

The amount of the reduction in future contributions to a plan is the lower of surplus or present value of the future service cost to the entity for each year over the shorter of the expected life of the plan or the entity. Future service costs should assume no benefit changes and a stable workforce, unless there are specific commitments that will change these items.

If there is a future minimum funding requirement, and that contribution exceeds the future service cost in any year, the present value of the excess reduces the amount of the asset available as a reduction in future contributions.

How Do I Account for Actuarial Gains and Losses?

Actuarial gains and losses arise from changes in the present value of a defined benefit obligation, or in the fair value of related plan assets. Such gains and losses are caused, for example, by changes in rates of employee turnover, early retirement, altered rates of mortality, and changes in the estimates of these items for future periods.

When measuring a defined benefit liability, recognize a portion of actuarial gains and losses as income or expense if the net cumulative unrecognized actuarial gains and losses at the end of the reporting period exceed the greater of 10 percent of the fair value of any plan assets or 10 percent of the present value of the defined benefit obligation. These 10 percent boundaries create a corridor within which actuarial gains and losses are likely to vary over time, and which do not require ongoing recognition.

Calculate and apply these limits separately for each defined benefit plan.

It is allowable to recognize these gains and losses in other comprehensive income, as long as the entity does so for all defined benefit plans and all actuarial gains and losses. Also, do not reclassify these gains and losses to profit or loss in a later reporting period.

How Do I Account for Actuarial Gains and Losses If I Have a Surplus?

If an entity has a surplus in a defined benefit plan, and it cannot recover the surplus under the plan terms through a reduction in future contributions, then take the following steps to recognize actuarial gains or losses in the current period:

- ○ *Actuarial losses.* Immediately recognize any net actuarial losses and past service cost of the current period to the extent that they exceed any *reduction* in the present value of any refunds from or reductions in future contributions to the plan. If there is no reduction, then immediately recognize the net actuarial losses and past service cost of the current period.
- ○ *Actuarial gains.* Immediately recognize any net actuarial gains of the current period, after reducing them by the past service cost of the current period, to the extent that they *exceed* any increase in the present value of any refunds from or reductions in future contributions to the plan. If there is no increase, then immediately recognize the net actuarial gains of the current period after deducting any past service cost of the current period.

How Do I Account for the Return on Plan Assets?

The expected return on plan assets is based on market expectations at the beginning of the period for returns over the life of the related obligations. The difference between the expected and actual rate of return on plan assets is an actuarial gain or loss.

EXAMPLE 18.4

The actuarial assumptions for Ambrosia Cuisine's defined benefit plan include an expected return of €150,000 in Year 1. The actual return during that period is €165,000, which produces an actuarial gain of €15,000.

How Do I Account for Past Service Cost?

Past service cost is the change in the present value of defined benefit obligations caused by employee service in prior periods. This cost arises from changes in post-employment benefits or other long-term employee benefits. The past service cost can be negative if an entity changes its benefits so that the present value of the obligation declines.

You should recognize past service cost as an expense on a straight-line basis over the average period until benefits vest. If benefits vest immediately, then recognize the associated expense immediately. There should be no need to amend the amortization schedule unless there is a benefit curtailment or settlement.

Example 18.5

Nicosia Thermal Energy operates a pension plan for its employees that provides a pension of 1 percent of final salary for each year of service, following a 10-year vesting period. Nicosia increases the pension to 1.5 percent of final salary. At the date of this change, the present value of the additional benefit for service up to that point for the past 10 years is:

Employees with more than 10 years of service	€180,000
Employees with less than 10 years of service (average remaining vesting period is four years)	92,000
	€272,000

Nicosia must recognize the €180,000 benefit increase immediately, because that benefit is entirely vested. It recognizes the €92,000 portion of the benefit on a straight-line basis over the next four years.

If the entity reduces benefits payable under a defined benefit plan, then recognize the resulting reduction in the benefit liability as past service cost over the average period until the benefits become vested. If there is a combination of benefit increases and decreases under a defined benefit plan, then treat the changes as a single net change.

Past service cost *does not* include:

- Benefit improvement estimates resulting from recognized actuarial gains, if there is an obligation to use plan surpluses for the benefit of plan participants
- Incorrect estimates of discretionary pension increases when there is a constructive obligation to grant the increases
- Increased benefits resulting from employee completion of vesting requirements
- Plan amendments that reduce benefits related to future service
- The impact of the difference between actual and previously assumed salary changes on the benefit obligation for prior years

 ## How Do I Account for Plan Assets?

You should deduct the fair value of any plan assets when calculating the amount to be recognized in the statement of financial position. If there is no market price available for making this determination, then estimate their fair value. For example, you can estimate the fair value by discounting the expected future cash flows arising from the plan assets.

When making this determination, do not include unpaid contributions from the entity to the fund or any nontransferable financial instruments issued by the entity and held by the fund. Also, reduce plan assets by any fund liabilities not relating to employee benefits, such as trade payables.

 ## How Do I Account for Reimbursements?

If it is certain that a third party, such as an insurance company, will reimburse some portion or all of an expenditure required to settle a defined benefit obligation, an entity should recognize the reimbursement amount as a separate asset and measure it at its fair value. You should present the reimbursement amount net of the related expense in the statement of comprehensive income.

 ## How Do I Account for Benefits Arising from a Business Combination?

An acquiring entity recognizes all assets and liabilities arising from post-employment benefits at the present value of the obligation, minus the fair value of any plan assets. The obligations include the following items that occurred before the acquisition date:

- ○ *Gains and losses.* Actuarial gains and losses
- ○ *Past service cost.* Past service cost caused by benefit changes or the introduction of a new plan

How Do I Account for Curtailments and Settlements?

A *curtailment* arises when an entity reduces the number of employees covered by a plan, or amends a benefit plan so that future service by employees will yield reduced benefits; a corporate restructuring is a common cause of a curtailment. A *settlement* occurs when an entity conducts a transaction that eliminates an obligation to pay future benefits; a common scenario is when employees receive a lump-sum cash payment in exchange for their rights to receive post-employment benefits.

You should recognize a gain or loss on a curtailment or settlement of a defined benefit plan when the event occurs, following the remeasurement of the obligation and/or assets using current actuarial assumptions. The gain or loss includes:

- ○ *Fair value.* Any change in the fair value of the plan assets
- ○ *Gains and losses.* Any actuarial gains and losses and past service cost not previously recognized
- ○ *Present value.* Any change in the present value of the defined benefit obligation

When a curtailment or settlement includes only some of the employees covered by a plan or when there is only a partial obligation settlement, you should recognize a proportionate share of the previously unrecognized past service cost and actuarial gains and losses. You calculate the proportionate share on the basis of the present value of the obligations before and after the event, unless there is another more rational basis.

EXAMPLE 18.6
Ambrosia Cuisine discontinues its Canola Oil production facility; the employees of that segment will earn no further benefits. Under current actuarial assumptions as of the curtailment date, Ambrosia has a

defined benefit obligation with a present value of €100,000, plan assets having a fair value of €75,000, and net cumulative unrecognized actuarial gains of €5,000. The curtailment reduces the present value of the obligation by €10,000, to €90,000. Ten percent of the net cumulative unrecognized actuarial gains relate to the part of the obligation that was eliminated by the curtailment. These changes result in the post-curtailment figures in the following table:

	Prior to Curtailment	Curtailment Gain	Post Curtailment
Obligation present value	€100,000	€(10,000)	€90,000
Plan assets fair value	(75,000)	—	(75,000)
	25,000	(10,000)	15,000
Unrecognized actuarial gains	5,000	500	4,500
Net liability in statement of financial position	€30,000	€(9,500)	€10,500

Ambrosia records the curtailment gain with the following entry:

Accrued pension cost	9,500	
Curtailment gain		9,500

What Defined Benefit Plan Amounts Appear in Profit or Loss?

Recognize the net total of these amounts in profit or loss:

Actuarial gains and losses	Interest cost
Current service cost	Net actuarial gains or losses
Effect of any curtailments or settlements	Past service cost
Expected return on plan assets and reimbursement rights	

How Frequently Should I Review Plan Assets and Obligations?

You should measure the present value of defined benefit obligations and the fair value of plan assets with sufficient regularity to ensure that the amounts shown in the financial statements do not differ materially from the amounts that would be determined through measurement at the end of the reporting period.

When Can I Recognize an Asset under a Defined Benefit Plan?

You can recognize an asset when a defined benefit plan has been overfunded, or in some cases when you have recognized an actuarial gain. You can do this when the entity has the ability to use the surplus, the surplus arises from past contributions, and the entity either will receive a cash refund or a reduction in future contributions, or can use the surplus to offset another plan that is in a deficit funding situation.

What Characteristics Should Actuarial Assumptions Have?

All actuarial assumptions used by an entity should be unbiased and mutually compatible. An actuarial assumption is unbiased if it is prudent and not excessively conservative. Actuarial assumptions are mutually compatible if they reflect the economic relationships between such factors as inflation, salary raise percentages, discount rates, and the return on plan assets. Further, an entity should base any financial assumptions on market expectations for the period over which it expects to settle the obligations.

Do I Need an Actuary to Measure Benefit Obligations?

The use of a qualified actuary is encouraged, but not required, to measure post-employment benefit obligations.

What Are Demographic and Financial Actuarial Assumptions?

Actuarial assumptions are divided into demographic and financial assumptions. *Demographic assumptions* typically include mortality, employee turnover rates, disability, early retirement, and claim rates. *Financial assumptions* typically include the discount rate, future salary and benefit levels, future medical costs, claim administration costs, and the expected rate of return on plan assets.

What Are the Actuarial Assumptions for Salaries, Benefits, and Medical Costs?

An entity must calculate its post-employment benefit obligations using a number of actuarial assumptions for salaries, benefits, and medical costs. The following assumptions should be addressed:

- ○ *Plan benefits.* Benefits noted in the plan, or from constructive obligations exceeding those noted in the plan. Medical cost assumptions should account for estimated future changes in the cost of medical services, based on the entity's own historical data (adjusted for demographics), supplemented if necessary by data from other entities. Future medical cost assumptions should include a consideration of changes in the health status of participants, technological advances, health care utilization levels, and employee contributions.
- ○ *Salaries.* Estimated future salary changes based on such factors as inflation, seniority, and labor market supply and demand.
- ○ *State benefits.* Estimated future changes in the amount of any state benefits impacting the defined benefit plan if the changes were enacted before the end of the reporting period or evidence indicates that the state benefits will change in a predictable manner.

What Discount Rate Should I Use for Actuarial Assumptions?

You should refer to the market yields at the end of the reporting period on high-quality corporate bonds when determining the discount rate on post-employment benefit obligations. If there is no deep market for such bonds, then use the market yields at the end of the reporting period for government bonds. In either case, use corporate or government bonds whose currency and term are consistent with the currency and estimated term of the post-employment benefit obligations. It may be necessary to

estimate the discount rate for longer maturities by extrapolating the current market rate along the yield curve.

 ## How Do I Calculate the Interest Cost Associated with a Defined Benefit Obligation?

You calculate the interest cost associated with a defined
benefit obligation by multiplying the discount rate at the
start of the period by the present value of the defined benefit obligation throughout the period.

 ## What Present Value Method Should I Use for a Defined Benefit Plan?

Use the projected unit credit method (PUC method) to calculate the present value of defined benefit obligations, related current service cost, and past service cost. Under the
PUC method, each period of service creates an additional
unit of benefit entitlement; you measure each unit individually, then aggregate the units to reach the final obligation
amount.

EXAMPLE 18.7

Under Wilkerson Supercomputer's defined benefit
plan, a lump-sum benefit is payable upon termination
of an employee's service and equals 2 percent of an
employee's final salary for each full year of service.
Mr. Bond has a salary in Year 1 of £80,000, which Wilkerson assumes will increase at a compounded rate of
5 percent per year. Wilkerson uses an annual discount
rate of 8 percent. The following table shows the increase in the obligation to Mr. Bond over a four-year
period, where the pay increases result in a pay level
of £92,610 at the end of Year 4:

Year	1	2	3	4
Benefit attributed to:				
- Prior years		0	1,852	3,704	5,556
- Current year (2% of final salary)	1,852	1,852	1,852	1,852
- Current year and prior years	1,852	3,704	5,556	7,408
Opening obligation:	—	1,470	3,176	5,145

- Interest on opening obligation at 8%	–	118	254	412
- Current service cost*	1,470	1,588	1,715	1,852
Closing obligation	1,470	3,176	5,145	7,409
Discount rate	0.79383	0.85734	0.92593	1.0000

*The current service cost is the current year benefit multiplied by the present value discount rate.

 ## How Do I Attribute Benefit to Periods of Service?

The general rule is to attribute benefit to periods of service in accordance with the plan's benefit formula. However, if employee service in later years leads to a materially higher benefit level than in earlier years, then attribute benefit on a straight-line basis from the date when employee service first leads to benefits under the plan, until the date when further employee service leads to no material additional plan benefits (other than from additional salary increases).

EXAMPLE 18.8

The Hercules Shoe Company has a defined benefit plan that pays retirees €2,000 for each year of service, payable on their retirement date. Under the terms of the plan, Hercules must attribute €2,000 to each year. The current service cost is the present value of €2,000, while the present value of the defined benefit obligation is the present value of €2,000, multiplied by the number of years of employee service through the end of the reporting period.

Hercules offers a different plan to the employees in a labor union, under which they receive a monthly pension payment equaling 0.5 percent of their final full-year wages for each year of service, with pension payments starting at age 70. Under the terms of this second plan, Hercules recognizes a benefit equal to the present value, at the expected retirement date of each employee, of a monthly pension of 0.5 percent of the estimated final salary, which is payable from the expected retirement date to the expected date of
(Continued)

(Continued)
death. The current service cost is the present value of this benefit, while the defined benefit obligation is the present value of monthly pension payments, multiplied by the number of years of employee service through the end of the reporting period.

Hercules offers a third plan to its management group, under which it pays a lump-sum benefit of €200,000 that vests after 20 years of service. There is no further benefit for service exceeding the 20-year vesting period. In this case, Hercules attributes €10,000 to each of the first 20 years of each manager's employment. Hercules adjusts the current service cost in each of the 20 years for the probability that managers will not complete the service period.

Hercules also has a post-employment medical plan that reimburses 5 percent of retiree medical expenses if employees work for the company at least 10 but less than 20 years, and reimburses 40 percent of these costs if they work for the company for 20 years or more. The 20-year vesting period leads to a materially higher benefit level, so for employees expected to stay with the company that long, Hercules attributes the benefit on a straight-line basis for 20 years, which is 2.0 percent (40% ÷ 20 years) of the present value of the expected medical costs. For those employees expected to leave after 10 years but before 20 years, Hercules attributes 0.5 percent (5% ÷ 10 years) of the present value of the expected medical costs. Hercules attributes no benefit for those employees it expects to leave within 10 years.

 ## Do I Recognize an Expense prior to Employee Vesting?

Yes. The entity accrues an obligation under a defined benefit plan even if employees are not yet vested in the plan. This creates a constructive obligation. In measuring the constructive obligation, the entity should consider the probability that some employees will not stay with the company long enough to be vested.

Similarly, if post-employment benefits are conditional upon a specific event occurring, the entity should still recognize the obligation, taking into consideration the probability that the event will occur.

EXAMPLE 18.9

The Iberian Tile Company has a defined benefit plan under which it pays all employees €500 for each year of service, with payment occurring on their date of retirement. This benefit is available only to those employees recording at least 15 years of service with the company.

Based on past employment histories, Iberian estimates that 50 percent of its employees will record 15 years of service, so it discounts the €500 annual benefit by 50 percent in determining the present value of the obligation.

Should I Account for a Constructive Obligation under a Defined Benefit Plan?

Yes. A constructive obligation arises when an entity has no realistic alternative to paying employee benefits, such as when altering an informal practice would cause unacceptable damage to employee relations.

How Do I Account for Other Long-Term Employee Benefits?

Other long-term employee benefits include sabbatical leave, long-term disability benefits, and deferred compensation paid 12 months or more after the period in which they are earned. There is little uncertainty related to these benefits, so accounting for them is simplified. The principal simplifications are that an entity immediately recognizes both actuarial gains and losses, as well as all past service costs.

To account for other long-term employee benefits, recognize as a liability the net total of the present value of the defined benefit obligation, minus the fair value of plan assets from which obligations are to be settled. Also, recognize as expense or income the net total of the current service cost, interest cost, expected return on plan assets and reimbursements rights, actuarial gains and losses, and any curtailments or settlements.

If other long-term employee benefits are for long-term disability and the benefit level depends on the length of service, then recognize the benefit over the service period, factoring in the probability that payment will be required and the period of time over which the entity expects to make payments. If the benefit level is the same irrespective of service period, then recognize the expected cost when a disability event occurs.

How Do I Account for Termination Benefits?

You should recognize termination benefits as a liability and an expense when the entity commits to either terminating employment before the normal retirement date or providing termination benefits due to an offer to encourage voluntary redundancy; if the latter, measure termination benefits based on the number of employees you expect to accept the offer. An entity is committed to a termination only when it has a detailed formal plan for doing so and it is not realistically possible to withdraw from the plan. The formal plan should include the location and function of the affected employees, as well as the approximate number to be terminated, the termination benefits for each job classification, and when the entity will implement the plan.

If termination benefits are due for payment more than 12 months after the reporting period, then record their present value using a discount rate that is based on market yields at the end of the reporting period on high-quality corporate bonds. If there is no deep market in such bonds, then use the market yields on government bonds instead.

If there is some uncertainty about how many employees will accept an offer of termination benefits, this is a reportable contingent liability. See the Provisions and Contingencies chapter for more information.

Can I Offset the Assets and Liabilities of Different Plans?

You can offset the assets and liabilities of different plans for presentation purposes only when an entity has an enforceable right to use a surplus from one plan to settle an obligation under another plan, and intends to do so on a net basis, or to simultaneously realize the surplus in one plan and settle the obligation in another one.

What Information Do I Disclose about a Multi-Employer Plan?

If there is not sufficient information to account for the entity's share of a defined benefit plan, then disclose that the plan is a defined benefit plan and the reason why sufficient information is not available to enable the entity to account for the plan as such. If a surplus or deficit in the plan may affect the amount of future contributions to the plan, then also disclose any available information about the surplus or deficit, the basis for determining it, and the implications for the entity.

What Information Do I Disclose for a Plan under the Control of a Single Entity?

An entity participating in a defined benefit plan that is under the control of a single entity should disclose the following:

- ○ *Chargeback methodology.* The agreement or policy for charging the net defined benefit cost, or that there is no agreement or policy for doing so
- ○ *Contribution methodology.* The policy for calculating contribution payments
- ○ *General.* Information about the plan as a whole

What Information Do I Disclose for a Defined Benefit Plan?

Disclose the following information for an entity's defined benefit plans. This information can be presented in total for all plans, individually, or in other groupings that are more useful.

- ○ *Accounting policy.* The accounting policy for recognizing actuarial gains and losses.
- ○ *Actuarial assumptions.* The actuarial assumptions in use at the end of the reporting period, including discount rates, expected rates of return on plan assets and on reimbursement rights, salary rates of increase, medical cost trends, and other material actuarial assumptions.
- ○ *Comparative periods.* The present value of the defined benefit obligation, the fair value of plan assets, and

the surplus or deficit in the plan for the current annual period and the previous four annual periods. For the same periods, also note the experience adjustments separately for the plan liabilities and assets, expressed as either an amount or a percentage of the period-end liabilities and assets, respectively.

○ *Contributions.* The best estimate of contributions the entity expects to be paid into the plan during the annual period beginning after the reporting period.

○ *Fair value proportions.* The percentage or amount that each major category of plan assets constitutes of the fair value of total plan assets; this should at least include equity instruments, debt instruments, and the entity's own financial instruments or property.

○ *Funding.* The obligation, split into amounts arising from unfunded plans and from wholly or partly funded plans.

○ *General.* The nature of the plan and the financial effects of any changes in the plan during the period.

○ *Other comprehensive income items.* The amount recognized in other comprehensive income for actuarial gains and losses, and the cumulative amount of actuarial gains and losses so recognized.

○ *Profit or loss items.* The amount recognized in profit or loss for the current service cost, past service cost, interest cost, expected return on plan assets, expected return on reimbursement rights, actuarial gains and losses, the effect of curtailments or settlements, and the line items in which they are included.

○ *Rates of return.* The basis for determining the overall expected rate of return on assets, incorporating the effect of major categories of plan assets. Also separately note the actual rates of return on plan assets and any reimbursement rights recognized as an asset.

○ *Reconciliation – assets.* Reconciliation of the opening and closing balances of the fair value of plan assets and reimbursement rights, showing the separate effects attributable to the expected return on plan assets, actuarial gains and losses, effects of foreign exchange rates, employer contributions, plan participant contributions, benefits paid, business combinations, and settlements.

○ *Reconciliation – general.* Reconciliation of the present value of the defined benefit obligation and the fair value of plan assets to these categories recognized in the statement of financial position, showing net actuarial gains and losses not recognized in the statement, the past service cost not recognized in the statement, any amount not recognized as an asset, and the fair value of any reimbursement right recognized as an asset.

○ *Reconciliation–obligations.* Reconciliation of the opening and closing balances of the present value of the defined benefit obligation, showing the separate effects attributable to current service cost, interest cost, plan participant contributions, actuarial gains and losses, effects of foreign exchange rates, benefits paid, past service cost, business combinations, and curtailments or settlements.

○ *Sensitivity analysis.* The effect of a one percentage point increase and decrease in the assumed medical cost trend rate on both the aggregate of the current service cost and interest cost components of post-employment medical costs, and the accumulated post-employment benefit obligation for medical costs. Keep all other assumptions constant for this analysis.

CHAPTER 19

SHARE-BASED PAYMENTS

 When Do I Recognize a Share-Based Payment?

When you pay for goods or services with an entity's shares, you should recognize the goods or services when you receive them. If the received goods or services do not qualify as assets, then recognize them as expenses.

If the transaction is settled with a share-based payment, then record the offsetting credit in equity. If the transaction is a cash-settled, share-based payment transaction, then record the offsetting credit as a liability.

 How Do I Account for an Equity-Settled, Share-Based Payment Transaction?

In general, if you settle a share-based payment with an equity instrument, measure the goods or services received at the fair value of the goods or services received. If you cannot reliably estimate this fair value, then measure them at the fair value of the equity instruments issued. The treatment of two subsets of these transactions differs somewhat:

- ○ *Employee services.* Measure the fair value of employee services received in exchange for equity at the fair value of the equity instruments granted at their grant date.
- ○ *Suppliers.* Preferably, measure the transaction at the fair value of the goods or services received. If this measurement is not reliable, then measure instead based on the fair value of the equity instruments granted as of the date when the goods are delivered or services rendered.

EXAMPLE 19.1

The Wilkerson Supercomputer Company orders a specially designed computer chip from a supplier and receives delivery on July 31. The supplier has agreed to accept 10,000 of Wilkerson's ordinary shares as payment. The chips are custom-designed for Wilkerson, so it is impossible to directly determine their value. Instead, Wilkerson assigns a value to the transaction based on the market price of its shares on July 31 (the delivery date) of €5.50. Thus, Wilkerson records an expense of €55,000 on the delivery date.

How Do I Determine the Fair Value of a Granted Equity Instrument?

If you measure a share-based payment based on the fair value of the equity instrument granted, then determine fair value using one of the following two methods, in declining order of preference:

1. *Market prices.* Take into account the terms and conditions attached to the granted equity instrument, since they may vary from the equity instruments for which market prices are available.
2. *Valuation technique.* Use a valuation technique to estimate what the price would have been on the grant date between knowledgeable and willing parties.

If there are vesting conditions attached to an equity instrument, do not take them into account when estimating the fair value of the equity at the measurement date. Instead, adjust the number of equity instruments used to measure the transaction, based on the best available estimate of the number of such instruments that will vest. You should revise this estimate if subsequent information indicates that the number of equity instruments likely to vest differs from previous estimates.

On the vesting date, alter the current estimate of the number of equity instruments to match the actual amount that does.

What If I Cannot Determine the Fair Value of a Granted Equity Instrument?

In rare cases, it is not possible to measure a share-based transaction based on the fair value of the underlying equity instruments. If so, measure them at their *intrinsic value,* both at the initial service date and at the end of each subsequent reporting period and the final settlement date. Intrinsic value is the difference between the price a party must pay for the right to receive shares and the fair value of those shares.

If there is any change in the intrinsic value between the various measurement dates, record the difference in profit or loss. The final settlement date for share options is either the exercise date, the forfeiture date, or the end of the option's life.

Meanwhile, measure the goods or services received based on the number of equity instruments that vest or are exercised. For share options, recognize an amount for goods and services received during the vesting period that is based on the number of share options that you expect to vest, which you should update periodically if there is better information and eventually match to the actual number exercised. If settlement occurs during the vesting period, recognize at once all remaining unrecognized amounts.

If, upon settlement, you pay some additional amount, record the payment as an equity reduction; however, if the payment exceeds the intrinsic value of the equity instruments, recognize the excess as an expense.

After the vesting date, and *only* when the equity instruments are measured at their intrinsic value, reverse all amounts recognized for goods or services received, if the related share options are forfeited or lapse.

EXAMPLE 19.2

The Quack's Roast Duck franchise chain pays for the services of a legal firm with share options. Each option has an exercise price of €10 and a fair value of €15. The intrinsic value of each option is €5, which is the difference between its fair value and exercise price.

How Does Vesting Impact the Recognition of Services?

If an entity settles a share-based payment in equity and the equity vests immediately, then the entity presumes that the related services also have been completed, and should recognize the full amount of the transaction at once.

If an entity settles a share-based payment in equity and the equity *does not* vest at once, then the entity presumes that the related services will be provided over the vesting period, and accordingly recognizes the services over the vesting period. There are three conditions under which you can estimate the vesting period:

- ○ *Fixed period.* If the vesting period is fixed in the agreement, then use the stated vesting period over which to recognize the related expense.
- ○ *Market condition.* If the vesting period is dependent upon a market condition, then estimate the expected vesting period, ratably recognize the expense over that period, and do not subsequently revise it.
- ○ *Performance condition.* If the vesting period is based upon the completion of a performance condition, then estimate the vesting period at the grant date, using the most likely outcome. You should revise the vesting period if subsequent information indicates that a different vesting period is more likely.

How Do I Account for a Reload Feature?

A reload feature automatically grants additional share options whenever an option holder exercises previously granted options using an entity's shares to satisfy the exercise price. If a share option contains a reload feature, do not include it in an estimate of the fair value of options granted. Instead, account for it as a new option grant.

What Happens to Equity Instruments That Are Forfeited or Not Exercised?

There is no subsequent adjustment to total equity after the vesting date of an equity instrument. Thus, if an employee does not exercise share options or a supplier forfeits vested shares, you should not reverse the related amounts recognized for services received.

What Happens If I Modify the Terms of an Equity Instrument?

You sometimes may modify the terms and conditions of an equity instrument, such as altering an option exercise price or the vesting period. These changes can alter the fair value of the equity instrument. The primary measurement concept is to always recognize goods and services received based, at a minimum, on the fair value of the equity instruments on their grant date, unless vesting is not yet complete. This applies even if the instruments are later modified, cancelled, or replaced. In addition, you should recognize instrument modifications that incrementally *increase* the fair value of the instruments. Here are the key accounting issues related to modifications of terms:

- ○ *Extra payments.* If the entity makes any payment to an employee or supplier upon the settlement of the instrument, account for it as an equity deduction. If the payment exceeds the fair value of the equity instrument, then recognize the incremental difference as an expense.
- ○ *Liability component.* If a share-based payment arrangement contains a liability component, then remeasure the liability's fair value at the settlement date. If there is a payment to settle the liability, account for it as a liability extinguishment.
- ○ *Replacements.* If an entity grants new equity instruments to an employee and identifies them on the grant date as replacements for cancelled instruments, then recognize the incremental increase (if any) of the fair value of the new instruments on their grant date over the old instruments immediately prior to their cancellation.
- ○ *Settlement.* If an equity instrument is settled during the vesting period, treat it as vesting acceleration and immediately recognize all remaining expenses that otherwise would have been recognized later in the vesting period.

This answer assumes that the modifications are being applied to an equity instrument granted to an employee. If the grant is to a supplier, the accounting treatment is the same, except that you replace the grant date with the date when the entity obtains goods or services from the supplier.

EXAMPLE 19.3

Mr. Smith is the president of World Audio Distributors. World's board of directors granted him 100,000 restricted stock units (RSUs) on January 1 of Year 1, and they will fully vest on December 31 of Year 3. The RSUs initially were valued at £3.60 each, or £360,000 in total. Since Mr. Smith is assumed to be providing services during the vesting period, the company charges £10,000 to compensation expense in each of the 36 months.

After 10 months, the board of directors decides to modify the terms of the RSUs, so that they vest immediately. At this point, £260,000 of the related expense remains unvested, so World must charge the remaining £260,000 to expense as of the date of the modification.

How Do I Account for the Repurchase of a Vested Equity Instrument?

If an entity repurchases a vested equity instrument, account for the payment as a deduction from equity. If the payment exceeds the fair value of the equity instruments that the entity purchased as of the repurchase date, then recognize the excess as an expense.

How Do I Account for a Cash-Settled, Share-Based Payment Transaction?

When an entity settles a share-based payment in cash, measure the goods or services received at the fair value of the offsetting liability. You should remeasure the liability's fair value at the end of each reporting period and at final settlement, and recognize in profit or loss any incremental changes in fair value following each measurement.

If employees must render services in exchange for cash-settled, share-based payments, then recognize the services received and the offsetting liability as the employees render the services. Again, you should remeasure the fair value of the instruments at the end of each reporting period and at settlement, and recognize any incremental changes in profit or loss.

EXAMPLE 19.4

The Acme Roadrunner Tire Company grants 10,000 restricted share units (RSUs) to its chief executive officer, Mr. Coyote, under which Acme will pay Mr. Coyote, in cash, the net increase in the RSUs during their vesting period. The grant date is January 1, and the vesting date is December 31 of the same year. On January 1, Acme's stock sells for £5. On April 30, the share price has increased to £6, so Acme records compensation expense of £10,000. On October 31, the share price has dropped back to £5, so Acme reverses the £10,000 charge to compensation expense. On December 31, the settlement date, the share price has risen to £7, so Acme records compensation expense of £20,000 and pays the amount in cash to Mr. Coyote.

EXAMPLE 19.5

Hephaestus Construction issues two grants to its chief executive officer, Ms. Charis. The first is share appreciation rights worth €50,000 that vest immediately and that require cash payment. Since Ms. Charis has no service period requirement, Hephaestus should recognize the full amount of the compensation expense at once.

The second grant is for share appreciation rights worth €100,000 that vest over 36 months, and which will be paid in cash. Due to the implied 36-month service period, Hephaestus should recognize the €100,000 compensation expense ratably over 36 months.

 ### How Do I Account for a Share-Based Payment Transaction with Cash Alternatives?

An entity may enter into a share-based payment transaction where either the entity or the payee can opt for payment in cash or in the entity's equity. You should account for such transactions as cash-settled, share-based payments (see the preceding question) if the entity has incurred a cash settlement liability. If there is no such liability, then treat it as an equity-settled, share-based payment (see How Do I Account for an Equity-Settled, Share-Based Payment Transaction?).

An entity may grant a payee the right to choose whether the transaction is settled in cash or in equity instruments. This is a compound financial instrument, where you treat the right to receive a cash payment as the debt component and the right to receive an equity instrument as the equity component. The accounting treatment varies, depending upon whether the payee is an employee or a supplier:

○ *Employee.* If the transaction is with an employee, measure both components at their fair value on the measurement date, taking into account all terms and conditions of the grant.
○ *Supplier.* If the transaction is with a supplier, measure the equity component as the difference between the fair value of the goods or services received and the fair value of the debt component as of the receipt date.

For either scenario, on the settlement date, remeasure the liability to its fair value. If the settlement is with an equity instrument, rather than cash, then transfer the liability to equity. If the settlement is with cash, then the offsetting entry is to the liability.

In other circumstances, the entity, rather than the payee, has the right to choose whether the transaction is settled in cash or in equity instruments. Accounting for this is a four-step process:

EXAMPLE 19.6

Indonesian Linens buys a flax-spinning machine for €500,000. The supplier can choose payment in the form of either 100,000 Indonesian ordinary shares in one year, or a cash payment in three months that equals the market price of 80,000 Indonesian shares. Indonesian estimates that the one-year option has a fair value of €600,000, and the three-month option has a fair value of €450,000.

Upon receipt of the equipment, Indonesian should credit a liability account for €450,000 and credit an equity account for €50,000. The €50,000 represents the difference between the value of the spinning machine and the fair value of the liability.

1. Determine whether you have an obligation to settle in cash. This may be the case if there is a past practice of always settling in cash, or if the entity is legally prohibited from issuing more shares. If so, then account for the transaction as a cash-settled, share-based transaction (see How Do I Account for a Cash-Settled, Share-Based Payment Transaction?).
2. If there is no obligation to settle in cash, but the entity pays in cash, then deduct the payment from equity.
3. If there is no obligation to settle in cash, and the entity pays with an equity instrument, then there is no further accounting transaction.
4. If the entity picks the payment alternative with a higher fair value, then record the excess value given as an additional expense.

How Do I Disclose Share-Based Payments?

The disclosure of information about share-based payments is generally to give the users of an entity's financial statements an understanding of the extent and type of such arrangements. More specifically, disclose the following:

○ *Description.* Summary of each type of share-based arrangement in existence during the reporting period, and their general terms and conditions.
○ *Expenses.* The total expense recognized in the reporting period related to share-based payment transactions, where the goods and services received under such arrangements are recognized at once as an expense. Separately disclose that portion of the expense caused by transactions accounted for as equity-settled, share-based transactions.
○ *Fair value.* If the fair value of goods or services received was measured directly, then disclose how this determination was made. If the fair value was measured based on the value of equity instruments issued, then disclose the weighted average fair value of the equity instruments granted during the period, as well as the following:

• *Options.* If share options were granted, note the pricing model used, inputs to the model, volatility assumptions and the usage of historical volatility information, and whether other option features were incorporated into the fair value calculation.

- *Other equity instruments.* If equity instruments other than options were granted, note how fair value was determined, the inclusion of dividends in the fair value calculation, and whether other instrument features were incorporated into the fair value calculation.
- *Modified arrangements.* If equity instruments were modified during the period, explain the modifications, the incremental fair value of changes caused by the modifications, and how the incremental fair value of the modifications were measured.

○ *Liabilities.* For any liabilities caused by share-based transactions, note the total period-end carrying amount, as well as the total intrinsic value of liabilities at the end of the period when the payee's right to payment has vested.

○ *Option pricing.* The number and weighted average exercise prices of share options, broken out for the options outstanding at the beginning and end of the period, those exercisable at the end of the period, and those options granted, forfeited, exercised, and expired during the period.

○ *Options exercised.* If share options are exercised during the period, then note the share price on the exercise date; if exercised throughout the period, then disclose the weighted average share price during the period.

○ *Options future details.* If share options are outstanding at the end of the reporting period, then note the range of possible exercise prices and the weighted average of the remaining contractual lives of those options.

CHAPTER 20

INCOME TAXES

What Is an Accounting Profit?

Accounting profit is profit or loss *before* deducting income tax expense.

What Is Taxable Profit and Can It Vary?

Taxable profit is the profit (or loss) upon which income taxes are payable. The composition of taxable profit varies by taxation authority, so it will vary depending upon the rules of the taxation authorities within which an entity is located or does business.

What Is the Tax Base?

The tax base of an asset is the amount that will be deductible for tax purposes against any taxable economic benefits generated by the asset. If the economic benefits are nontaxable, then an asset's tax base equals its carrying amount.

EXAMPLE 20.1

Bonifacio Bakeries owns an automated baking oven that cost €100,000 that it is depreciating on the straight-line basis over 10 years. After three years, it has depreciated €30,000 of the baking oven's cost. The remaining €70,000 cost will be deductible in future periods. The baked goods that Bonifacio produces with the baking oven generate taxable revenue. Consequently, the remaining €70,000 cost of the baking oven is the tax base of the asset, to be deducted against future revenue.

The tax base of a liability is its carrying amount minus any amount related to that liability that will be deductible for tax purposes in the future. If an entity receives revenue in advance, its tax base for the resulting liability will be its carrying amount, less any amount that will not be taxable in the future.

Example 20.2
The Ginseng Plus retail chain records accrued expenses of €5,000. Ginseng reports its taxable results on a cash basis, so there is no tax base for the accrued expenses. If Ginseng reported its taxable results on an accrual basis, the accrued expenses would have a tax base of €5,000.

    What Is a Temporary Difference?

A temporary difference is the difference between the carrying amount of an asset or liability in the statement of financial position and its tax base. A temporary difference can be either of the following:

- ○ *Deductible.* A deductible temporary difference is a temporary difference that will yield amounts that can be deducted in the future when determining taxable profit or loss.
- ○ *Taxable.* A taxable temporary difference is a temporary difference that will yield taxable amounts in the future when determining taxable profit or loss.

In both cases, the differences are settled when the carrying amount of the asset or liability is recovered or settled.

Example 20.3
Celtic Pottery Company has a taxable temporary difference when it depreciates an automated glazing machine using accelerated depreciation for tax purposes, and straight-line depreciation to determine its accounting profit.   Celtic also has a taxable temporary difference when it deducts rent expenses on a cash payment basis to calculate its tax profit, but records them as a prepaid expense to calculate its accounting profit.

EXAMPLE 20.4

Industrial Environmental has a deductible temporary difference when it deducts retirement benefit costs to calculate its accounting profit, but does not deduct them for tax profit purposes until it pays the benefits.

Similarly, Industrial Environmental has another deductible temporary difference when it recognizes research costs as an expense to determine its accounting profit, but cannot include them in the tax profit calculation until a later period.

EXAMPLE 20.5

Meridian Vacuum Company has an accounting profit of €500,000, as well as €60,000 of taxable temporary differences and €30,000 of deductible temporary differences. Its taxable income is:

Accounting profit	€500,000
Taxable temporary differences	(60,000)
Deductible temporary differences	30,000
Taxable profit	€470,000

Meridian is subject to a 30 percent income tax rate. It records the following income tax entry:

Income tax expense – current	141,000	
Income tax expense – deferred	9,000	
Deferred tax asset	9,000	
Deferred tax liability		18,000
Payables – income taxes		141,000

Because of temporary differences, the tax expense that an entity incurs in a reporting period usually comprises both current tax expense or income, and deferred tax expense or income.

 ## What Are Deferred Tax Assets and Liabilities?

A deferred tax liability is income taxes payable in a future period, while a deferred tax asset is income taxes recoverable in a future period and is caused by a deductible temporary difference and the carryforward of either unused tax losses or unused tax credits.

EXAMPLE 20.6

Electro Tram has the following assets and liabilities at the end of its fiscal year (in millions):

	Carrying Amount	Tax Base	Temporary Difference
Cash	€3,500	€3,500	€ 0
Accounts receivable	8,000	8,500	(500)
Inventory	6,500	7,500	(1,000)
Plant and equipment	11,000	9,250	1,750
Accounts payable	2,000	2,000	0
			€ 250

In the table, the plant and equipment has a different valuation for tax purposes than its carrying amount. Electro Tram also has made provisions for receivable bad debts of €500,000 and for inventory obsolescence of €1 million, neither of which are allowed in the current year for tax purposes, but which can be used in the future. These issues result in a net difference between Electro Tram's carrying amounts and tax base of €250,000. Since the income tax rate is 35 percent, Electro Tram records a deferred tax provision of €87,500.

How Do I Account for the Tax Effects of Research and Development?

This varies by tax jurisdiction. Research and development costs may not be permitted as a deduction in determining taxable profit or loss until a later period. If so, this is a deductible temporary difference that results in a deferred tax asset.

How Do I Recognize a Tax Liability?

You should record the current tax for current and prior periods as a liability, if not already paid. If you have paid more than the tax amount due in the current and prior periods, then record the excess as an asset.

How Do I Recognize a Carryback Tax Loss?

If you record a tax loss that you can carry back to recover taxes paid in a previous period, you can recognize the eligible tax loss as an asset in the current period.

How Do I Recognize Taxable Temporary Differences?

Recognize a deferred tax liability for all taxable temporary differences, except when the liability arises from the initial recognition of goodwill, or the recognition of an asset or a liability that does not arise from a business combination and affects neither accounting profit nor taxable profit or loss.

EXAMPLE 20.7

Masterson Brick Company has an asset that cost £15,000 and has a carrying amount of £10,000. Cumulative tax depreciation on the asset is £9,000, and the tax rate is 35 percent.

Masterson's tax base in the asset is £6,000, which is the cost of £15,000 minus cumulative tax depreciation of £9,000. To recover the carrying amount of £10,000, Masterson must earn offsetting taxable income of £10,000; however, it can deduct only the remaining tax depreciation of £6,000. Thus, Masterson will pay income taxes of £1,400 (£4,000 × 35% tax rate) when it recovers the asset's carrying amount.

The difference between the carrying amount of £10,000 and the tax base of £6,000 is a taxable temporary difference of £4,000. Consequently, Masterson recognizes a deferred tax liability of £1,400 (£4,000 × 35% tax rate), which represents the income taxes it must pay when it recovers the asset's carrying amount.

A temporary difference may arise when an entity includes income or expense in accounting profit in one period, but in taxable profit in a different period. This results in a *timing difference*.

EXAMPLE 20.8

Ram-Jet International incurs a large amount of development costs for its hypersonic ramjet engine. In the current year, it capitalized £28 million of development costs and will amortize the costs over future periods to determine its accounting profit. However, the tax jurisdiction in which Ram-Jet is located requires that all development costs be deducted as incurred to derive taxable profit.

The £28 million of development costs have no tax base, since Ram-Jet has already deducted them from its taxable profit. The temporary difference is the difference between the carrying amount of £28 million and their tax base of zero.

What Temporary Differences Arise in a Business Combination?

When an entity acquires assets and liabilities in a business combination, it recognizes them at their fair values as of the acquisition date. It will record temporary differences when the tax bases of the acquired assets and liabilities are either not affected by the business combination or are affected differently.

EXAMPLE 20.9

When Meridian Vacuum Company acquired High Suction Ltd., it increased the carrying amount of High Suction's production equipment to fair value. However, the tax base of the production equipment remained at the previous owner's tax base. This creates a taxable temporary difference that results in a deferred tax liability.

How Does a Business Combination Affect Existing Deferred Tax Assets?

If an entity is about to enter into a business combination as the acquirer, it should review its existing deferred tax assets to see if there is a changed probability of recovering a tax asset. For example, the acquiring entity may find that it can use previously unused tax losses against the future taxable profits of the acquiree. If so, the acquiring entity recognizes a change in the deferred tax asset in the same period as the business combination, but not as part of the accounting for the business combination. Thus, any such change has no impact on the acquiring entity's measurement of goodwill or bargain purchase gains associated with the business combination.

 ## How Does a Business Combination Affect Acquired Deferred Tax Assets?

An acquiring entity can recognize acquired deferred tax benefits after the business combination, if the recognition of acquired deferred tax benefits results from new information about facts and circumstances that existed at the acquisition date. The acquiring entity must apply these changes to the reduction of any goodwill relating to that acquisition. If the goodwill carrying amount is zero, then the acquiring entity should recognize any remaining deferred tax benefits in profit or loss.

The acquiring entity should recognize all other acquired deferred tax benefits that are realized in profit or loss.

 ## Can I Recognize Temporary Differences Related to Goodwill?

Many tax jurisdictions do not recognize a reduction in the carrying amount of goodwill as a deductible expense for calculating taxable profit. This results in a tax base of zero. Although there is a difference between the tax base and carrying amount of goodwill, the recognition of a deferred tax liability is not allowed. Similarly, you cannot recognize a reduction in a deferred tax liability resulting from a goodwill impairment loss.

However, it is possible to recognize a deferred tax liability for a *taxable* temporary difference relating to goodwill, if it does not arise from the initial recognition of goodwill.

EXAMPLE 20.10

The Arthur Bates Compton consulting firm (ABC) recognizes €1,000,000 of goodwill as a result of a business combination. The tax jurisdiction in which it is
(Continued)

(*Continued*)
located allows it to deduct the goodwill for tax purposes at a rate of 10 percent per year. In the first year, this means the tax base of the goodwill is €1,000,000 immediately following the business combination and €900,000 at the end of the year. If the carrying amount of ABC's goodwill at the end of the first year remains unchanged at €1,000,000, then a taxable temporary difference of €100,000 has arisen; this difference does not relate to the initial recognition of goodwill, so ABC can recognize the deferred tax liability.

 ## What Is the Tax Treatment of Goodwill That Is Less Than Its Tax Base?

If the carrying amount of goodwill from a business combination is less than its tax base, record a deferred tax asset. Recognize it to the extent that it is probable that taxable profit will be available against which the deductible temporary difference could be utilized.

 ## Does Fair Value Accounting Create Temporary Differences?

In some tax jurisdictions, an entity's revaluation of an asset to fair value affects the tax profit or loss in the current period. The entity adjusts the tax base of the asset, and therefore there is no temporary difference.

In other tax jurisdictions, an entity's revaluation of an asset to fair value does not affect the tax profit or loss in the current period. In this case, the entity does not adjust the tax base of the asset, which results in a temporary difference and creates a deferred tax liability or asset. The temporary difference arises even if the entity does not intend to dispose of the asset, or if the tax on capital gains is deferred if the entity invests the proceeds from asset disposal in similar assets.

 ## Does a Temporary Difference Arise from the Initial Recognition of an Asset or a Liability?

A temporary difference can arise upon the initial recognition of an asset or a liability. A common reason is that some portion of an asset is not deductible for tax purposes; if so, an entity recognizes any deferred tax liability or asset, and recognizes the resulting deferred tax expense or income in profit or loss.

If the initial asset or liability recognition arises from a business combination, then the entity recognizes any deferred tax liability or asset, which in turn affects the amount of the goodwill or bargain purchase option that it recognizes as part of the business combination.

Finally, if the initial recognition of an asset or liability does not affect accounting profit or taxable profit, and is not caused by a business combination, then an entity cannot recognize any resulting deferred tax liability or asset at any time, nor can it recognize subsequent changes in the unrecognized deferred tax liability or asset as it depreciates.

EXAMPLE 20.11

The Smith & Wilberforce Pop-Gun Factory intends to acquire a conveyor belt that costs £40,000, use it for four years, and then dispose of it. Smith's controller assumes there will be no residual value. The tax rate is 35 percent. In the tax jurisdiction in which Smith is located, depreciation of the conveyor belt is not deductible for tax purposes. When it disposes of the conveyor, any capital gain will not be taxable, nor will any capital loss be deductible.

After one year, Smith has depreciated £10,000 of the conveyor's cost, leaving a carrying value of £30,000. Smith earns taxable income of £30,000, and pays £10,500 of income taxes. Smith does not recognize the deferred tax liability of £10,500 because it results from the initial recognition of the conveyor.

How Do I Recognize Deductible Temporary Differences?

An entity recognizes a deferred tax asset for all deductible temporary differences if it is probable that taxable profit will be available against which the temporary difference can be utilized. However, this does not apply if the deferred tax asset arises from the initial recognition of an asset or liability in a transaction that affects neither accounting profit nor taxable profit or loss, or that is a business combination.

EXAMPLE 20.12

The Unibody Plastics Company recognizes a liability of €100,000 for accrued warranty costs on its children's toy products. The product warranty costs are not deductible for tax purposes until Unibody actually pays a warrant claim. The tax rate is 35 percent.

The tax base of the accrued liability is zero, while the carrying amount of the liability is €100,000. This results in a deductible temporary difference of €100,000. Thus, Unibody recognizes a deferred tax asset of €35,000 (€100,000 × 35% tax rate), provided that it is probable that Unibody will earn a sufficiently large taxable profit in the future to benefit from this reduction in tax payments.

Here are other examples of deductible temporary differences resulting in deferred tax assets:

- ○ *Business combination costs.* An entity recognizes identifiable assets and liabilities acquired in a business combination at their fair values. When an entity recognizes a liability at the acquisition date but does not deduct the related cost in the calculation of taxable profits until a later period, this creates a deferred tax asset. A deferred tax asset also arises when an entity recognizes the fair value of an acquired asset at less than its tax base.
- ○ *Fair value situations.* An entity may revalue an asset to its fair value without making a corresponding adjustment for tax purposes. This creates a deductible temporary difference if the asset's tax base exceeds its carrying amount.
- ○ *Research costs.* These costs are deducted for the purpose of calculating accounting profit as the entity incurs them, but it may be deducted for tax profit calculations only in a later period. Thus, the carrying amount of the research costs is zero, but the tax base (the amount that the taxing jurisdiction will allow as a future deduction) may be substantial. The difference is a deferred tax asset from which the entity will benefit whenever it is allowed to recognize the related expense.
- ○ *Retirement benefit costs.* These costs are deducted for the purpose of calculating accounting profit as the entity provides service to employees, but may be deducted for tax profit calculations only when

contributions are paid by the entity. Thus, the tax base of the liability is usually zero, which results in a deferred tax asset from which the entity will benefit when it eventually pays the contributions.

 ## When Is It Probable That There Will Be Sufficient Taxable Profit to Utilize Deductible Temporary Differences?

Deductible temporary differences should be recorded only if it is probable that there will be sufficient future taxable profits to offset them. This situation is probable when there are sufficient taxable temporary differences relating to the same tax jurisdiction and taxable entity that are expected to reverse in the same period as the expected reversal of the deductible temporary differences, or in periods in which a tax loss can be carried back or forward from the deferred tax asset. In these situations, recognize the deferred tax asset in the same period in which the deductible temporary difference arises.

If there are insufficient taxable temporary differences relating to the same tax jurisdiction and taxable entity, then recognize the deferred tax asset only to the extent that it is probable that the entity will have sufficient taxable profit relating to the same tax jurisdiction in the same period as the reversal of the deductible temporary difference, or in periods in which a tax loss can be carried back or forward from the deferred tax asset. Alternatively, the entity can recognize the deferred tax asset to the extent that tax planning opportunities (see next question) will create taxable profit in the appropriate periods.

 ## What Is Tax Planning?

A tax planning opportunity is an action an entity must take to create or increase taxable income in a period before the expiration of a tax loss or tax credit carryforward. Examples of tax planning are:

- *Asset swap.* Selling an asset that generates nontaxable income and using the funds to buy another asset that generates taxable income.
- *Asset sale.* Selling an asset that has appreciated, and for which the tax base has not been adjusted to reflect the appreciation. A variation on this approach is sale and leaseback transactions (see the Leases chapter).

○ *Deduction deferral.* Delaying the recognition of some deductions from taxable profit that can be deferred.
○ *Recognition basis.* Electing to recognize interest income for the calculation of taxable profit on either a received or receivable basis.

When Do I Recognize Unused Tax Losses and Unused Tax Credits?

Recognize a deferred tax asset for the carryforward of unused tax losses and unused tax credits to the extent that it is probable that future taxable profit will be available against which the unused tax losses and credits can be utilized.

The existence of unused tax losses is considered strong evidence that future taxable profit may not be available. Thus, when there is a history of recent losses, recognize a deferred tax asset arising from unused tax losses or credits only to the extent that the entity has sufficient taxable temporary differences, or if there is convincing evidence that sufficient taxable profit will be available to offset the unused tax losses or credits.

Consider the following criteria when assessing the probability of a future taxable profit against which to offset unused tax losses or credits:

○ *Recurrence.* Do unused tax losses result from causes that are unlikely to recur?
○ *Sufficient differences.* Are there sufficient taxable temporary differences that will result in taxable amounts against which unused tax losses or credits can be used prior to expiration?
○ *Tax planning.* Are tax planning opportunities available that will create a taxable profit in a period when unused tax losses or credits can be utilized?
○ *Timing.* Is it probable that the entity will have taxable profits before the unused tax losses or credits expire?

Do not recognize a deferred tax asset to the extent that it is not probable that taxable profit will be available for use against unused tax losses or credits.

When Do I Reassess Unrecognized Deferred Tax Assets?

Reassess unrecognized deferred tax assets at the end of each reporting period. You should recognize a previously unrecognized deferred tax asset to the extent that it has become probable that future taxable profit will allow for the recovery of the deferred tax asset.

How Do I Account for the Tax Impact of Investments in Other Entities?

When there is a difference between the carrying amount and the tax base of an entity's investment in a subsidiary, branch, associate, or joint venture, this is a temporary difference. Examples of situations where this temporary difference can arise are:

- ○ *Carrying amount.* When the entity reduces the carrying amount of its investment in an associate to what it estimates is the recoverable amount
- ○ *Exchange rates.* When the entities are based in different countries and there are changes in foreign exchange rates
- ○ *Profits.* When there are undistributed profits from a subsidiary, branch, associate, or joint venture

A parent entity should recognize a *deferred tax liability* for all taxable temporary differences involving its investments in subsidiaries, branches, associates, and joint ventures, unless the parent can control the timing of the reversal of a temporary difference *and* the temporary difference probably will not reverse in the foreseeable future. The parent entity can control the timing of the reversal of a temporary difference if it can control the dividend policy of the other entity.

A parent entity should recognize a *deferred tax asset* for all deductible temporary differences involving its investments in subsidiaries, branches, associates, and joint ventures, but only to the extent that it is probable that the temporary difference will reverse in the foreseeable future and that a taxable profit will be available against which the temporary difference can be utilized.

If an entity's taxable profit or loss is determined in a different currency, then changes in the exchange rate create temporary differences. The entity should recognize this deferred tax liability or asset, and charge or credit the resulting deferred tax to profit or loss.

How Do I Measure Tax Liabilities and Assets?

Measurements for tax liabilities and assets are as follows:

- ○ *For current and prior periods.* Measure tax liabilities and assets at the amount you expect to pay to or be paid by the taxing authority.

○ *For future periods.* Measure deferred tax assets and liabilities at the tax rates that you expect to apply when the asset is realized or the liability is settled.

In both cases, base the measurements on the tax rates that have been substantively enacted by the end of the reporting period.

When different tax rates apply to different amounts of taxable income, measure deferred assets and liabilities at the average rate that you expect to apply to the taxable profit or loss of the periods in which the differences should reverse.

When measuring deferred tax assets or liabilities, assume the tax consequences that will arise from the manner in which you expect to recover or settle the carrying amounts of the items under consideration.

EXAMPLE 20.13

The Kirkwall Ocean Kayak Company owns a baking oven in which it hardens polyethylene kayak molds. The oven has a carrying amount of £40,000 and a tax base of £30,000. Kirkwall will incur a tax rate of 25 percent if it sells the oven, while a tax rate of 35 percent applies to other income.

Kirkwall recognizes a deferred tax liability of £2,500 (£10,000 × 25% tax rate) if it expects to sell the oven without further use, or a deferred tax liability of £3,500 (£10,000 × 35% tax rate) if it expects to retain the oven and recover its carrying amount through continuing use.

Some tax jurisdictions require a different tax rate if the entity pays dividends, or may make some taxes refundable or payable in the event of a dividend payment. If so, measure current and deferred tax assets and liabilities at the tax rate that applies to undistributed profits.

EXAMPLE 20.14

The Ajax Machining Company operates in a tax jurisdiction where income taxes are payable at a 40 percent rate on undistributed profits, with a 10 percent tax refund when profits are distributed. Thus, the tax rate on distributed profits is 30 percent. Taxable income for the year is €1 million. There is a net temporary tax difference for the year of €80,000.

Ajax recognizes a current tax liability and income tax expense of €400,000. Since there is no dividend declaration, Ajax does not recognize any tax that would be recoverable in the event of a future dividend. Ajax does recognize a deferred tax liability and deferred tax expense of €32,000 (€80,000 net temporary tax difference × 40% tax rate). This is the amount of income taxes that Ajax expects to pay when it settles the tax difference.

Two months later, Ajax's board of directors recognizes €250,000 of the prior year's taxable income as dividends payable, which triggers an income tax recovery of €25,000 (€250,000 × 10% tax rate reduction). Ajax records the income tax recovery as an income tax reduction and a current tax asset.

How Do I Account for Tax Withholdings on Dividends?

If a tax jurisdiction requires that an entity remit a portion of any dividends on behalf of shareholders, then you should charge the amount remitted to the tax authorities to equity as part of the dividends.

How Do I Measure Taxes on the Revaluation of Nondepreciable Assets?

You should recognize a deferred tax liability or asset if you revalue a nondepreciable asset. Measure the deferred tax liability or asset based on the tax consequences following from recovery of the asset's carrying amount via its sale. Thus, use the tax rate specified by the tax jurisdiction applicable to the *sale* of an asset, if it differs from the rate for *using* the asset.

Should I Discount Deferred Tax Assets and Liabilities?

No. Discounting a deferred tax asset or liability requires a present value analysis that contains detailed payment and/or payout schedules. Given the uncertainty and complexity of future tax scenarios, it is difficult to create reliable discounted information, and so it is not required to report deferred tax assets or liabilities in this manner.

When Should I Review the Carrying Amount of Deferred Tax Assets?

Review the carrying amount of deferred tax assets at the end of each reporting period. You should reduce the carrying amount of a deferred tax asset to the extent that it is no longer probable that sufficient taxable profit will be available for offset against the deferred tax asset.

It is allowable to later reverse this reduction to the extent that it becomes probable that sufficient taxable profit will become available for offset.

What Events Alter the Carrying Amount of Deferred Tax Assets and Liabilities?

You should alter the carrying amount of deferred tax assets and liabilities to match any changes in the amount of related temporary differences. In addition, change the carrying amounts when there is a change in tax rates, a change in the expected manner of asset recovery, or a reassessment of the recoverability of deferred tax assets.

How Do I Recognize Current and Deferred Taxes in Profit or Loss?

You should recognize current and deferred taxes as income or expense, except to the extent that the tax arises from a business combination or a transaction or event that is recognized outside profit or loss (e.g., in other comprehensive income or equity).

EXAMPLE 20.15

The Chemical Detection Consortium recognizes €5,000 per month of royalties on its patented bomb detection technology, even though it only receives a single cash payment of €60,000 at the end of each calendar year. Thus, €5,000 appears in accounting profit every month, and €60,000 in December's taxable income.

What Situations Result in Tax Asset or Liability Recognition outside of Profit or Loss?

You should recognize current taxes and deferred taxes outside of profit or loss if the tax relates to items that are recognized outside of profit or loss. Thus, if an item is recognized in other comprehensive income, then also recognize the related current and deferred taxes in other comprehensive income. Similarly, if an item is recognized in equity, then also recognize the related current and deferred taxes in equity.

Examples of items recognized in other comprehensive income are revaluation changes for property, plant, and equipment, as well as foreign exchange differences caused by translating the financial statements of a foreign operation.

Examples of items recognized in equity are adjustments to the opening equity balance caused by a change in accounting policy or the correction of an error, as well as the initial recognition of the equity portion of a compound financial instrument.

If it is difficult to determine the amount of current and deferred tax relating to items recognized outside of profit or loss, then use a reasonable pro rata allocation of the current and deferred tax. This situation can arise, for example, when there are graduated rates of income tax and you cannot determine the rate at which a specific component of taxable profit or loss has been taxed.

 How Do Tax Status Changes Alter Income Tax Recognition?

An entity may experience a change in its tax status, such as when it gains or loses tax incentives by moving to a different location. If so, include these tax effects in profit or loss for the period, unless the consequences relate to transactions and events that will alter equity or other comprehensive income.

 How Do I Account for the Taxes Related to an Asset Revaluation?

If you revalue an asset for tax purposes, and the revaluation is related to an accounting revaluation from another period, then recognize the tax effects of the asset revaluation and the tax base adjustment in other comprehensive income in the period in which they occur. If the revaluation for tax purposes is not related to an accounting revaluation from another period, then recognize the tax effects of the adjustment in profit and loss.

Example 20.16

The Guttering Candle Company revalues its property from £15 million to a new value of £18 million. The tax base of the property was £13 million. The tax rate is 25 percent. Guttering calculates a deferred tax liability related to the property of £1.25 million. This is based on the difference between the new revaluation of £18 million and the tax base of £13 million, multiplied by the 25 percent tax rate.

How Do I Account for Taxes Arising from Share-Based Payments?

Some tax jurisdictions grant to an entity a tax deduction for remuneration paid with various forms of equity, such as shares or share options. If so, there may be a timing difference between the receipt of services and equity grants, which results in a deductible temporary difference that the entity can record as a deferred tax asset.

The amount of the tax deduction granted by the tax jurisdiction may not be ascertainable at once, since, for example, it may be based on the entity's share price on the date a share option is exercised. If so, the entity should estimate the amount of the deferred tax asset based on information available at the end of the period (such as the entity's share price at that time).

If the amount of the tax deduction exceeds the amount of the related remuneration expense, then record the excess of the current or deferred tax in equity.

Can I Offset Current Tax Assets and Liabilities?

You can offset current tax assets and current tax liabilities only when the entity has a legally enforceable right to do so and intends to settle them on a net basis or to settle both simultaneously.

Can I Offset Deferred Tax Assets and Liabilities?

You can offset deferred tax assets and deferred tax liabilities only when the entity has a legally enforceable right to do so, and these assets and liabilities relate to income taxes levied by the same tax jurisdiction on either the same taxable entity or different entities that intend to settle these assets and liabilities on a net basis or to settle both simultaneously.

Where Do I Present Tax Income or Expense?

You should present tax expense or income related to profit or loss from ordinary activities in the statement of comprehensive income.

What Tax Income or Expense Information Should I Disclose?

You should separately disclose the major components of tax income or expense. These components may include:

- Adjustments recognized in the period for current tax of prior periods
- Benefits arising from a previously unrecognized tax loss, tax credit, or temporary difference of a prior period used to reduce current tax expense
- Benefits from a previously unrecognized tax loss, tax credit, or temporary difference from a prior period that reduces deferred tax expense
- Changes in a pre-acquisition deferred tax asset caused by a business combination
- Current and deferred tax for items charged or credited to equity
- Current tax income or expense
- Deductible temporary differences, unused tax losses, and unused tax credits for which no deferred tax asset is recognized
- Deferred tax assets and the reason for recognizing them when utilizing them depends on future taxable profits exceeding those arising from the reversal of existing taxable temporary differences and the entity has recorded a recent loss
- Deferred tax benefits acquired in a business combination and recognized after the acquisition date,

along with the description of the event causing the recognition

- Deferred tax expense from the write-down or reversal of a previous write-down of a deferred tax asset
- Deferred tax income or expense for changes in tax rates or new taxes
- Deferred tax income or expense relating to the origination and reversal of temporary differences
- Explanation of changes in the tax rate compared with the previous period
- For discontinued operations, the tax expense relating to the discontinuance gain or loss, and the profit or loss from the ordinary activities of the discontinued operation for all periods presented
- For each type of temporary difference, unused tax loss (and unused tax credit), the amount of the deferred tax assets and liabilities recognized for each period presented, and the amount of deferred tax income or expense recognized in profit or loss
- Income tax consequences of proposed or declared dividends to shareholders that are not recognized as a liability
- Income tax for each component of other comprehensive income
- Potential income tax consequences resulting from the payment of dividends
- Reconciliation between tax income or expense and accounting profit
- Tax income or expense relating to changes in accounting policies or errors that are included in profit or loss
- Temporary differences for investments in subsidiaries and other entities for which deferred tax liabilities have not been recognized

PART IV

SPECIAL TRANSACTIONS

CHAPTER 21

BUSINESS COMBINATIONS

 What Is a Business Combination?

A business combination is a transaction in which the acquirer obtains control of another business (the acquiree). A *business* is an integrated set of activities and assets that can provide a return to investors in the form of dividends, reduced costs, or other economic benefits. A business typically has inputs, processes, and outputs. A development-stage entity may not yet have outputs, in which case you can substitute other factors, such as having begun operations and having plans to produce output, and having access to customers who can purchase the outputs.

A business combination is not the formation of a joint venture, nor does it involve the acquisition of assets that do not constitute a business.

 What Is Goodwill?

Goodwill is an asset that is not individually identified, is separately recognized, and represents the future economic benefits arising from other assets acquired in a business combination.

 How Do I Account for a Business Combination?

You should use the *acquisition method* to account for a business combination. Specifically, follow these five steps:

1. *Identify the acquirer.* This is the entity that gains control of the acquiree.
2. *Determine the acquisition date.* This is when the acquirer gains control of the acquiree, which is usually the deal closing date, but could be another date if so stated in the purchase agreement.

3. *Recognize and measure identifiable assets acquired and liabilities assumed.* These must be part of the business combination transaction, rather than from separate transactions. Measure these assets and liabilities at their fair values as of the acquisition date. More specifically:

   a. *Employee benefits.* Recognize a liability for any employee benefits assumed.
   b. *Held-for-sale assets.* Measure an acquiree's assets designated as held for sale at their fair value, less costs to sell.
   c. *Income taxes.* Recognize a deferred tax asset or liability associated with the other assets acquired and liabilities assumed.
   d. *Indemnifications.* The acquiree provides an indemnification to the acquirer for various issues related to the acquired business. For example, the acquiree may provide an indemnification against excessive accounts receivable bad debts. This is an indemnification asset, which the acquirer recognizes at its fair value at the same time it recognizes the indemnified item. However, do not recognize an indemnification if the related asset is not recognized.
   e. *Reacquired rights.* Measure a reacquired right as an intangible asset having a term tied to the duration of its remaining contractual term, irrespective of the potential for a contract extension.
   f. *Share-based payments.* Measure a liability or equity instrument to replace similar acquiree share-based payments.

4. *Recognize and measure any noncontrolling interest in the acquiree.* Measure this noncontrolling interest either at its proportionate share of the acquiree's net assets or at its fair value.

5. *Recognize and measure either goodwill or the gain from a bargain purchase.* Measure goodwill as follows:

   Consideration paid, measured at fair value on the acquisition date
   Plus noncontrolling interests in the acquiree
   Plus fair value of acquirer's previously held equity interest in the acquiree
   Minus identifiable assets and liabilities acquired.

A bargain purchase occurs when the above calculation yields a negative goodwill amount. When this occurs, first review the goodwill calculation to ensure that all items were included. If they were, then recognize the gain resulting from the bargain purchase in profit or loss as of the acquisition date.

EXAMPLE 21.1

Wilson Ross, a publicly held consulting firm, acquires Finnegan Beagle, which is also a publicly held consulting firm. The price to buy Finnegan is £7 million. Wilson identifies assets at Finnegan having a fair value of £8 million, intangible assets with a value of £1 million, as well as £2 million of liabilities and £500,000 of contingent liabilities. Wilson also owned an existing stake in Finnegan that has a fair value on the acquisition date of £3 million. Wilson calculates the goodwill associated with the business combination as follows:

+ Purchase price	£7,000,000
+ Liabilities	2,000,000
+ Contingent liabilities	500,000
+ Existing stake in Finnegan	3,000,000
− Assets	(8,000,000)
− Intangible assets	(1,000,000)
= Goodwill	£3,500,000

If the acquirer pays with noncash assets or liabilities, it should remeasure them as of the acquisition date and recognize any gains or losses in profit or loss. However, if the acquirer retains control of the assets or liabilities (as can happen if they are transferred to the acquiree rather than its owners), then they are measured at their carrying value, which precludes the recognition of any gain or loss by the acquirer in consolidation.

How Do I Account for Contingent Consideration?

If there is additional consideration payable by the acquirer based on conditions not yet met, the acquirer recognizes its fair value as of the acquisition date.

EXAMPLE 21.2

Rotary Mower Company, maker of the world's only lawn mower that runs on a Wankel rotary engine, acquires Turbofan Concepts, maker of the only jet-engine powered lawn mower (for really big lawns). Rotary Mower includes in the purchase agreement a contingent consideration payment of £4 million, payable over the next four years, if Turbofan achieves specific levels of profitability in each period. Rotary's management believes that Turbofan will meet these targets, so it recognizes the full amount of the contingent consideration as of the acquisition date.

 ## Do I Include Expected Costs in Assumed Liabilities?

If you expect to incur a cost as a result of a business combination, but there is no obligation to do so, then do not include it in the initial accounting for the business combination.

EXAMPLE 21.3

Amundsen Salvage acquires Scott Reclamation. Amundsen expects to sell off one of Scott's salvage tugboats and terminate the employment of its crew, but is under no obligation to do so. Thus, Amundsen does not assume a liability for the tugboat elimination as part of its accounting for the business combination.

 ## How Do I Account for an Acquiree's Contingent Liabilities?

A contingent liability is a possible obligation, arising from past events, whose existence will be confirmed only by uncertain future events that are not entirely under an entity's control. It also may be an obligation, arising from past events, that it is not possible to reliably measure. The acquirer should recognize a contingent liability if it can reliably measure the fair value of the liability as of the acquisition date, even if there is not a probable outflow of resources required to settle it.

What If an Acquisition Occurs in Stages?

An entity may already have a noncontrolling equity inter-est in an acquiree and then acquires a controlling interest in the acquiree. This is called a *step acquisition*. In this situ-ation, the acquirer should remeasure its existing equity in-terest in the acquiree as of the date when it obtains control over the acquiree, and recognize any gain or loss in profit or loss.

If the acquirer had recognized any changes in the value of its noncontrolling interest in other comprehen-sive income, it should now shift that amount into profit or loss.

EXAMPLE 21.4

Iberian Tile acquires 100 percent of Tango Mural Company in two stages, as noted in the following table:

Acquisition Date	Percent Acquired	Purchase Payment	Net Assets Fair Value
January 1, 20 ×1	15%	€2,000,000	€12,000,000
July 1, 20 ×2	85%	13,000,000	14,000,000
Totals	100%	€15,000,000	

Iberian calculates the goodwill from the two trans-actions as follows:

Acquisition Date	(A) Purchase Payment	(B) Percent Acquired	(C) Net Assets Fair Value	A − (B x C) Goodwill
January 1, 20 ×1	€2,000,000	15%	€12,000,000	€200,000
July 1, 20 ×2	13,000,000	85%	14,000,000	1,100,000
				€1,300,000

The before-and-after statements of financial posi-tion for Iberian and Tango, with adjustments, are as follows:

(*Continued*)

(Continued)

	(A) Iberian	(B) Tango	(C) Adjustments	A + B +/– C Consolidated
Cash	€400,000	€150,000		€550,000
Accounts receivable	9,250,000	7,000,000		16,250,000
Property, plant, and equipment	8,200,000	5,700,000	+ €2,000,000 (Note 1)	15,900,000
Investment in Tango	2,000,000	0	– €2,000,000 (Note 2)	0
Goodwill	0	0	+ €1,300,000 (Note 3)	1,300,000
Total assets	€19,850,000	€12,850,000		€34,000,000
Accounts payable	1,900,000	850,000		2,750,000
Revaluation surplus	0	0	+ €1,300,000 (Note 4)	1,300,000
Retained earnings	7,500,000	5,100,000		12,600,000
Issued equity	10,450,000	6,900,000		17,350,000
Liabilities and equity	€19,850,000	€12,850,000		€34,000,000

(1) Add back excess of €14,000,000 fair value on acquisition date over initial net assets (cash + accounts receivable + PP&E – accounts payable).

(2) Eliminate minority interest, since now own 100% of Tango.

(3) See preceding goodwill calculation table.

(4) Iberian's share of the increase in the net assets of Tango, per the preceding goodwill calculation table.

What Is the Measurement Period?

The measurement period is the period following the acquisition date. The acquirer uses the measurement period to adjust the provisional amounts that it initially recognizes for a business combination. This typically includes the finalization of the identification of the acquiree's assets and liabilities, noncontrolling interests, and goodwill. The measurement period does not exceed one year from the acquisition date.

What If the Initial Measurement Is Not Completed in the Initial Reporting Period?

If the acquirer cannot complete the accounting for a business combination within the initial reporting period, then it reports provisional amounts for any incomplete items. During the measurement period, the acquirer should retrospectively adjust the initial provisional amounts as it obtains new information that affects the measurement of the business combination. This can involve the recognition of additional assets or liabilities.

The measurement period ends as soon as the acquirer either:

○ Finishes collecting information about the facts and circumstances existing at the acquisition date or
○ Determines that no more information is obtainable; or one year passes from the acquisition date.

How Do I Adjust for a Provisional Measurement?

If you recognize a provisional amount for an asset, liability, or noncontrolling interest and later need to alter it, the offsetting adjustment is to goodwill.

You also should revise comparative information for previous periods presented in the financial statements, so that adjustments are reflected in all comparative periods. If a change is to an asset that is being depreciated or amortized, retrospectively adjust the depreciation and amortization to reflect the revisions to the provisional amount.

How Do I Account for Acquisition-Related Costs?

An acquirer incurs a variety of acquisition-related costs to complete a business combination. Examples of these costs are advisory fees, finder's fees, legal and accounting expenses, valuation services, and the costs of maintaining an internal acquisitions department. You should charge all of these costs to expense in the period incurred.

How Do I Subsequently Measure a Business Combination?

You should subsequently measure most assets and liabilities acquired through a business combination normally, in accordance with the applicable international accounting standards most applicable to those items. However, the following items require special measurement:

○ *Reacquired rights.* Amortize the carrying amount of these rights over the remaining contractual period of the contract in which the right was granted.

○ *Contingent liabilities.* Until settled, measure at the higher of the amount initially recognized less any cumulative amortization, or the amount that would be recognized as noted in the Provisions and Contingencies chapter.

○ *Indemnification assets.* Measure at the end of every subsequent period on the same basis as the indemnified asset or liability, altered by any contractual limitations. If you are not measuring it at its fair value, use management's assessment of its collectibility. You should derecognize it once the acquirer collects it, sells it, or loses the right to it in some other manner.

○ *Contingent consideration.* If there is a change in contingent consideration resulting from events *after* the acquisition date, it is not a measurement period adjustment. You should account for contingent consideration in one of three ways:

1. *Equity.* If the consideration originally was classified as equity, also make subsequent settlement entries to equity.

2. *Financial instruments.* If the consideration originally was classified as a financial instrument, then measure it at its fair value, and recognize the gain or loss in either profit or loss or other comprehensive income. See the Financial Instruments: Recognition and Measurement chapter for more information.

3. *Other assets and liabilities.* Account for them as indicated in the Provisions and Contingencies chapter.

What Information Do I Disclose about a Business Combination?

Generally, you should disclose sufficient information so that an entity's financial statement users can evaluate the nature and financial effect of a business combination occurring either in the current reporting period or following the period but before the period's financial statements are authorized for issuance. More specifically, disclose the following:

○ *Assets.* The amounts recognized for each major class of assets acquired.

○ *Bargain purchase.* If the combination is a bargain purchase transaction, note the amount of the gain, where in the financial statements it is recorded, and why the transaction resulted in a gain.

- *Consideration.* Fair value, as of the acquisition date, of the consideration paid, broken down by class of consideration.
- *Contingent consideration.* The recognized amount of contingent consideration arrangements and indemnification assets, a description of these arrangements, how the payment amounts were determined, and an estimate of the undiscounted range of outcomes. If there is no maximum payment, note this. If it is not possible to determine a range of possible payments, note this and the reasons why the determination cannot be made.
- *Contingent liabilities.* All standard disclosures for recognized contingent liabilities. See the Provisions and Contingencies chapter for more information.
- *Control method.* How the acquirer attained control over the acquiree.
- *Date.* The acquisition date.
- *Description.* The name and description of the acquiree.
- *Equity interest.* The percent of voting equity interest acquired.
- *Financial results – acquiree.* The acquiree's revenue and profit or loss since the acquisition date.
- *Financial results – consolidated.* The combined entity's revenue and profit or loss in the current period, adjusted as though all acquisitions in the year had been as of the beginning of the fiscal year.
- *Goodwill – detail.* The factors making up goodwill, such as intangible assets not qualifying for separate treatment, and expected synergies from the business combination.
- *Goodwill – deductible.* The amount of goodwill that you expect will be deductible for tax purposes.
- *Liabilities.* The amounts recognized for each major class of liabilities assumed.
- *Noncontrolling interests.* If the acquirer does not own 100 percent of the acquiree, note the amount of the noncontrolling interest, how that amount is measured, and the valuation methods and inputs used to calculate the value of the noncontrolling interests.
- *Reasons.* The main business reasons for the acquisition.
- *Receivables.* For acquired receivables, their aggregate fair value, the gross amounts receivable, and the best estimate of receivables that will not be collected.
- *Separate transactions.* If there are transactions recognized separately from the business combination, provide a description of each transaction, how it was accounted for, the amounts recognized, and the

financial statement line item in which it is located. If it settles a pre-existing relationship, note the method used to determine the settlement amount. Also note the amount of acquisition-related costs, identified by the amounts expensed and not expensed.

○ *Staged combination.* If a business combination has occurred in several stages, note the fair value of the acquirer's equity interest just prior to the acquisition date, the gain or loss it recognized when it remeasured to fair value just prior to the acquisition date, and where that gain or loss is recognized.

If a business combination is completed after the reporting period but before the financial statements are authorized for issuance, disclose all of the preceding information to the extent practicable. If not practicable, note which disclosures were not made, and why.

In addition, you should disclose information that allows financial statement users to evaluate the effects of adjustments recognized in the current period relating to business combinations that occurred in either the current or previous reporting periods. Specifically, disclose the following for each material business combination, and in aggregate for those business combinations that are individually immaterial:

○ *Contingent consideration.* For each reporting period until settled, note the recognized changes in contingent consideration, the reasons for and amounts of any changes in the range of undiscounted outcomes, and the valuation methods and inputs used to measure the contingent consideration.

○ *Gains and losses.* Note the amounts of and reasons for any recognized gains or losses related to the assets acquired and liabilities assumed as part of a business combination, if they are relevant to understanding the financial statements.

○ *Provisional items.* If the accounting for a combination is provisional, then state why it is incomplete and which specific items are incomplete, and describe any adjustments made during the reporting period.

○ *Reconciliation.* Reconcile the carrying amount of goodwill at the beginning and end of the period, highlighting changes in the gross amount, impairment losses, additional goodwill recognized, adjustments caused by tax asset recognition, inclusion in a held-for-sale group, net exchange rate differences, and any other reconciling items.

CHAPTER 22

CHANGES IN ACCOUNTING POLICIES, ESTIMATES, AND ERRORS

 ### What Is a Change in Accounting Estimate?

A change in accounting estimate is an assessment of the current and future status of the benefits and obligations associated with assets and liabilities, resulting in a modification of the carrying amount of either an asset or a liability, or the periodic consumption of an asset.

 ### What Is a Material Omission or Misstatement?

An omission or misstatement is material if it could influence the economic decisions that users of financial statements make. The size or nature of the item (or both) may be relevant to the determination.

 ### What Is a Prior-Period Error?

A prior-period error is an omission from, or a misstatement of, prior-period financial statements that was caused by the failure to use, or the misuse of, information that was available when the financial statements were authorized for issuance and that could be expected to have been obtained. Examples of a prior-period error are fraud, calculation mistakes, factual misinterpretations or oversights, and mistakes in applying accounting policies.

 ### What Is a Retrospective Application?

A retrospective application is the application of a new accounting policy as if that policy had always been applied.

What Is a Retrospective Restatement?

A retrospective restatement is the correction of financial statements as if a prior-period error had never occurred.

 When Is a Retrospective Policy Change Impractical?

It is impractical to implement a retrospective policy change when the entity cannot apply it after making reasonable efforts to do so. It is impractical to make a change for a specific prior period when its effects are not determinable, or it requires assumptions about what management's intent would have been in that period, or it requires an estimate of significant amounts *and* it is impossible to distinguish the information about the estimates on the measurement dates that would have been available when the financial statements for that period were authorized for issuance.

 What Is a Prospective Application?

A prospective application is the application of a new accounting policy to transactions after the date of the policy change, with recognition of the effect of changes in accounting estimates in the current and future periods.

 Can I Avoid Implementing an International Financial Reporting Standard (IFRS) That Has an Immaterial Impact?

If the effect of applying an IFRS is immaterial, then you do not need to apply it. However, do not depart from an immaterial IFRS in order to create a particular presentation of the financial statements.

 What Controls Should I Use for IFRS Implementations Having an Immaterial Impact?

There are cases where the decision to not implement an IFRS will be highly judgmental; one person may rule in favor of doing so, and another may not. Other cases are more clearly in favor of implementation, but an entity does not do so, either because it is unaware of the standard or because someone wants to avoid the financial reporting consequences of the implementation. The following controls can mitigate these issues:

- *Formal review.* Create a review committee that examines how standards apply to an entity and whether they are immaterial. Document its proceedings to show how the group voted on each issue.
- *Scheduled reviews.* Schedule a review of all new or updated standards at least once a year. Consider consulting with an auditing firm for advice, since auditing firms are most likely to be cognizant of changes that may impact the entity.

 ## When Can I Change an Accounting Policy?

It is acceptable to change an accounting policy only when required by an IFRS, or when the change will result in financial statements that provide more relevant information.

An accounting policy is not considered to be changed when you apply a new policy to transactions, conditions, or events that have not occurred previously or are immaterial.

 ## What Controls Should I Use for Changing an Accounting Policy?

The key issue when revising an accounting policy is whether the change results in more relevant information in the financial statements. Some policy changes have a significant impact on reported results, and so are worthy of considerable review prior to implementation. This should involve a discussion not only among the entire management team, but also with the company auditors. Furthermore, document the basis for the change and archive the document, to ensure that the entity can justify its position at a later date.

 ## How Do I Account for a Change in Accounting Policy?

If an accounting policy change is mandated by an IFRS, then account for it in accordance with any specific transitional provisions noted in the IFRS. If there are no specific transitional provisions listed in the IFRS, then apply the change retrospectively to all financial statements presented. If you voluntarily change an accounting policy, then apply the change retrospectively to all financial statements presented. Early application of an IFRS is not considered a voluntary change in accounting policy.

EXAMPLE 22.1

Celtic Pottery Company originally tracked its hand-thrown ceramic products in inventory on an individual basis. However, with increased sales volume, this method proves impractical to continue, so Celtic elects to change its accounting method to the first-in, first-out (FIFO) method.

Celtic presents two years of financial statements. For Year 1, the impact of the change was an inventory increase of £28,000, and in Year 2 the impact was an inventory decrease of £12,000. The changes to Celtic's income statement are as follows:

	Year 1			Year 2		
	Prior to Adjustment	Adjustment	Restated	Prior to Adjustment	Adjustment	Restated
Revenue	£2,475,000		£2,475,000	£3,100,000		£3,100,000
Cost of sales	1,485,000	£(28,000)	1,457,000	1,860,000	£+12,000	1,872,000
Other expenses	750,000		750,000	868,000		868,000
Net profit*	£240,000	£(28,000)	£268,000	£372,000	£12,000	£360,000

*No impact on income taxes is assumed in this example.

When making a retrospective adjustment to the financial statements for prior periods, adjust the opening balance of each affected equity account (usually retained earnings) for the earliest prior period presented, as though the new policy had always been applied.

Do not implement a retrospective accounting policy if it is impractical to determine either the period-specific or cumulative effects of the change. If this is the case, apply the policy to the carrying amounts of assets and liabilities as of the beginning of the earliest period for which this treatment is practicable.

What Activities Involve Accounting Estimates?

Many business activities involve accounting estimates, since their ultimate outcomes may not be resolved for some time. Examples of transactions requiring estimates are reserves for bad debts, inventory obsolescence, and warranty obligations, as well as the useful lives of property, plant, and equipment, and the fair value of financial assets or liabilities.

A change in measurement basis is a change in accounting policy, not a change in accounting estimate. However, when it is difficult to distinguish between changes in accounting policy and a change in accounting estimate, treat the issue as a change in accounting estimate.

 Does a Change in Accounting Estimate Require a Retrospective Application?

No. The revision of an estimate does not relate to prior periods.

 How Do I Account for a Change in Accounting Estimate?

It may be necessary to change an accounting estimate if there is new information about the circumstances on which the most recent estimate was based. Recognize a change in accounting estimate for transactions and other events and conditions beginning in the period of the change. If the change in estimate alters the carrying amount of assets or liabilities, recognize these changes in the period of the change.

EXAMPLE 22.2

Glass Lamination International uses vacuum deposition to deposit a thin-film coating on periscope lenses. It originally depreciates the vacuum deposition equipment using an estimated useful life of 10 years, with no residual value. Thus, it depreciates the €10,000,000 carrying amount of the equipment at the rate of €1,000,000 per year.

(Continued)

> (*Continued*)
> After five years, Glass Lamination determines that the equipment now has a remaining useful life of eight years. It therefore depreciates the remaining carrying amount of €5,000,000 at a revised rate of €625,000 per year. There is no retrospective change in prior periods.

 ## What Controls Do I Use for a Change in Estimate?

A change in estimate is subject to manipulation, since it can result in the deferral of expense recognition. To avoid this problem, consider shifting asset and liability evaluations to an outside firm. Also, document the reasons for all changes in estimate, and require the approval of a senior manager prior to implementation.

 ## How Do I Account for the Correction of an Accounting Error?

Correct a prior-period material error retrospectively. Restate the amounts for the prior periods in which the error occurred, or, if the error occurred before the earliest period presented, restate the opening balances of the affected accounts for the earliest period presented. Exclude the correction of a prior-period error from the current reporting period's profit or loss.

If it is impracticable to determine the period-specific or cumulative effect of an error, then do not make a retroactive restatement. Instead, restate the opening balances of the current accounts for the earliest period for which the restatement is practicable.

EXAMPLE 22.3

Bonifacio Bakeries acquires Corsican Chestnut Flour. Two years later, Bonifacio discovers that it has not amortized any of the intangible assets that it booked as a result of the acquisition. The amortization expense should have been €30,000 in the first year (a partial year) and €75,000 in the second year. The changes to Bonifacio's income statement are as follows:

	Year 1			Year 2		
	Prior to Adjustment	Adjustment	Restated	Prior to Adjustment	Adjustment	Restated
Revenue	€5,220,000		€5,220,000	€5,612,000		€5,612,000
Cost of sales	3,760,000		3,760,000	4,040,000		4,040,000
Gross margin	1,460,000		1,460,000	1,572,000		1,572,000
Amortization	0	€30,000	30,000	0	€75,000	75,000
Other expenses	897,000		897,000	882,000		882,000
Other income before taxes	563,000		533,000	690,000		615,000
Income taxes	195,000	(10,000)	185,000	240,000	(25,000)	215,000
Net profit	€368,000	€20,000	€348,000	€450,000	€50,000	€400,000

Bonifacio adds the following disclosure to its financial statements:

The amortization of intangible assets acquired as part of the Corsican Chestnut Flour acquisition was not included in the financial statements for Year 1 or Year 2. The financial statements for the past two years have been restated to correct this error. The effect of the restatement on those financial statements is summarized below:

	Year 1	Year 2
Increase in amortization expense	€(30,000)	€(75,000)
Decrease in income tax expense	10,000	25,000
Decrease in profit	€(20,000)	€(50,000)
Decrease in equity	€(20,000)	€(50,000)

What Information Do I Need for a Retrospective Application?

If you plan to retrospectively apply a change in accounting policy or adjust an accounting error, the following information must have been available in the prior periods that you plan to adjust:

○ Evidence of circumstances that existed when the transaction, condition, or event occurred
○ Evidence that would have been available when the prior-period financial statements were authorized for issuance

It is not acceptable to use hindsight when applying a change in accounting policy or an accounting error, since this implies the use of information and knowledge of circumstances that were not available when the original financial statements were assembled.

How Do I Disclose the Application of a Policy Mandated by an IFRS?

When applying an IFRS that has an effect on past, present, or future financial statements, disclose the following:

○ Title of the IFRS
○ Whether the change is made in accordance with the transitional provisions of the IFRS
○ The nature of the policy change
○ The transitional provisions of the change, and any provisions that may affect future periods
○ The amount of the adjustment for the current and prior periods (if practicable), and the adjustment amount for each line item affected, including basic and diluted earnings per share (if applicable)
○ The adjustment amount for periods prior to those presented (if practicable)
○ Why retrospective application is not possible for a prior period or for periods before those presented, as well as from what period the policy change was applied

It is necessary to disclose this information only once, when initially applying the IFRS.

How Do I Disclose a Voluntary Change in Accounting Policy?

When a voluntary accounting policy change affects past, present, or future financial statements, disclose the following:

○ The nature of the policy change

○ The reasons why the change provides more reliable and relevant information

○ The amount of the adjustment for the current and prior periods (if practicable), and the adjustment amount for each line item affected, including basic and diluted earnings per share (if applicable)

○ The adjustment amount for periods prior to those presented (if practicable)

○ Why retrospective application is not possible for a prior period or for periods before those presented, as well as from what period the policy change was applied

It is necessary to disclose this information only once, when initially applying the voluntary policy change.

How Do I Disclose an Issued But Not Yet Effective IFRS?

If you have not applied an IFRS that has been issued but is not yet effective, disclose this fact, as well as an assessment of the impact of the IFRS on the entity's financial statements when the change is first applied. The assessment is based on any known or reasonably estimable information.

Although not mandatory, consider also disclosing the title of the new IFRS, the nature of the impending change, the date of conversion to the IFRS, and either a discussion of the initial impact of the change on the entity's financial statements or a disclosure that the initial impact is not yet known or reasonably estimable.

How Do I Disclose a Change in Accounting Estimate?

Disclose the nature and amount of a change in an accounting estimate that affects the current period or is expected to impact future periods. Do not disclose this information for future periods if it is impractical to estimate the effect, but disclose that fact.

How Do I Disclose a Prior-Period Error?

If there is a prior-period error, disclose the nature of the error, the amount of the correction for each line item affected in each prior period presented, and the change in basic and diluted earnings per share (if applicable). Also note the amount of the correction at the beginning of the earliest period presented. If it is impracticable to have a retrospective restatement, disclose the circumstances causing that condition, when the error was corrected, and how it was corrected.

It is necessary to disclose this information only once, when initially applying the error correction.

CHAPTER 23

DISCONTINUED OPERATIONS AND NONCURRENT ASSETS HELD FOR SALE

 What Is a Discontinued Operation?

A discontinued operation is a component of an entity that either has been disposed of already, or is held for sale. It also falls into one of the following three categories:

1. *Separate business.* It is a separate and major line of an entity's business, or comprises a geographical area of operations.
2. *Disposal plan.* It is part of a plan to dispose of a separate and major line of an entity's business, or a geographical area of operations.
3. *Resale acquisition.* It is a subsidiary that the entity originally acquired exclusively to resell it.

EXAMPLE 23.1

Tongan Motors suffers an apparently permanent and substantial decline in its automobile sales along the Pacific Rim, due to an increase in mass transit systems in Tongan's markets. Accordingly, Tongan plans to stop producing its Copra sedan by the end of the year and close the Koloyai facility that produces the car. Tongan should account for the Copra product line as a discontinued operation.

 When Should I Classify a Noncurrent Asset as Held for Sale?

You should classify a noncurrent asset as held for sale if you expect that its carrying amount will be recovered through its sale, rather than through its continuing use by the entity. You can assign this classification only if the asset's sale is highly probable and it is ready for immediate sale in its present condition.

For an asset sale to be highly probable, management must be committed to sell it and actively searching for a buyer to acquire it at a price that is reasonable in relation to its fair value. Further, the transaction should qualify for recognition within one year of the classification date.

EXAMPLE 23.2

Magellanic Company, maker of custom sea-going rowboats for the fishing industry, acquires Ramsgate Rowboats and elects to merge both entities in Ramsgate's facilities, leaving empty its warehouse complex in Margate. Magellanic advertises the Margate facility for sale at a below-market price. Magellanic can classify its Margate facility as held for sale, since it is ready for immediate sale and that sale is highly probable.

There is a real estate market crash one week later, and building prices in Ramsgate drop by 50 percent. Magellanic does not reduce its offer price to the new market rate. Since the offer price is well above the market price, the warehouse is no longer available for immediate sale, and Magellanic should discontinue its classification as held for sale.

 ## When Should I Classify a Subsidiary as Held for Sale?

You should classify all of the assets and liabilities of a subsidiary as held for sale when you are committed to a sales plan involving loss of control of the subsidiary, even if you will retain a noncontrolling interest after the sale. You should use this classification for a subsidiary only if you expect that its carrying amount will be recovered through its sale, rather than through its continuing operations, and also if the subsidiary's sale is highly probable and it is ready for immediate sale in its present condition.

When Should I Classify a Noncurrent Asset as Held for Distribution to Owners?

You should classify an asset as held for distribution to owners when the entity is committed to distribute the asset to the entity's owners, the assets are available for immediate distribution, and the distribution is highly probable. Further, you should expect the distribution to be completed within one year.

 ## What If I Cannot Meet the Held-for-Sale Criteria until after the Reporting Period?

If you cannot meet the designated criteria (see first question) for reporting a noncurrent asset as held for sale, then you cannot assign this classification to the asset in the financial statements related to that period. However, if you can meet the criteria after the reporting period but before the statements are authorized, then disclose this fact in the accompanying notes.

 ## What If a Sale Transaction Takes Longer Than One Year?

If circumstances prolong the sale period to beyond one year, it is still acceptable to use the held-for-sale designation, as long as the cause of the delay is beyond the entity's control and the entity remains committed to selling the asset.

EXAMPLE 23.3

Hermigua Hydroelectric wants to sell its El Guro hydroelectric facility, which requires regulatory approval from the government of the Canary Islands. The government will not consider any approval request until Hermigua can document a firm purchase commitment from a third party. Hermigua believes it is highly probable that it will obtain such a commitment within one year. Since government approval may cause a delay and that delay is beyond Hermigua's control, there is a valid exception to the one-year limitation, and Hermigua can continue to classify the El Guro facility as held for sale.

EXAMPLE 23.4

Masterson Brick Company decides to sell a brick production facility and classifies it as held for sale. Masterson markets the property at a competitive price. It fails to find a buyer, and market conditions deteriorate during the ensuing year. Masterson continues to drop its offer price to match the market rate. In this scenario, market conditions are beyond Masterson's control, and so it can continue to designate the facility as held for sale, so long as it continues to offer the facility at or below the market price.

 ## How Should I Classify an Asset to Be Abandoned?

If you plan to abandon a noncurrent asset, do not classify it as held for sale. However, if it is a separate major business line or operational area, or a subsidiary acquired exclusively for resale, then classify it as a discontinued operation as of the date when you stop using it.

 ## How Do I Classify an Asset Acquired with the Intent of Disposal?

If you acquire an asset exclusively in order to dispose of it, then classify it as held for sale as of the acquisition date, but only if you can sell it within one year and you can meet all other criteria for the held-for-sale classification within three months of the acquisition date.

 ## How Do I Account for Assets Classified as Held for Sale?

If you classify an asset as held for sale, apply the following accounting to it:

○ *Carrying cost.* Measure the asset at the lower of its carrying amount or its fair value less costs to sell, and charge any impairment loss to profit or loss. If it will take longer than one year to sell an asset classified as held for sale, then measure the costs to sell at their present value. Later, if there is a gain on any subsequent increase in the asset's fair value less costs to sell, recognize the gain only to the extent of any cumulative impairment loss.

If you classify an asset as held for sale that you acquired as part of a business combination, then measure it at its fair value less costs to sell.

If you classify an asset as held for distribution to owners, measure it at the lower of its carrying amount or its fair value less costs to distribute (which are any incremental costs directly attributable to the distribution, not including finance costs and income tax expenses).

○ *Depreciation.* Stop depreciating the asset as of the classification date.

○ *Assets and liabilities.* If it is a multi-asset group, present the related assets and liabilities separately in the statement of financial position.

EXAMPLE 23.5

Pilkington Pottery designates its Kitchener Ceramics subsidiary as held for sale. At this point, Pilkington must measure the subsidiary at the lower of its carrying amount or its fair value less costs to sell. The carrying amount of the Kitchener subsidiary is 2 million Canadian dollars. Its fair value is 1.8 million Canadian dollars, and the costs to sell are 100,000 Canadian dollars. Thus, Pilkington should record an impairment loss of 300,000 Canadian dollars in profit or loss, which is Kitchener's fair value less its costs to sell.

How Do I Depreciate Held-for-Sale Assets and Discontinued Operations?

Do not depreciate a noncurrent asset while it is classified as held for sale, and do not depreciate a discontinued operation while it retains that classification.

What If an Asset No Longer Meets the Held-for-Sale Criteria?

If an asset no longer meets the criteria for being designated as held for sale, then stop classifying it as such.

At the time of conversion away from the held-for-sale designation, measure the asset at the lower of its recoverable amount or its carrying amount before it was classified as held for sale, adjusted for any depreciation or revaluations that otherwise would have taken place while it was held for sale. Thus, no longer being held for sale subjects an asset to a "catch up" event for depreciation in arrears. The entity records this adjustment in profit or loss as soon as the asset no longer meets the held-for-sale criteria.

If an entity removes a single asset or liability from a disposal group that is currently classified as held for sale, the remaining assets and liabilities in the disposal group must still qualify as held for sale, or else they too must be treated as just noted, at the lower of their recoverable amounts or their carrying amounts before being classified as held for sale, adjusted for any depreciation or revaluations that otherwise would have taken place while they were held for sale.

What Controls Should I Use for the Classification of Held-for-Sale Items?

The principal control problem with the held-for-sale and discontinued operations designations is that you stop depreciating their carrying cost as of the classification date, which increases net profits. Managers could use these designations to alter reported results in the short term, even though a reclassification back to the original designation eventually will be required if there is no sale, which causes a depreciation "catch up" transaction.

To keep this profit manipulation from occurring, the accounting staff should notify the audit committee whenever either designation is applied, as well as when it is removed. The audit committee should have an annual procedural requirement to review this information to see if management is using the designation to manipulate the entity's results.

How Do I Disclose the Results of Discontinued Operations and Held-for-Sale Items?

Generally, an entity should disclose information that enables users of its financial statements to evaluate the financial effects of discontinued operations and held-for-sale items. Specifically, you should disclose the following information in the statement of comprehensive income:

○ *Adjustments to discontinued operations.* Any current-period changes to previously classified discontinued operations that are related to their disposal in a prior period. Examples are the resolution of purchase price adjustments, indemnification issues, product warranty obligations, and benefit plan obligations.

○ *Assets.* Separately present the major classes of assets of a disposal group in the statement of financial position. Do not offset these assets against the liabilities of the disposal group. Separate asset disclosure is not necessary if it relates to a newly acquired subsidiary that was classified as held for sale upon acquisition. Also, do not separately present this information for prior periods if the held-for-sale classification occurred in the current period.

○ *Cash flows.* The net cash flows related to the operating, investing, and financing activities of the discontinued operation. Present this information either in the notes to the financial statements or within the statement of comprehensive income.

○ *Ended classification.* If you no longer classify an operation as held for sale, then reclassify its operational results back into the entity's continuing operations for all periods presented, and describe the amounts for prior periods as being re-presented. Any gain or loss on remeasurement of such an operation also is included in profit or loss from continuing operations.

○ *Income linked to owners.* The income from discontinued operations and separately from continuing operations that is attributable to the owners of the parent entity. Present this information either in the notes to the financial statements or within the statement of comprehensive income.

○ *Liabilities.* Separately present the major classes of liabilities of a disposal group in the statement of financial position. Do not offset these liabilities against the assets of the disposal group. Separate liability disclosure is not necessary if it relates to a newly acquired subsidiary that was classified as held for sale upon acquisition. Also, do not separately present this information for prior periods if the held-for-sale classification occurred in the current period.

○ *Profit or loss summary.* The post-tax profit or loss on discontinued operations, and the post-tax gain or loss on either the adjustment to fair value less costs to sell, or on final disposition.

○ *Profit or loss detail.* Break down the summary-level profit or loss into the revenue, expenses, pre-tax profit or loss, related income tax, and pre- and post-tax gain or loss on either the adjustment to fair value less costs to sell, or on final disposition. Present this information either in the notes to the financial statements, or separately identified within the statement of comprehensive income. Also present the same information for the discontinued operation in all previous periods presented, even if the operation was not discontinued in the earlier periods.

EXAMPLE 23.6

The following is a sample layout of a statement of comprehensive income, with the results of discontinued operations included:

Continuing operations	
Revenue	1,000
Cost of sales	600
Gross profit	400
General and administrative expenses	300
Profit before tax	100
Income tax expense	40
Profit from continuing operations	60
Discontinued operations	
Profit from discontinued operations	20
Profit for the period	80
Profit attributable to:	
Owners of the parent	
Profit from continuing operations	15
Profit from discontinued operations	0
Profit attributable to owners of the parent	15
Noncontrolling interests	
Profit from continuing operations	45
Profit from discontinued operations	20
Profit attributable to noncontrolling interests	65
Total profit from all sources	80

When identifying noncurrent assets classified as held for sale in an entity's statement of financial position, enter them as a separate line item after current assets, entitled "Noncurrent assets classified as held for sale." When identifying liabilities that are associated with such assets, enter them as a separate line item entitled, "Liabilities directly associated with noncurrent assets classified as held for sale."

In addition to the above information, which is disclosed within an entity's financial statements, also disclose the following information in the accompanying notes:

- *Classification change.* If an asset or disposal group is no longer classified as held for sale, the reason for the change, and the effect of the change on the results of operations for both the current period and prior periods presented in the financial statements
- *Description.* A description of the noncurrent asset or disposal group that is held for sale
- *Fair value changes.* Any gain or loss from changes in the fair value of the asset or disposal group
- *Sale information.* The circumstances of the expected sale, including its manner and timing
- *Segment.* The reportable segment (if applicable) in which the noncurrent asset or disposal group is presented

CHAPTER 24

EFFECTS OF FOREIGN EXCHANGE RATE CHANGES

 What Is a Functional Currency?

A functional currency is the currency used in the primary economic environment where an entity operates. This is the environment in which an entity primarily generates and expends cash. You should consider the following *primary* factors in determining an entity's functional currency:

- ○ The currency that primarily influences sales prices (usually the currency in which prices are denominated and settled)
- ○ The currency of the country whose competition and regulations primarily influence sales prices
- ○ The currency that primarily influences labor and other costs of goods sold (usually the currency in which prices are denominated and settled)

Less critical deciding factors are the currency in which an entity retains receipts from its operations, and the currency in which debt and equity instruments are issued.

When determining the functional currency of an entity's foreign operation, consider the following factors:

- ○ *Autonomy.* Whether the operation is essentially an extension of the reporting entity, or can operate with a significant degree of autonomy. The functional currency is the reporting entity's in the first case, and the local currency in the latter.
- ○ *Proportion of transactions.* Whether the foreign operation's transactions with the reporting entity constitute a high or low proportion of the operation's activities. The functional currency is the reporting entity's in the first case, and the local currency in the latter.

○ *Proportion of cash flows.* Whether cash flows from the foreign operation directly affect the cash flows of the reporting entity and are available for remittance. The functional currency is the reporting entity's if so, and the local currency if not.

○ *Debt service.* Whether the foreign operation's cash flows can service its debt obligations without funds transfers from the reporting entity. The functional currency is the reporting entity's if funds transfers are needed, and the local currency if not.

EXAMPLE 24.1

Chillo Ice Cream Company, based in the United Kingdom, has a subsidiary in Chile, to which it ships its products for sale through a number of retail outlets. The local subsidiary only sells the imported ice cream and then remits receipts back to corporate headquarters, so Chillo should treat British pounds as the functional currency of its Chilean operation.

Chillo also owns Sorvete Firma, which is located in Brazil. Sorvete manufactures its own ice cream, markets it throughout Brazil, accumulates cash reserves and borrows funds in Brazilian reals, and rarely remits funds back to corporate headquarters. In this case, the functional currency for Sorvete is Brazilian reals.

If the preceding indicators present such mixed results that the functional currency is not obvious, then management should use its judgment to select the functional currency most representative of the economic effects of the situation.

 ## What Is an Exchange Rate?

An exchange rate is the ratio at which two currencies are exchanged. The *spot exchange rate* is the exchange rate at which a currency can be delivered immediately. The *closing rate* is the spot exchange rate at the end of a reporting period.

 ## If There Are Several Possible Exchange Rates, Which Do I Use?

If there are several possible exchange rates that can be applied to a transaction, use the one at which the transaction's future cash flows or balance could have been settled if it had occurred on the measurement date.

If there is temporarily no exchange rate between the two currencies, use the first subsequent rate at which exchanges could be made.

 ## How Do I Initially Account for a Foreign Currency Transaction?

A foreign currency transaction is either denominated in or requires settlement in a foreign currency.

EXAMPLE 24.2

Katana Cutlery, a South Korean company, buys titanium for its super-sharp commercial knives from Canada; the purchase is denominated in Canadian dollars. It also has a loan from a Japanese bank that is denominated in yen. It buys the ebony for its knife handles from Sri Lanka, and the purchase is denominated in Sri Lankan rupees. Since all of these transactions are settled in currencies other than Katana's functional currency of the South Korean won, they are all classified as foreign currency transactions.

To initially account for a transaction denominated in a foreign currency, in an entity's functional currency, apply the spot exchange rate between the functional currency and the foreign currency as of the transaction date.

EXAMPLE 24.3

Bergschrund Designs is a German exporter of climbing equipment, whose functional currency is the euro. On November 30, it sells an order of ice climbing gear to a U.S. outdoor retail chain that is denominated in U.S. dollars, in the amount of $80,000. The spot rate on the November 30 shipment date was €1:$1.25, so Bergschrund records the following entry in euros (calculated as $80,000 ÷ $1.25 exchange rate):

Accounts receivable	€64,000	
Sales		€64,000

(Continued)

(Continued)

The receivable is still outstanding on December 31, which is Bergschrund's fiscal year-end. On December 31, the exchange rate has changed to €1:$1.15, so the receivable is now worth €69,565 (calculated as $80,000 ÷ $1.15 exchange rate). This represents a foreign exchange gain of €5,565, which Bergschrund records with this entry:

Accounts receivable	€5,565	
Foreign currency exchange gain		€5,565

The customer wires payment to Bergschrund on the following day, when the exchange rate remains at €1:$1.15. Bergschrund records the following entry to recognize the receipt of cash:

Cash	€69,565	
Accounts receivable		€69,565

Is It Acceptable to Apply an Average Exchange Rate Instead of the Spot Exchange Rate?

It is acceptable to use an average exchange rate that approximates the spot exchange rate, such as a weekly or monthly average. However, an average rate is not acceptable if the exchange rate fluctuates significantly.

How Does an Entity Incorporate Exchange Rates into Its Financial Statements?

When preparing financial statements, an entity should follow these three general steps in order to properly incorporate the effects of foreign exchange rates:

1. Determine the entity's functional currency.
2. Translate foreign currency items into the functional currency. If an entity has a number of subsidiaries,

associates, or joint venture investments, it must convert the results and financial position of each of these entities into the reporting entity's functional currency.

3. Report the effects of this translation.

If the financial statements of a foreign operation are as of a different date than those of the reporting entity, it is best to have the foreign operation prepare additional statements matching the date used by the reporting entity. If this is not possible, then use a different date, but with no more than three months difference, and make adjustments for the effects of significant transactions occurring between the different dates. When there is a date differential, translate the foreign entity's assets and liabilities at the exchange rate at the end of the foreign operation's reporting period.

 ## What Happens If I Change the Functional Currency?

Changing an entity's functional currency should be a rare event, triggered only by a change in the underlying transactions, events, and conditions relevant to the entity's currency.

If an entity changes its functional currency, it applies the steps just noted in the preceding question to the new functional currency, from the date of the change. This will yield new translated amounts for nonmonetary items, which you then treat as their new historical costs.

Switching to a new functional currency does *not* trigger a shift of any exchange differences previously recognized in other comprehensive income to profit or loss.

 ## Can I Record Foreign Exchange Rate Changes in Revenue?

No. An entity records revenue at the initial point of sale and does not change it again, no matter what happens to foreign exchange rates between the initial sale and the settlement of payment terms. The reason is that the time period between the initial sale date and the payment date is a financing decision, not a sales decision, and so any foreign exchange gains or losses incurred during that interval should not be reflected in sales.

How Do I Translate a Foreign Entity's Goodwill?

If a foreign entity has recorded goodwill (which arises from an acquisition) in its accounting records, treat it as a normal asset of the foreign entity. This means that it is expressed in the foreign operation's functional currency, and is translated to the reporting entity's functional currency at the closing rate at the end of the reporting period of the reporting entity.

 ## What Is a Monetary Item?

A monetary item is an item containing a right to receive or deliver either a fixed or determinable number of units of currency.

EXAMPLE 24.4

Hadrian's Brewery has a pension liability of £100,000, a cash dividend payable of £20,000, and accounts receivable of £400,000. These are all monetary items, because they are to be settled in cash.

Hadrian's also has a deposit of £10,000 on a future hops delivery, £1,000,000 of goodwill, £250,000 of barley inventory, and £2,500,000 of brewing equipment. These are all nonmonetary items, because they will not be settled in cash.

 ## How Do I Account for Foreign Currency Items in Subsequent Periods?

Use the following transactions to account for foreign currency items in subsequent periods:

- *Foreign currency monetary item.* Translate it at the end of each reporting period using the closing rate at the end of the period.
- *Nonmonetary item at historical cost.* If measured in a foreign currency, translate it using the exchange rate on the transaction date.
- *Nonmonetary item at fair value.* If measured in a foreign currency, translate it using the exchange rate on the date of fair value determination.

EXAMPLE 24.5

Gaelic Fire Candy obtains a $1,000,000 mixer for the corn syrup used in its blisteringly hot candies from a supplier in the United States on October 31, when the British pound to U.S. dollar exchange rate is £1:$1.50. Gaelic also sells $200,000 of its signature Combustion Candy to a U.S. retail chain on November 30, when the exchange rate is £1:$1.65. Both the payable and receivable are not yet settled as of year-end, when the closing exchange rate is £1:$1.40. Gaelic's functional currency is the British pound.

The accounts payable for the corn syrup mixer is a foreign currency monetary item, and so must be translated at the end of the period, using the closing rate. On the October 31 purchase date, Gaelic records the mixer as an asset, having a carrying cost of £666,667 (calculated as $1,000,000 payment due ÷ $1.50 exchange rate), along with a matching account payable. At year-end, Gaelic has not yet settled the payable, so it recognizes a foreign exchange loss of £47,619 (calculated as [$1,000,000 payment due ÷ $1.40] – £666,667).

The account receivable for the Combustion Candy sale is a foreign currency monetary item, and so must be translated at the end of the period, using the closing rate. On the November 30 sale date, Gaelic records the sale at £121,212 (calculated as $200,000 ÷ $1.65 exchange rate), along with a matching account receivable. At year-end, Gaelic has not yet settled the receivable, so it recognizes a foreign exchange gain of $£21,645 (calculated as [$200,000 receivable ÷ $1.40] – £121,212).

How Do I Account for Exchange Differences between Periods?

You should recognize the difference between exchange rates on the settlement or translation of items differently, based on the type of transaction. Here are the scenarios:

- ○ *Monetary items.* For foreign exchange rate differences between the end of the current reporting period and their initial recognition, recognize the differences in profit or loss in the period in which they arise.

○ *Nonmonetary items.* When you recognize a gain or loss on a nonmonetary item in other comprehensive income, then also recognize any exchange-rate component of that gain or loss in other comprehensive income. When you recognize a gain or loss on a non-monetary item in profit or loss, then also recognize any exchange-rate component of that gain or loss in profit or loss.

○ *Net investment in a foreign operation.* If there is an exchange rate difference on a monetary item that is part of a net investment in a foreign operation, then recognize the difference in the profit or loss of either the reporting entity or the foreign operation, as appropriate. If the reporting entity issues consolidated results that include the foreign operation as a subsidiary, it instead recognizes the difference in other comprehensive income, and then reclassifies it to profit or loss when it disposes of the net investment.

What Items Are Considered a Net Investment in a Foreign Operation?

An equity investment is clearly a net investment in a foreign operation. In addition, if an entity has a monetary item either payable to or receivable from a foreign operation for which there is no planned or likely settlement in the near future, then treat it as a net investment in a foreign operation. A loan also may be considered a net investment in a foreign operation. Do not treat a trade receivable or payable in this manner.

How Do I Account for a Cumulative Exchange Difference after Disposing of a Foreign Operation?

When you dispose of all or part of a foreign operation, you should reclassify from other comprehensive income to profit or loss the cumulative amount of the exchange differences relating to that operation.

If a foreign operation being disposed of has noncontrolling interests, then derecognize the cumulative amount of the exchange difference relating to those noncontrolling interests, but do not reclassify the exchange differences to profit or loss.

If an entity disposes of only a portion of a foreign operation, then it should reclassify to profit or loss only that portion of the cumulative amount of exchange difference that it has disposed of.

Besides the outright sale or liquidation of a business, a disposal also is considered to have occurred when a reporting entity loses control of a subsidiary that includes a foreign operation, or loses significant influence over an associate that includes a foreign operation, or loses joint control over a jointly controlled entity that includes a foreign operation.

If you write down the carrying amount of a foreign operation, this does not constitute a disposal, and so you should not recognize in profit or loss any cumulative foreign exchange difference because of a write-down.

EXAMPLE 24.6

Bonifacio Bakeries originally paid €4,000,000 for Cleveland Croissants, an American pastry company. On December 31, Bonifacio sells Cleveland Croissants to Detroit Doughnuts for $6,000,000. On that date, the exchange rate is €1:$1.25. Bonifacio's functional currency is the euro, so it translates the $6,000,000 sale price into €4,800,000 (calculated as $6,000,000 ÷ $1.25 exchange rate), which is a profit of €800,000 over its original purchase price.

In addition, Bonifacio previously accumulated an exchange reserve of €150,000 related to its transactions with Cleveland Croissants. On December 31, it shifts this exchange loss into profit or loss. Thus, Bonifacio records a gain on the disposition of €800,000 and an exchange loss of €150,000.

How Do I Translate from a Functional Currency to a Presentation Currency?

A presentation currency is the currency in which an entity presents its financial statements. If this currency is not the same as an entity's functional currency, it translates its financial statements into the presentation currency using the following procedure:

1. Translate assets and liabilities at the closing rate on the date of the statement of financial position.

2. Translate revenue and expenses at the exchange rates on the transaction dates. It is acceptable to use an average exchange rate, unless the rates fluctuate significantly.
3. Recognize all resulting exchange differences in other comprehensive income. These differences arise from translating revenue and expenses at the exchange rates on the transaction dates, versus using the closing rate to translate assets and liabilities, as well as from translating opening net assets at a period-closing rate that differs from the previous period-closing rate.

EXAMPLE 24.7

Provence Panache, maker of stylish women's clothing, uses the euro as its functional currency, but wishes to use the U.S. dollar as its presentation currency. The exchange rate between euros and U.S. dollars at the beginning of the year was 1 euro to $1.25 U.S. dollars, changed to $1.75 U.S. dollars at the end of the year (closing rate), and averaged $1.50 U.S. dollars during the year. The conversion of its financial statements follows:

Profit and Loss Statement (P&L)

(000s)	In Euros	Comment	Exchange Rate	In U.S. $
Revenue	90,000	Average rate	1.50	135,000
Cost of sales	39,000	Average rate	1.50	58,500
Gross profit	51,000			76,500
Other expenses	34,000	Average rate	1.50	51,000
Profit	17,000			25,500

Balance Sheet

(000s)	In Euros	Comment	Exchange Rate	In U.S. $
Assets				
Cash	8,000	Closing rate	1.75	14,000
Accounts receivable	23,000	Closing rate	1.75	40,250
Inventory	18,000	Closing rate	1.75	31,500
Plant and equipment	11,000	Closing rate	1.75	19,250
Total Assets	60,000			105,000

Liabilities and Equity			
Accounts payable	19,000	Closing rate	33,250
Other liabilities	9,000	Closing rate	15,750
Retained earnings	17,000	From P&L	25,500
Exchange difference	–		4,250
Share capital	15,000	Closing rate	26,250
Liabilities and Equity	60,000		105,000

How Do I Translate from the Functional Currency of a Hyperinflationary Economy to a Presentation Currency?

Use the following procedure to translate the financial statements of an entity whose functional currency is located in a hyperinflationary economy to a different presentation currency:

1. Translate all assets, liabilities, equity items, revenue, and expenses at the closing rate on the date of the most recent statement of financial position.
2. Do not adjust comparative prior-year amounts for subsequent changes in the price level or exchange rates.

When an economy stops being hyperinflationary, an entity using the currency of that economy as its functional currency no longer restates its financial statements (see the Financial Reporting in Hyperinflationary Economies chapter). At that time, it should use as its historical costs for translation into the presentation currency the amounts restated to the price level on the date when it stopped restating its financial statements for hyperinflation.

What Information Do I Disclose about the Effects of Foreign Exchange Rate Changes?

A reporting entity should disclose the following information about the effects of foreign exchange rate changes:

○ *Change in functional currency.* When there is a change in the functional currency of either the reporting entity or a significant foreign operation, note the fact and why the entity changed the currency.

○ *Differences in other comprehensive income.* The net amount of exchange differences that it recognized in other comprehensive income. Also reconcile changes in the beginning and ending balances of these exchange differences.

○ *Differences in profit or loss.* The amount of exchange differences that it recognized in profit or loss.

○ *Different currency.* When the financial statements or other financial information is displayed in other than an entity's functional or presentation currency, then state that the financial statements comply with all IFRSs. If they do not, then identify the information as supplementary, the currency in which it is displayed, the functional currency, and the translation method used to create the supplementary information.

○ *Different presentation currency.* When the presentation currency differs from the functional currency, note this fact. Also disclose the functional currency, and why the entity is using a different presentation currency.

CHAPTER 25

FINANCIAL INSTRUMENTS: RECOGNITION AND MEASUREMENT

 What Is a Derivative?

A derivative is a financial instrument whose value changes in relation to changes in a variable, such as an interest rate, commodity price, credit rating, or foreign exchange rate. It also requires either a small or no initial investment, and it is settled at a future date. It allows an entity to speculate on or hedge against future changes in market factors at minimal initial cost. Examples of derivatives are call options, put options, forwards, futures, and swaps.

A nonfinancial instrument also may be a derivative, as long as it is subject to potential net settlement (not delivering or taking delivery of the underlying nonfinancial item) and it is not part of an entity's normal usage requirements.

EXAMPLE 25.1

Baroque Furniture Company enters into a contract to purchase gold at a fixed price on a future date. Baroque plans to sell a quantity of leftover gold from its gold-leaf operation on that future date, and intends to use the purchase contract to hedge the price it expects to be paid from the transaction. In this case, the gold purchase contract is a derivative transaction.

However, if Baroque simply had placed an order for the future delivery of gold, with the expectation of integrating the gold leaf into its faux-medieval furniture, then the transaction would not qualify as a derivative.

EXAMPLE 25.2

Acme Investments is a speculator. On January 1, Acme enters into a soybean futures contract to purchase a number of bushels of soybeans on November 30 and intends to net settle the contract at that time. There is no up-front cost to enter into the contract. On June 30, the fair value of the contract has increased by €50,000. Acme creates the following entry at that time:

Derivative asset	50,000	
Gain		50,000

What Is a Held-to-Maturity Investment?

A held-to-maturity investment is a nonderivative financial asset having either fixed or determinable payments and a fixed maturity, and that an entity has both the ability and the intention to hold to maturity. It does not include financial assets that the entity designates as being at fair value through profit or loss, as available for sale, or as loans or receivables.

An entity cannot classify any financial assets as held to maturity if it has sold or reclassified more than an insignificant amount of held-to-maturity investments before maturity during the current fiscal year or the two preceding years. This restriction does not include reclassifications that were so close to maturity or the asset's call date that changes in the market interest rate would not have significantly impacted the asset's fair value, or those for which the entity had already collected substantially all of the original principal, or those caused by an isolated event beyond the entity's control.

What Is an Available-for-Sale Investment?

An available-for-sale financial asset is a nonderivative asset that is designated as available for sale. It is not classified as held to maturity, or a loan, a receivable, or a financial asset at fair value through profit or loss.

> ### EXAMPLE 25.3
>
> Branxholm Industries invests £100,000 in an equity instrument that is traded on the New York Stock Exchange. Branxholm also has invested £75,000 in an equity instrument that is not actively traded; for this reason, it is not possible to derive a fair value. Branxholm also makes a strategic investment of £250,000 in the equity of a key supplier, which it does not intend to sell. Branxholm does not designate these investments as held for trading.
>
> Branxholm should designate all of these investments as available for sale.

 ## What Is a Financial Asset or Liability at Fair Value through Profit or Loss?

This is a financial asset or liability that is either:

1. Held for trading (acquired for short-term trading, or is a derivative); or
2. Designated as being at fair value through profit or loss.

An entity recognizes in profit or loss any changes in fair value of financial assets or liabilities carrying this designation. The designation can be applied only at initial recognition of the asset or liability.

 ## What Is a Financial Guarantee Contract?

A financial guarantee contract requires the issuer of the contract to make specific payments to the contract holder for a loss incurred by the holder if a debtor fails to pay under the terms of a debt instrument.

 ## What Is the Effective Interest Method?

The effective interest method is a technique for calculating the amortized cost of a financial asset or liability, and that allocates interest income or expense over the relevant period. The calculation includes all fees and points paid or received, transaction costs, and all premiums and discounts. The *effective interest rate*, which is used in the calculation, exactly discounts estimated future cash payments or receipts over the expected life of the instrument.

EXAMPLE 25.4

Svelte Equipment Company, which makes fine chrome-plated, weight-lifting equipment, acquires a debt security having a stated principal amount of €100,000, which the issuer will repay in three years. The debt has a coupon interest rate of 5 percent, which it pays at the end of each year. Svelte acquires the debt for €90,000, which is a discount of €10,000 to the principal amount of €100,000. Svelte classifies the investment as held to maturity and records this entry:

Held-to-maturity investments	90,000	
Cash		90,000

Based on a cash outflow of €90,000 to acquire the investment, three interest payments of €5,000 each, and a principal payment of €100,000 upon maturity, Svelte calculates an effective interest rate of 8.95 percent. Using this interest rate, Svelte calculates the following amortization table:

Year	(A) Beginning Amortized Cost	(B) Interest and Principal Payments	(C) Interest Income [A x 8.95%]	(D) Debt Discount Amortization [C − B]	Ending Amortized Cost [A + D]
1	90,000	5,000	8,055	3,055	93,055
2	93,055	5,000	8,328	3,328	96,383
3	96,383	105,000	8,617	3,617	100,000

Using the table, Svelte makes the following entries at the end of each of the next three years:

YEAR 1:

Cash	5,000	
Held-to-maturity investment	3,055	
Interest income		8,055

YEAR 2:

Cash	5,000	
Held-to-maturity investment	3,328	
Interest income		8,328

YEAR 3:

Cash	105,000	
Held-to-maturity investment		96,383
Interest income		8,617

 ## What Is Derecognition?

Derecognition is the removal of a previously recognized financial asset or liability from an entity's statement of financial position. You should derecognize a financial asset if either the entity's contractual rights to the asset's cash flows have expired or the asset has been transferred to a third party (along with the risks and rewards of ownership). If the risks and rewards of ownership have not passed to the buyer, then the selling entity must still recognize the entire financial asset and treat any consideration received as a liability.

EXAMPLE 25.5

Consolidated Green Products sells a financial asset. Part of the sales agreement is that Consolidated retains the right to repurchase the asset, but only at the asset's fair value on the date of repurchase. Since Consolidated cannot repurchase at a favorable price, it has not retained a reward of ownership, and so can derecognize the asset.

Consolidated recorded a carrying amount of €50,000 for the financial asset, and sells it for €49,500. It records the following entry:

Cash	49,500	
Loss on sale	500	
Asset		50,000

Exhibit 25.1 DERECOGNITION SCENARIOS

Action	Conditions
Derecognize the asset	The rights to related cash flows have expired, or the entity has transferred the right to receive cash flows or has transferred substantially all risks and rewards.
Continue to recognize the asset	The entity has retained substantially all risks and rewards, or it has not transferred the rights to the asset's cash flows and the rights to those cash flows have not expired.
Continue to recognize the asset to the extent of any continuing involvement	The entity has transferred some risks and rewards, but has retained control of the asset.

The proper derecognition treatment for various scenarios is covered in Exhibit 25.1.

What Is a Hedging Instrument?

A hedging instrument is a designated financial instrument whose fair value or related cash flows should offset changes in the fair value or cash flows of a designated hedged item. A *hedged item* is an asset, liability, commitment, highly probable transaction, or investment in a foreign operation that exposes an entity to changes in fair value or cash flows, and is designated as being hedged.

What Is an Embedded Derivative?

An embedded derivative is part of a financial instrument that also includes a nonderivative host contract. The embedded derivative requires that some portion of the contract's cash flows be modified in relation to changes in a variable, such as an interest rate, commodity price, credit rating, or foreign exchange rate. If a derivative is contractually transferable separately from the contract, then it is not an embedded derivative.

When Do I Separate an Embedded Derivative from the Host Contract?

If a contract contains an embedded derivative, an entity can designate the entire contract as being a financial asset or liability that it records at fair value through profit or loss.

It is allowable to separate an embedded derivative from the host contract only when its economic characteristics and risks vary from those of the host contract, when a separate instrument with the same terms would qualify as a derivative, *and* when the entity does not account for the combined instrument at fair value with changes in fair value recognized in profit or loss.

If an entity should separately account for an embedded derivative, but it cannot separately measure the derivative, then the entity should designate the entire contract as at fair value through profit or loss.

EXAMPLE 25.6

Acme Investments buys a convertible bond issued by Tongan Motors. The bond contains a debt instrument and an option to buy one share of Tongan equity after two years have passed, at a fixed price of €10 per share. Acme's total investment is €100,000, and the estimated fair value of the equity conversion option is €800. Acme should separate the equity conversion option from the bond and account for the option separately as a derivative with the following entry:

Investment	99,200	
Derivative asset	800	
Cash		100,000

 ### How Do I Initially Recognize a Financial Asset or Liability?

An entity initially recognizes a financial asset or liability only when the entity becomes a party to the contractual provisions of the instrument. At that time, it recognizes the asset or liability at its fair value. Also, if the entity is not recognizing the asset or liability at its fair value through profit or loss, it should add to the fair value those transaction costs directly attributable to the acquisition or issuance of the asset or liability.

EXAMPLE 25.7

The Conemaugh Cell Phone Company acquires 10,000 shares of Snowdonia Cellular for £52 each and incurs broker fees of £1 per share. Conemaugh classifies the shares as available for sale, so that it does not recognize changes in fair value in profit or loss. Conemaugh records the following entry, which includes the broker fees in the carrying amount of the available-for-sale asset:

Available-for-sale asset	530,000	
Cash		530,000

How Do I Subsequently Recognize a Financial Asset?

After initial recognition, an entity classifies its financial assets into the following categories for measurement purposes:

○ *Available-for-sale financial assets.* Measured at their fair value
○ *Financial assets at fair value through profit or loss.* Measured at their fair value
○ *Held-to-maturity investments.* Measured at their amortized cost using the effective interest method
○ *Loans and receivables.* Measured at their amortized cost using the effective interest method

If an entity invests in equity instruments that do not have a quoted market price in an active market, it should measure them at their cost.

How Do I Subsequently Recognize a Financial Liability?

After initial recognition, an entity measures all financial liabilities at their amortized cost using the effective interest method. However, it should not do so for financial liabilities designated as at fair value through profit or loss.

What Methods Are Available for Measuring Fair Value?

The best evidence for fair value is a quoted price in an active market. If this source is not available, then the next best evidence is a valuation technique that assumes an arm's-length exchange. All of the following valuation techniques are acceptable:

- Recent arm's-length market transactions between knowledgeable parties
- The current fair value of another instrument that is substantially the same
- Discounted cash flow analysis
- Option pricing models

If a valuation technique currently is used by market participants to price the instrument, and that technique provides reliable pricing estimates, then that is the preferred technique.

It is better to use a valuation technique that uses market information as inputs, rather than entity-specific information.

Example 25.8

Saint Nick & Elves, purveyors of fine crystal figurines, acquires 5,000 shares of Jackrabbit Ltd. for £15 per share and classifies them as at fair value through profit or loss. At the end of the year, the quoted price of Jackrabbit's shares declines to £13 per share. At the end of the following year, Saint Nick sells the shares for £16 each. Saint Nick records the following journal entries:

At initial stock purchase:

Assets at fair value through profit or loss	75,000	
Cash		75,000

At the end of Year 1:

Profit or loss	10,000	
Assets at fair value through profit or loss		10,000

(*Continued*)

> (*Continued*)
> At the end of Year 2:
>
> | | | |
> |---|---|---|
> | Cash | 80,000 | |
> | Assets at fair value through profit or loss | | 65,000 |
> | Gain | | 15,000 |

When measuring a financial liability that has a demand feature, its fair value must always be not less than the amount payable on demand, discounted from the first demand date.

How Do I Derecognize a Financial Asset or Liability?

Follow these seven steps to derecognize a financial asset or liability:

1. *Segregate assets.* Segregate a part of a financial asset for derecognition purposes if it comprises only specifically identified cash flows from a financial asset, or it comprises only a pro rata share of the cash flows from a financial asset, or it comprises only a fully proportionate share of specifically identified cash flows from a financial asset.

2. *Identify asset expiration or transfer.* Apply the derecognition steps either to the financial asset in its entirety or to the segregated parts of a financial asset that were segregated in the first step. Apply derecognition steps only when the entity's contractual rights to the cash flows from the financial asset expire, or it transfers the financial asset. A financial asset transfer occurs only when the entity transfers the contractual rights to receive cash flows from the financial asset, or it retains these rights but assumes an obligation to pay the cash flows to a recipient (and shifts the risks and rewards of ownership, as well as control over the asset, to the recipient). To determine whether the risks and rewards of ownership have shifted, it may be necessary to compare the entity's exposure to variability in the present value of future net cash flows both before and after the transfer.

3. *Segregate servicing rights.* If the entity transfers the financial asset but retains the right to service the asset for a fee, then recognize a servicing asset or liability for the contract.

4. *Recognize new asset or liability.* If the entity transfers the asset or liability but obtains a new financial asset or liability as part of the transfer, then recognize it at its fair value.

5. *Derecognize.* Derecognition varies depending on the status of the transferred or cancelled assets or liabilities, as follows:

    a. *Entire item.* If the entity derecognizes the entire financial asset or liability, it recognizes in profit or loss the difference between the carrying amount and the sum of any consideration received and any cumulative gain or loss that had been recognized in other comprehensive income.

    b. *Partial item.* If the entity derecognizes a portion of a financial asset or liability, it allocates the carrying amount of the total asset or liability between the parts to be recognized and derecognized, based on the fair values of the two parts on the transfer date. The amount it recognizes in profit or loss is based on the same calculation that would be used for the entire financial asset or liability.

    c. *Some continuing involvement.* If the entity has some continuing involvement with an asset or liability, it measures the transferred amounts based on the rights and obligations that it has retained. In this calculation, the retained liability is either the amortized cost of the rights and obligations retained by the entity (if measured at amortized cost) or their stand-alone fair value (if measured at fair value).

6. *Liability exchange.* If there is an exchange between an existing borrower and lender of debt instruments and the terms are substantially different, then the parties account for the original financial liability as a debt extinguishment, and recognize a new financial liability. The same accounting applies if there is a substantial modification of the terms of an existing financial liability. The difference between the carrying amount of the extinguished debt and the consideration paid for the replacement debt is recognized in profit or loss.

7. *Continuing income and expense recognition.* The entity continues to recognize any income earned or expense incurred on transferred assets and liabilities to the extent of its continuing involvement.

How Do I Account for Noncash Collateral Related to a Financial Asset Transfer?

When the transferor of a financial asset provides noncash collateral to the transferee, the two entities should use these rules to account for the collateral:

○ *Right to sell collateral.* If the transferee has the right to either sell or repledge the collateral, then the transferor reclassifies the collateral separately from other assets in its statement of financial position. The transferee does not recognize the collateral as an asset.

○ *Sells the collateral.* If the transferee sells the collateral, it recognizes the proceeds and a liability at fair value for its obligation to return the collateral.

○ *Contract default.* If the transferor defaults and so is not entitled to redeem the collateral, it derecognizes the collateral, while the transferee recognizes the collateral as an asset, at fair value.

Should I Offset Assets and Liabilities, or Income and Expenses, for Recognized Transferred Assets?

If an entity has transferred assets but continues to recognize them, then it should not offset the assets and associated liabilities. Further, it should not offset any income earned from the transferred assets against any expense it incurs on the associated liabilities.

When Can I Reclassify a Derivative or Other Financial Instrument?

An entity *cannot* reclassify a derivative or other financial instrument in the following circumstances:

Item	Action	Category Designation	Comments
Derivative	Out of	Fair value through profit or loss	While held or issued
Financial instrument	Out of	Fair value through profit or loss	If designated as such upon initial recognition
Financial instrument	Into	Fair value through profit or loss	After initial recognition

In addition, an entity *cannot* reclassify a derivative in either of the following circumstances:

- ○ It was already a designated and effective hedging instrument in a cash flow or net investment hedge and no longer qualifies as one; or
- ○ It becomes a designated and effective hedging instrument in a cash flow hedge or net investment hedge.

An entity *can* reclassify a derivative or other financial instrument in the following circumstances:

Item	Action	Category Designation	Comments
Financial asset	Out of	Fair value through profit or loss	If it is no longer held for sale in the near term. The entity does not reverse any previously recognized gains or losses. The reclassification is at its fair value at the reclassification date.
Financial asset	Out of	Fair value through profit or loss	If the entity has the intention and ability to hold the asset until maturity or the foreseeable future, and the asset would have met the definition of loans and receivables. The reclassification is at its fair value at the reclassification date.
Financial asset	Out of	Available for sale	Reclassify into loans and receivables if the asset would have met the definition of loans and receivables, and the entity has the intention and ability to hold the asset until maturity or the foreseeable future. The reclassification is at its fair value at the reclassification date.
Investment	Out of	Held to maturity	Reclassify into available for sale and remeasure at its fair value; happens only when there is a change in the intention or ability to hold the investment.

These reclassification restrictions are imposed in order to keep an entity from managing earnings by selectively reclassifying financial instruments.

How Do I Account for a Change in Carrying Cost Away from Fair Value?

If it becomes appropriate to carry a financial asset or liability at its cost or amortized cost rather than its fair value, then the entity uses the fair value on the conversion date as its new carrying amount. If the entity previously recognized any gains or losses in other comprehensive income, it recognizes the amounts under one of the following two methods:

- ○ *Fixed maturity asset.* If the financial asset has a fixed maturity, then amortize the gain or loss to profit or loss over the remaining life of the investment, using the effective interest method.
- ○ *No fixed maturity asset.* If the financial asset has no fixed maturity, recognize the gain or loss in profit or loss when the entity sells or disposes of the financial asset.

How Do I Account for a Gain or Loss Caused by a Financial Asset Fair Value Change?

If there is a gain or loss in the fair value of a financial asset, and it is not part of a hedging relationship, then you account for it as follows:

- ○ *Classified as at fair value through profit or loss.* If there is a gain or loss on a financial asset that is classified as at fair value through profit or loss, then recognize it in profit or loss.
- ○ *Classified as available for sale.* If there is a gain or loss on a financial asset or liability that is classified as available for sale, then recognize it in other comprehensive income, and in profit or loss upon derecognition.
- ○ *Carried at amortized cost.* If there is a gain or loss on a financial asset or liability that an entity carries at amortized cost, then recognize it in profit or loss upon derecognition, as well as through the amortization process.

What Events Lead to the Impairment or Uncollectibility of Financial Assets?

At the end of each reporting period, assess whether there is any objective evidence of financial asset impairment. Such evidence arises from a *loss event* that impacts the estimated future cash flows of the asset. The loss event actually may be the cumulative effect of several events. The event must already have occurred; a loss expected from a future event does not cause a loss event. All of the following are loss events that can cause financial asset impairment or uncollectibility:

- The issuer or obligor is in significant financial difficulty.
- There has been a default or delinquency in interest or principal payments.
- The entity has granted the borrower a concession for legal or economic reasons.
- The borrower will likely enter bankruptcy or another form of reorganization.
- There is no active market for the financial asset, due to financial difficulties. However, a loss event does not arise just because an entity's financial instruments are no longer publicly traded.
- There is a measurable decline in estimated future cash flows from a group of financial assets since their initial recognition, caused by either declines in the payment status of borrowers or regional economic conditions correlating with asset defaults in the group.
- There is a significant or prolonged decline in the fair value of an equity investment below its cost.

EXAMPLE 25.9

The Marley Mortgage Company notes a decrease in property prices in the London district where it normally issues mortgages. This condition correlates strongly with mortgage defaults, so Marley is experiencing a loss event.

How Do I Account for Impaired or Uncollectible Financial Assets?

The type of accounting for an impaired or uncollectible financial asset varies by the type of asset, as follows:

○ *Available-for-sale assets.* If a fair value decline has already been recognized in other comprehensive income, reclassify the cumulative loss into profit or loss to the extent of the impairment. The amount so reclassified is the difference between the acquisition cost of the financial asset (net of principal repayments and amortization) and the current fair value, minus any previously recognized impairment loss.

○ *Financial assets carried at cost.* Measure the amount of the loss as the difference between the asset's carrying amount and the present value of estimated future cash flows. For the discounting calculation, use the current market rate of return for similar assets.

○ *Loans, receivables, and held-to-maturity investments.* Measure the amount of the loss as the difference between the asset's carrying amount and the present value of estimated future cash flows. For the discounting calculation, use the effective interest rate used at initial recognition. Recognize the loss in profit or loss.

EXAMPLE 25.10

Klaxon Fire Alarm Company invests €50,000 in a debt security and classifies it as available for sale. The debt security decreases in value by €10,000, so Klaxon has an unrealized holding loss of €10,000 that it charges to equity. The issuer of the debt security then has such significant financial difficulties that it appears unlikely that it can repay the debt security. Klaxon's management decides that this constitutes objective evidence of impairment equaling the unrealized holding loss and uses the following entry to recognize the loss:

Impairment loss	10,000	
Equity		10,000

If an entity does not find that impairment is significant for an individual financial asset, it should include the asset in a group of assets having similar credit risk and assess the group for impairment. If it recognizes an impairment loss for an individual asset, it does not include that asset in an impairment assessment of a group of assets.

Can I Reverse a Financial Asset Impairment Loss?

It is allowable to reverse in a subsequent period an impairment loss on a debt instrument classified as available for sale or a financial asset carried at amortized cost. You can reverse the amount of an earlier impairment loss if the amount of the impairment subsequently declines, and the decline relates to an event occurring after the initial impairment recognition. You should recognize the reversal in profit or loss, up to the amount of the original impairment.

An impairment loss on a financial asset carried at cost, or on an equity instrument classified as available for sale, is not reversible.

 ### What Is Hedging?

Hedging is a risk reduction technique whereby an entity uses a derivative or similar instrument to offset future changes in the fair value or cash flows of an asset or liability. A *hedged item* can be any of the following individually or in a group with similar risk characteristics:

> Highly probable forecast transaction
> Net investment in a foreign operation
> Recognized asset
> Recognized liability
> Unrecognized firm commitment

Hedge effectiveness is the amount of changes in the fair value or cash flows of a hedged item that are offset by changes in the fair value or cash flows of a hedging instrument.

Hedge accounting involves matching a derivative instrument to a hedged item, and then recognizing gains and losses from both items in the same period.

EXAMPLE 25.11

Acme Investments has invested £100,000 in a hedged item and designates a derivative to hedge this investment. At the end of one year, Acme experiences a gain of £8,000 on the derivative and a loss of £10,000 on the hedged item. The net difference of the gain and loss is a £2,000 loss, which Acme records in profit or loss.

When Does a Hedging Relationship Qualify for Hedge Accounting?

A hedging relationship qualifies for hedge accounting only if it meets all of the following criteria:

- ○ *Documentation.* You formally designate a hedge at its inception, as well as document the hedging relationship, the entity's risk management objective, and its strategy for undertaking the hedge. The documentation should identify the hedging instrument, the item being hedged, the nature of the risk to be hedged, and how the entity plans to assess the hedging instrument's effectiveness in offsetting fair value or cash flow changes in the hedged item.
- ○ *Forecast probability.* If the hedge is a cash flow hedge, there is a highly probable forecast transaction that is the subject of the hedge. Also, the forecast transaction shows an exposure to cash flow variations that could impact profit or loss.
- ○ *Highly effective.* You expect the hedge to be highly effective in offsetting any changes in the fair value or cash flows attributable to the hedged risk.
- ○ *Measurement reliability.* It is possible to reliably measure the effectiveness of the hedge.
- ○ *Ongoing assessment.* You assess the hedge regularly and determine that it was highly effective throughout the financial reporting periods for which you designated the hedge.

How Do I Account for a Fair Value Hedge?

A fair value hedge is a hedge of an asset's or liability's exposure to changes in its fair value, which is attributable to a particular risk and could affect profit or loss.

You should record a gain or loss on remeasurement of the fair value hedge in profit or loss. Also, recognize in profit or loss the gain or loss on the hedged item that is attributable to the hedged risk, while also adjusting the carrying amount of the hedged item.

If there is an adjustment to the carrying amount of a hedged financial instrument for which you are using the effective interest method, then you should amortize the adjustment to profit or loss, using a recalculated effective interest rate. However, if it is not practical to use a recalculated effective interest rate, then amortize the adjustment using the straight-line method. No matter what recognition method is used, any adjustment should be fully amortized as of the maturity date.

You should discontinue hedge accounting if the hedging instrument expires or you sell, terminate, or exercise it. You also should discontinue hedge accounting if the entity revokes the hedging designation, or the hedge no longer meets the hedge accounting criteria.

EXAMPLE 25.12

Acme Investments buys a bond having a face value of £100,000 and paying interest of 4 percent, and records the purchase as an available-for-sale asset. The 4 percent rate paid by the bond matches the current market rate. If interest rates increase, the value of the bond will decline, so Acme enters into an interest rate swap, where it swaps the fixed interest payments it receives from the bond issuer for floating interest payments from a third party. Acme appropriately documents the interest rate swap as a hedge of the bond.

Market interest rates subsequently increase, reducing the fair value of the bond by £3,000, so Acme records the following entry:

Hedging loss (hedged item)	3,000	
Available-for-sale asset		3,000

Acme also records an increased value for the swap, which was positively impacted by the same increase in interest rates:

Swap asset	3,000	
Hedging gain (hedging instrument)		3,000

Since the changes in fair value of the bond and the interest rate swap exactly offset each other, there is no net gain or loss, and the hedge is 100 percent effective.

How Do I Account for an Unrecognized Firm Commitment Hedge?

When you designate an unrecognized firm commitment as a hedged item, you should subsequently recognize the cumulative change in the fair value of the commitment attributable to the hedged risk, along with a corresponding gain or loss that is recognized in profit or loss. You also should recognize changes in the fair value of the hedging instrument in profit or loss.

How Do I Account for a Cash Flow Hedge?

A cash flow hedge is a hedge exposure to cash flow variability. This variability is attributable to either a specific risk on a recognized asset or liability, or a highly probable forecast transaction.

You should account for a cash flow hedge by recognizing the portion of the gain or loss on the hedging instrument in other comprehensive income, but only to the extent of the gain or loss that is effective. You should record the ineffective part of the gain or loss on the hedging instrument in profit or loss.

If you do not expect that a loss previously recognized in other comprehensive income will be recovered in the future, then reclassify the amount you do not expect to recover into profit or loss. Similarly, you should reclassify a gain or loss previously recognized in other comprehensive income into profit or loss in the same period when the hedged forecast transaction affects profit or loss.

You should terminate cash flow hedge accounting in the following situations:

Termination Event	Resulting Accounting Action
Hedging instrument expires, is sold, is terminated, or is exercised	Retain cumulative gain or loss recognized in other comprehensive income until the forecast transaction occurs; then generally reclassify to profit or loss.
Hedging instrument no longer meets hedge accounting criteria	Retain cumulative gain or loss recognized in other comprehensive income until the forecast transaction occurs; then generally reclassify to profit or loss.
No longer expect forecasted transaction to occur	Reclassify any gains or losses recognized in other comprehensive income into profit or loss.
The entity revokes the hedging designation	Retain cumulative gain or loss recognized in other comprehensive income until the forecast transaction occurs; then generally reclassify to profit or loss. If the transaction is no longer expected to occur, reclassify to profit or loss.

EXAMPLE 25.13

Hermigua Hydroelectric orders a turbine from a supplier in the United States for $250,000, for delivery to its Canary Islands facility on November 30, which is 90 days in the future. Hermigua's functional currency is the euro. Currently, Hermigua expects to pay €180,000 for the turbine, which reflects the current Euro/dollar exchange rate. However, if the dollar strengthens against the euro within the next 90 days, Hermigua will have to pay more euros for the purchase.

To avoid this exchange rate risk, Hermigua enters into a forward contract to purchase $250,000 on November 30 for €180,000. Hermigua appropriately designates the forward contract as a hedge of its exposure to increases in the dollar exchange rate.

After one month, the dollar has increased in value against the euro, so that the $250,000 would require €185,000 on the open market, which represents a €5,000 increase in the value of the forward contract. Hermigua records the change in value with this entry:

Forward asset	5,000	
Equity		5,000

Hermigua settles the forward contract on November 30 with this entry:

Cash	5,000	
Forward asset		5,000

Hermigua then pays €185,000 for the turbine on November 30 and reduces the carrying amount of the machine with the following entry, which shifts the deferred gain from equity to the cost of the turbine:

Equity	5,000	
Machinery		5,000

How Do I Account for a Net Investment Hedge?

A hedge of a net investment relates to an investment in a foreign operation. Hedge accounting can be applied only to the foreign exchange differences arising between the functional currencies of the foreign operation and the parent entity. The parent entity can hedge an amount equal to or less than the carrying amount of the net assets of the foreign operation.

You should account for the net investment hedge by recognizing the portion of the gain or loss on the hedging instrument in other comprehensive income, but only to the extent of the gain or loss that is effective. You should record the ineffective part of the gain or loss on the hedging instrument in profit or loss.

If the entity disposes of the foreign operation, then you should shift the related amount of the gain or loss previously recognized in other comprehensive income into profit or loss.

EXAMPLE 25.14

Tongan Motors invests 50 million Singapore dollars in an automobile production facility in Singapore, which it plans to sell in five years, likely at an amount that will recoup its original investment. To hedge the investment, Tongan borrows 50 million Singapore dollars and designates the loan as a hedge of the net investment.

Over the next five years, there is a 500,000 Singapore dollar foreign currency gain on the loan. Tongan defers the gain in equity, and then uses it to offset the 500,000 Singapore dollar foreign exchange loss when it sells the Singapore facility at the end of five years.

Can I Designate a Nonderivative Instrument as a Hedging Instrument?

You can designate a nonderivative financial asset or liability as a hedge of only a foreign currency risk.

How Do I Designate a Nonfinancial Item as a Hedged Item?

If you want to designate a nonfinancial asset or liability as being hedged, you can hedge it only for either foreign currency risks or all risks. The reason for this restricted treatment is that it is difficult to isolate and measure the various portions of cash flow or fair value changes attributable to the various types of risk.

Can I Hedge a Held-to-Maturity Investment?

You cannot hedge the interest-rate risk or prepayment risk of a held-to-maturity investment. However, you can hedge the credit risk and risk of changes in foreign currency associated with a held-to-maturity investment.

How Do I Account for Intra-Entity Hedging Instruments?

It is not possible to designate as a hedging instrument an instrument that originates within a consolidated group. You must eliminate these transactions upon consolidation.

Can I Assign a Portion of a Hedging Instrument to a Hedging Relationship?

You normally assign an entire hedging instrument to a hedging relationship. However, it is allowable to separate the interest element and spot price of a forward contract, as well as to assign only the change in intrinsic value of an option contract, excluding the change in its time value. It is also allowable to assign a portion of a hedging instrument to a hedging relationship.

It is not allowable to assign a hedging instrument to a hedging relationship for only a portion of the time period when the hedging instrument remains outstanding.

Can I Designate a Portion of a Financial Item as a Hedged Item?

You can hedge the risks associates with a portion of a financial asset's or financial liability's cash flows or fair value, as long as you can measure the effectiveness of the hedge.

Can I Cluster Similar Assets and Liabilities into Groups of Hedged Items?

You can aggregate similar assets or similar liabilities and hedge them as a group. However, you can do so only if the individual items in each group share the risk exposure that you are designating as being hedged. Also, you can create such a group only if you expect the change in fair value attributable to the hedged risk for each item in the group to be proportional to the overall change in fair value attributable to the hedged risk of the group as a whole.

Can a Hedging Instrument Hedge More Than One Type of Risk?

You can designate a single hedging instrument to be a hedge of more than one type of risk, but only if you can clearly identify the risks being hedged, can demonstrate the effectiveness of the hedge, and can specifically designate the hedging instrument and different risk positions.

What Information Should I Disclose about Financial Instruments in the Statement of Financial Position?

You should disclose the following information either within the statement of financial position or its accompanying notes:

- ○ *Carrying amounts.* The carrying amounts of each of these categories of financial instruments:

  - Financial assets at fair value through profit or loss.
  - Held-to-maturity investments.
  - Loans and receivables.
  - Available-for-sale financial assets.
  - Financial liabilities at fair value through profit or loss.
  - Financial liabilities measured at amortized cost.

- ○ *Loan or receivable at fair value through profit or loss.* If it designates either an individual or group of loans or receivables as at fair value through profit or loss, then disclose:

  - Maximum exposure to credit risk of the loan or receivable at the end of the period.
  - Amount of mitigation by related credit derivatives.
  - Amount of change in the fair value of the loan or receivable that is attributable to changes in credit risk, both during the period and cumulatively.

- Changes in market conditions causing market risk, such as changes in a benchmark interest rate, commodity price, or foreign exchange rate.
- Changes in the fair value of any related credit derivatives, occurring both during the period and cumulatively since designation.

○ *Financial liability at fair value through profit or loss.* If it designates a financial liability as at fair value through profit or loss, then disclose:

- Amount of the change in the fair value of the liability attributable to changes in credit risk, both during the period and cumulatively.
- Changes in market conditions causing market risk, such as changes in a benchmark interest rate, commodity price, or foreign exchange rate.
- Difference between the liability's carrying amount and the amount the entity is required to pay at maturity.

○ *Credit risk method.* The methods used to compile disclosure information about valuation changes caused by credit risk. If the entity does not believe that this disclosure faithfully represents the fair value change, then state the reasons for this conclusion.

○ *Reclassification.* The amount reclassified into and out of each category and the reason for doing so, if the entity has reclassified a financial asset. If the entity has reclassified a financial asset out of either the fair value through profit or loss or the available-for-sale categories, then it should disclose:

- The amount reclassified both into and out of each category.
- The carrying amounts and fair values of all financial assets that were reclassified in the current and previous periods.
- The fair value gain or loss on a financial asset recognized in profit or loss or other comprehensive income, both in that reporting period and the previous period.
- The fair value gain or loss that would have been recognized in profit or loss or other comprehensive income in the absence of reclassification. Report this information for each period starting with reclassification and continuing until derecognition.
- The effective interest rate and estimated cash flows that the entity expects to recover, as of the reclassification date.

○ *Derecognition.* If financial assets are transferred but the entity cannot derecognize them, then disclose the following for each class of such assets:

- The nature of the assets.
- The remaining risks and rewards of ownership to which the entity is still exposed.
- The carrying amounts of those assets and liabilities that it still recognizes.
- The total carrying amount of the original assets, the amount it continues to recognize, and the carrying amount of any related liabilities.

○ *Collateral.* The carrying amount of any financial assets that the entity has pledged as collateral, and the terms and conditions of such pledges. If the entity holds collateral and can sell or repledge it, then disclose the fair value of collateral held, the fair value of collateral sold or repledged, whether it has an obligation to return the collateral, and the terms and conditions linked to its use of the collateral.

○ *Credit loss allowance.* Reconcile the changes in any allowance account for credit losses for each class of financial assets.

○ *Compound instruments.* The existence of any compound financial instruments (containing both liability and equity components) that contain multiple embedded derivatives whose values are interdependent.

○ *Defaults and breaches.* The details of any loan defaults during the period on any principal, interest, sinking fund, or redemption terms, as well as the carrying amount of loans payable in default at the end of the period. Also, discuss whether defaults were remedied, or the renegotiated terms of any loans, before the financial statements were authorized for issuance.

What Information Should I Disclose about Financial Instruments in the Statement of Comprehensive Income?

You should disclose the following information either within the statement of comprehensive income or its accompanying notes:

○ *Gains or losses.* The net gains or losses on financial assets or liabilities for the following categories:

- For at fair value through profit or loss financial assets and liabilities, separately show the gains or losses on financial assets and liabilities in profit or loss upon initial recognition, and for those classified as held for trading.
- For available-for-sale financial assets, separately disclose the amount recognized in other comprehensive income and the amount reclassified from equity to profit or loss.
- Held-to-maturity investments.
- Loans and receivables.
- Financial liabilities measured at amortized cost.

○ *Interest income and expense.* Separately show total interest income and total interest expense, using the effective interest method, for financial assets and liabilities that are not at fair value through profit or loss.

○ *Fee income and expense.* Separately show the fee income and expense arising from financial assets or liabilities not at fair value through profit or loss, and from fiduciary activities requiring the holding or investing of assets on behalf of others.

○ *Impairment information.* Any interest income on impaired financial assets, and the amount of any impairment loss for each class of financial asset.

What Information Should I Disclose about Hedging?

You should disclose the following information separately for fair value hedges, cash flow hedges, and hedges of net investments in foreign operations:

○ *Hedge description.* Each type of hedge, the financial instruments designated as hedging instruments, their fair values at the end of the reporting period, and the nature of the risks that the entity is hedging

○ *Cash flow hedges.* Specifically for cash flow hedges, the periods when cash flows are forecasted to occur and when they should affect profit or loss, any forecasted transactions for which hedging previously was used but is no longer expected, and the following amounts recognized during the reporting period:

- The amount recognized in other comprehensive income

- The amount reclassified from equity to profit or loss, showing the amounts in each line item in the statement of comprehensive income
- The amount removed from equity and included in the initial cost of a nonfinancial asset or liability that was a hedged highly probable forecast transaction
- The amount of hedging ineffectiveness recognized in profit or loss

○ *Fair value hedges.* Gains or losses on the hedging instrument, as well as on the hedged item attributable to the hedged risk

○ *Hedges of net investments in foreign operations.* The amount of hedging ineffectiveness recognized in profit or loss

 ## What Information Should I Disclose about Fair Value?

You should separately disclose, for each class of financial assets and financial liabilities, the following information:

○ *Fair values.* The fair value of each class of financial assets and liabilities.
○ *Methods and assumptions.* The methods and assumptions used to determine the fair values of each class of financial assets and liabilities. This may include, for example, assumptions about interest rates, credit losses, and prepayment rates.
○ *Active market reliance.* Whether fair values are determined based on published price quotations from an active market, or whether they are estimated using a valuation technique.
○ *Assumption changes.* If a valuation technique is used to determine fair value and altering a supporting assumption to a reasonably possible alternative causes a significant valuation change, then state this fact and note the resulting change.
○ *Profit or loss impact.* If a valuation technique was used to determine fair value, disclose the total amount of the fair value change recognized in profit or loss during the period.
○ *Initial valuation reconciliation.* If there is a difference between the fair value at initial recognition of a financial instrument and the transaction price, then describe the accounting policy for recognizing the difference in profit or loss, and present a

reconciliation of the aggregate difference not yet recognized from the beginning to the end of the period.

There is no need to disclose fair value information when the carrying amount of a financial instrument reasonably approximates its fair value, and when an equity instrument's fair value cannot be measured reliably. However, in the latter case, disclose the fact that fair value information has not been disclosed and why, describe the instruments, note their carrying values, describe the market for them, note how the entity intends to dispose of them, and, if derecognized, state their carrying amounts at derecognition and the gain or loss recognized.

What Information Should I Disclose about Financial Instrument Risks?

In general, you should disclose enough information about the risks associated with financial instruments so that an entity's financial statement users can evaluate the type and size of these risks to which it is exposed. More specifically, disclose this information separately for each type of risk:

- ○ *Qualitative.* The type of risk and how it occurs, any changes in it from the previous period, and the entity's risk-specific policies and procedures to manage and measure it
- ○ *Quantitative.* The summary-level quantitative exposure at the end of the period, based on information provided internally to key management personnel, as well as risk concentrations if not otherwise apparent

Also disclose the following information by class of financial instrument:

- ○ *Credit risk.* The maximum exposure to credit risk at the end of the period without accounting for any collateral held. Also describe the collateral held, and state the credit quality of financial assets neither past due nor impaired, and the carrying amount of renegotiated financial assets that otherwise would be past due or impaired.
- ○ *Noncurrent financial assets.* The age of those financial assets that are past due at the end of the period, those financial assets considered impaired and the factors the entity uses in making this assessment,

and for both cases the collateral held as security (and its estimated fair value).

○ *Collateral.* If the entity takes possession of any collateral or calls on guarantees during the period, state the nature and carrying amount of these assets, and if not readily convertible into cash, the collateral disposition or usage policies.

In addition, an entity should disclose a maturity analysis for any financial liabilities it holds, showing remaining contractual maturities, and describe how it manages this liquidity risk.

Further, disclose a sensitivity analysis for each type of market risk to which the entity has an exposure at the end of the period. This analysis should reveal how profit or loss and equity would have been altered by changes in specific risk variables that were reasonably possible at the end of the period. The disclosure should include the methods and assumptions used in making the analysis, as well as any changes in these methods and assumptions from the previous period, and why they were altered. If the sensitivity analysis is unrepresentative of the risk inherent in a financial instrument, then disclose that fact and the reason why; this situation can arise when year-end exposure levels vary from those during the year.

CHAPTER 26

FINANCIAL INSTRUMENTS: PRESENTATION

 ### What Is a Financial Asset?

A financial asset can be any of these four items:

1. Cash
2. Equity of another entity
3. A contractual right to receive cash or similar from another entity or a potentially favorable exchange of financial assets or liabilities with another entity
4. A contract probably to be settled in the entity's own equity and that is a nonderivative under which the entity may receive a variable amount of its own equity instruments, or a derivative that probably will be settled other than through the exchange of cash or similar for a fixed amount of the entity's equity

Examples of financial assets are cash, investments in the bonds and equity issued by other entities, receivables, and derivative financial assets.

 ### What Is a Financial Liability?

A financial liability can be either of these two items:

1. A contractual obligation to deliver cash or similar to another entity, or a potentially unfavorable exchange of financial assets or liabilities with another entity
2. A contract probably to be settled in the entity's own equity and that is a nonderivative under which the entity may deliver a variable amount of its own equity instruments, or a derivative that probably will be settled other than through the exchange of cash or similar for a fixed amount of the entity's equity

Examples of financial liabilities are accounts payable, loans issued by the entity, and derivative financial liabilities.

What Assets and Liabilities Are Not Financial Instruments?

Physical assets, such as inventory, property, plant, and equipment, are not financial instruments, nor are leased assets, intangible assets, prepaid expenses, warranty obligations, or constructive obligations.

When Do I Classify a Financial Instrument as an Equity Instrument?

An equity instrument is a contract containing a residual interest in the assets of an entity, after deducting all of its liabilities. A financial instrument is an equity instrument (rather than a financial liability) if it meets both of these conditions:

- ○ There are no contractual obligations to deliver cash or similar to the other entity or to engage in a potentially unfavorable exchange of financial assets and liabilities.
- ○ If it will be settled with the entity's own equity, it is a nonderivative instrument requiring no obligation to deliver a variable amount of its own equity or a derivative instrument that only the issuer can settle by exchanging a fixed amount of cash or similar for a fixed amount of its own equity.

Examples of equity instruments are ordinary shares and warrants to purchase a fixed number of an entity's shares in exchange for a fixed amount of cash.

When Do I Classify a Puttable Instrument as an Equity Instrument?

A puttable instrument is a financial instrument that either gives its holder the right to put the instrument back to its issuer for cash or similar, or that is automatically put back to the issuer upon either the occurrence of an uncertain future event or the death or retirement of its holder. You should classify a puttable instrument as an equity instrument if it has all of these features:

○ *Cash flow derivation.* The cash flows attributable to the instrument are based on the profit or loss, or change in assets of the entity over the life of the instrument.

○ *Identical features.* All financial instruments in the most subordinate class of instruments have identical features.

○ *Liquidation rights.* The holder is entitled to a pro rata share of the entity's net assets if it liquidates.

○ *Restricted features.* Other than the obligation for the issuer to redeem the puttable instrument for cash or similar, it contains no other obligation to deliver or exchange financial assets under unfavorable conditions.

○ *Subordinate.* The puttable instrument is in a class of instruments subordinate to all others, such that it has no claim priority.

Further, the issuer must have no other financial instrument or contract that restricts the residual return to puttable instrument holders, nor can the instrument or contract have cash flows based substantially on the profit or loss or change in assets of the entity.

If a puttable instrument ceases to have all of these features, you shall reclassify it as a financial liability as of the date when its features no longer qualify it to be an equity instrument. Your entity shall measure the puttable instrument at its fair value on the reclassification date and recognize in equity any difference between the carrying amount of the former equity instrument and the fair value of the new financial liability.

If the reverse occurs and a former financial liability becomes an equity instrument, you should measure it at the carrying value of the financial liability as of the reclassification date.

How Do I Classify a Puttable Instrument Requiring a Cash Payment?

If a puttable instrument requires the issuer to pay cash or similar to the holder, then classify it as a financial liability. This is the case even when the payment amount is based on an index or some other benchmark that is subject to change and also when the entity has the option of paying in cash or its own shares, but the value of the shares substantially exceeds the amount of the cash payment.

This classification is common for mutual funds and unit trusts, which allow their unit holders the right to redeem their interests for cash.

 ## Do I Classify an Instrument Having Liquidation Rights as an Equity Instrument?

A financial instrument may include an obligation for the issuer to deliver to the holder a pro rata share of its net assets upon liquidation. You should classify this instrument as an equity instrument only if it contains *all* of these features:

- *Identical features.* All financial instruments in the most subordinate class of instruments have identical features.
- *Liquidation rights.* The holder is entitled to a pro rata share of the issuer's net assets upon the issuer's liquidation.
- *Subordinate.* The financial instrument is in a class of instruments subordinate to all others, such that it has no claim priority.

Further, the issuer must have no other financial instrument or contract that restricts the residual return to instrument holders, nor can the instrument or contract have cash flows based substantially on the profit or loss or change in assets of the entity.

If a financial instrument ceases to have all of these features, you shall reclassify it as a financial liability as of the date when its features no longer qualify it to be an equity instrument. You shall measure the instrument at its fair value on the reclassification date, and recognize in equity any difference between the carrying amount of the former equity instrument and the fair value of the new financial liability.

If the reverse occurs and a former financial liability becomes an equity instrument, you should measure it at the carrying value of the financial liability as of the reclassification date.

 ## How Do I Classify a Preference Share?

If a preference share requires mandatory redemption of a fixed amount on a future date or gives the holder the right to redeem the instrument on a future date, then classify it as a financial liability.

How Do I Classify an Instrument that Settles in a Variable Number of Shares?

A financial instrument may require settlement in however many of an entity's shares are required to match a specific amount of cash or the market value of a commodity on the settlement date. You should classify this financial instrument as a financial liability, because the entity must use a variable amount of its own equity to settle the contract.

Conversely, if a financial instrument requires settlement by delivering a fixed amount of an entity's equity in exchange for a fixed amount of cash or similar, you should classify it as an equity instrument. For example, an option to buy a fixed number of an entity's shares at a fixed price is an equity instrument.

EXAMPLE 26.1

A key helium supplier to Düsseldorf Airship has the option of requiring payment from Düsseldorf either in cash or in Düsseldorf's stock, based on Düsseldorf's share price on the invoice due date. This is a financial liability, since it may require payment in a variable amount of Düsseldorf stock.

How Do I Account for an Equity Instrument?

You should add any consideration received for an equity instrument directly to equity. You should not recognize changes in the fair value of an equity instrument in the financial statements.

EXAMPLE 26.2

The Nero Fiddle Company sells warrants to the Great White Investment Company for €15,000, which gives Great White the right to purchase 5,000 Nero shares for €50,000. Nero records the warrant sale with this entry:

Cash	15,000	
Equity		15,000

How Do I Account for a Financial Liability?

You should recognize the present value of the redemption amount of a financial liability, even if the liability is contingent upon the counterparty's right to redeem. If the underlying contract expires without delivery, you should reclassify the carrying amount of the financial liability to equity.

How Do I Classify a Contingent Settlement Provision?

A financial instrument may contain a provision that is beyond the control of both the issuer and the holder, such as a payment based on changes in the consumer price index. You should classify such an instrument as a financial liability, unless the contingent settlement provision is not genuine or the issuer is required only to settle the obligation in the event of the issuer's liquidation, and contains all of these features:

○ *Cash flow derivation.* The cash flows attributable to the instrument are based on the profit or loss or change in assets of the entity over the life of the instrument.
○ *Identical features.* All financial instruments in the most subordinate class of instruments have identical features.
○ *Liquidation rights.* The holder is entitled to a pro rata share of the entity's net assets if it liquidates.
○ *Restricted features.* Other than the obligation for the issuer to redeem the instrument for cash or similar, it contains no obligation to deliver or exchange financial assets under unfavorable conditions.
○ *Subordinate.* The financial instrument is in a class of instruments subordinate to all others, such that it has no claim priority.

Further, the issuer must have no other financial instrument or contract that restricts the residual return to instrument holders, nor can the instrument or contract have cash flows based substantially on the profit or loss or change in assets of the entity.

How Do I Classify a Derivative Containing a Choice of Settlement Options?

If a derivative financial instrument allows its holder a choice of settlement options (such as in cash or shares), you should classify it as either a financial asset or financial liability. You can classify it as an equity instrument only if all settlement alternatives would classify it as an equity instrument.

How Do I Classify Compound Financial Instruments?

If a nonderivative financial instrument contains both a liability and an equity component, then you should classify them separately. For example, a convertible bond is a compound financial instrument that contains both a financial liability and an equity instrument. In this case, you should split the instrument in two and classify part as a debt instrument with an early settlement provision and part as warrants to purchase shares.

When assigning values to the financial liability and equity components of a compound financial instrument, you should assign the residual amount to the equity component after deducting from the fair value of the entire instrument the amount calculated for the liability component.

EXAMPLE 26.3

Snowdonia Cellular issues a £10,000 convertible bond that gives its holder the right to convert it into Snowdonia shares and receives £10,000 in proceeds. Snowdonia discounts the bond's cash flows using market interest rates for similar bonds that are not convertible. The result of this discounting calculation is that Snowdonia's bond, without the equity component, has a fair value of £9,500. Snowdonia then assigns the residual value of the bond to its equity component, using this entry:

Cash	10,000	
Financial liability		9,500
Equity		500

Do not subsequently reclassify the liability and equity components of a convertible instrument, even if there is a change in the probability that the holder will exercise the conversion option. Instead, do not alter the initial accounting for the instrument until the entity's obligation to make future payments is extinguished, either through exercise of the conversion option or maturity of the instrument.

 ## How Do I Classify Treasury Shares?

When an entity buys back its own shares, you should deduct them from equity without recording any gain or loss on the transaction.

EXAMPLE 26.4

Branxholm Industries sells 100 shares for £40 per share, and records this entry:

Cash	4,000	
Equity		4,000

Branxholm later buys back 100 shares for £30 per share, and records this entry:

Equity	3,000	
Cash		3,000

 ## How Do I Account for Financial Instrument Dividends, Gains, Losses, and Transaction Costs?

If there are dividends, gains, losses, or transaction costs related to a financial instrument, you should account for them as follows.

- ○ *Dividends.* Recognize dividend payments on shares recognized as a liability as expenses (similar to interest on a bond). Recognize dividend payments on shares recognized as equity as a debit to equity, net of any related income tax effect.
- ○ *Gains and losses.* Recognize gains and losses associated with redemptions or refinancings of financial liabilities in profit or loss, but recognize them as changes in equity if associated with equity instruments.
- ○ *Transaction costs.* Recognize transaction costs related to an equity transaction as an equity deduction, net

of any related income tax effect. This deduction is only for those costs directly attributable to the equity transaction. Recognize as expense the costs of an equity transaction that is abandoned. If you issue a compound financial instrument, allocate the transaction costs to both components in proportion to the allocation of proceeds.

When Can I Offset a Financial Asset and a Financial Liability?

You can present the net amount of a financial asset and a financial liability in the statement of financial position just when the entity not only has the legal right to set off the recognized amounts but also intends to settle on a net basis or to settle both items simultaneously.

Example 26.5

Grasp & Sons Door Handle Corporation has a legal right to set off cash flows due from Open Sesame Door Company, and it intends to do so. Payables to and from the two companies are noted next.

Payable Date	Payable to Open Sesame	Receivable from Open Sesame	Presentation Offset
March 31	£150,000	£100,000	(£50,000)
April 30	25,000	0	None
May 15		25,000	None
May 31	82,000	0	None
June 30	75,000	100,000	25,000

Grasp & Sons can offset only the payables and receivables that are due on March 31 and June 30, since these are the only dates on which payments and receipts are due simultaneously.

CHAPTER 27

GOVERNMENT GRANTS

 **What Is a Government Grant
or Government Assistance?**

A *government grant* is governmental assistance in the form
of transfers or resources in return for past or future compliance with certain conditions relating to an entity's
activities. A grant does not include any government
assistance that cannot be valued. *Government assistance* is
governmental action to provide an economic benefit to an
entity under certain qualifying criteria, such as free technical or marketing advice or loan guarantees. This does not
include indirect support, such as the imposition of trading
restrictions on an entity's competitors.

 **How Do I Account for a Government
Grant?**

You should recognize a government grant in profit or loss
on a systematic basis over the periods in which the entity
incurs and recognizes the expenses that the grant is intended to offset. Recognition of a grant solely upon receipt
is acceptable only when there is no basis for allocating the
grant to additional periods.

Example 27.1

The government of the Austrian province of Tirol
pays €3,000,000 to Finstertal Fisheries to repopulate
its fish farm that was destroyed when an avalanche
overran the Finstertal Reservoir. It will take three
years to repopulate the fish farm. Finstertal will incur
costs of €1,500,000, €800,000, and €400,000 in the
three-year period to repopulate the farm. Based
on this expenditure pattern, Finstertal should recognize the grant in the following manner:

(Continued)

(*Continued*)

Year	Costs	Proportion of Total Expense	Allocation to Grant
1	€1,500,000	55%	€1,650,000
2	800,000	30%	900,000
3	400,000	15%	450,000
	€2,700,000	100%	€3,000,000

If a grant is a receivable based on compensation for expenses already incurred or to give immediate financial support, then you should recognize it in profit or loss as soon as it becomes a receivable.

If a grant is related to a depreciable asset, then recognize the grant over the periods in which and in similar proportions to what the entity recognizes for depreciation expense for that asset.

EXAMPLE 27.2

Nicosia Thermal Energy receives a grant from the Cypriot government of €20,000,000 to construct a photovoltaic array in the plains near Skilloura. Nicosia plans to depreciate the array over 10 years, using the straight-line method of depreciation.

Nicosia should recognize the grant over the same 10 years used for the depreciation period, in the same proportion used for the straight-line depreciation method. Thus, the appropriate amount of the grant to recognize each year is €2,000,000.

If a grant is related to a nondepreciable asset (such as land), then recognize the grant over the period during which the entity must fulfill any obligations attached to the grant. If a government transfers a nonmonetary asset (such as land or property) to an entity, the entity should account for the asset and the grant at their fair value. It is also possible to record both the grant and asset at their nominal value.

If a government issues a grant accompanied by a number of conditions, then it may be appropriate to allocate parts of the grant to different subsets of the conditions, and then recognize portions of the grant based on the different allocations.

EXAMPLE 27.3

Arona Agricultural Products is granted 1,000 acres of unimproved land on the south coast of Tenerife Island by the Canary Islands government, on the condition that it improve the land with sufficient irrigation and road systems to support banana plants. The land has a fair value of €20,000,000. Arona estimates that the improvement project will require three years and cost €8,000,000, with half of the expenditure in the first year, and the remainder spread over the following two years. Arona should recognize the grant in the following manner:

Year	Costs	Proportion of Total Expense	Recognition of Grant
1	€4,000,000	50%	€10,000,000
2	2,000,000	25%	5,000,000
3	2,000,000	25%	5,000,000
	€8,000,000	100%	€20,000,000

EXAMPLE 27.4

Hermigua Hydroelectric receives a consolidated grant of €15,000,000 from the Canary Islands government, under which it must build and maintain a hydroelectric dam for the next 20 years, and also build electrical transmission lines from the dam to several local villages. Once the lines are built, Hermigua has no further obligation to maintain them. Of the grant amount, €12,000,000 is for building the dam and €3,000,000 is for the transmission lines.

For accounting purposes, Hermigua should split the grant into two pieces:

⊙ *Hydroelectric dam.* It should recognize €600,000 per year for 20 years to match the mandated service period of the dam.
⊙ *Transmission lines.* It should recognize €3,000,000 as soon as it completes construction of the transmission lines.

Do not recognize a government grant unless there is reasonable assurance that the entity will comply with the accompanying conditions, and that the entity will receive the grant. Even receipt of a grant does not provide evidence that the attached conditions have been fulfilled.

The accounting for a grant is the same, irrespective of its form (such as cash, or the reduction of a liability, for example, loan forgiveness).

A below-market interest rate on a government loan is a grant. In such a situation, measure the grant as the difference between the initial carrying value of the loan and the proceeds the entity receives.

How Do I Account for a Grant Repayment?

If an entity must repay a government grant, then account for it as a change in accounting estimate. If there is an unamortized deferred credit related to the grant, then apply the repayment against that amount. If the repayment exceeds the unamortized deferred credit (or if there is no credit), then recognize the repayment at once in profit or loss.

If the repayment is related to an asset, then increase the carrying amount of the asset or reduce the deferred income balance by the repayment amount. Then recognize immediately in profit or loss the cumulative additional depreciation that the entity would have recognized in the absence of the grant.

How Do I Present Grants Related to Assets?

You should present government grants related to assets in the statement of financial position either:

1. As deferred income that the entity recognizes in profit or loss over the useful life of the asset; or
2. By deducting them to calculate the carrying amount of the asset, and reducing the related depreciation expense.

How Do I Present Grants Related to Income?

You should report a government grant related to income either as a credit in the statement of comprehensive income or as a deduction in reporting the related expense.

What Government Grant Information Should I Disclose?

You should disclose the following information:

- *Accounting policy.* The policy used by the entity for government grants, including the methods of presentation used in the financial statements
- *Assistance.* Any government assistance from which the entity has directly benefited
- *Conditions.* Any unfulfilled conditions and other contingencies related to government assistance
- *Extent of grants.* The nature and extent of grants that the entity recognizes in its financial statements

CHAPTER 28

INSURANCE CONTRACTS

 What Is an Insurance Contract?

An insurance contract is a contract in which one party, the insurer, accepts significant insurance risk from another party, the policyholder, to compensate the policyholder if a specific uncertain future event impacts the policyholder. Examples of insurance contracts are insurance against property theft, insurance against professional liability, life insurance, disability insurance, fidelity bonds, product warranties, and credit insurance. Self-insurance is not an insurance contract.

 How Do I Account for a New Insurance Policy?

If you are the insurer and you sell an insurance policy, then you can either defer revenue over the policy period and match expenses to the deferrals, or recognize the entire amount at once using a fair value approach, depending upon how your internal accounting policies are structured.

EXAMPLE 28.1

Inverness Insurance writes a policy for £10,000 and expects to pay an £8,000 claim on the policy in Year 4. There is a 10 percent commission on the policy, payable at once. Inverness expects a 3 percent return on its investment of the initial policy payment (less the commission payout). If Inverness's accounting policies require the ratable recognition of related revenue and expenses over the policy term, its results will be as follows:

(Continued)

(Continued)

	Year 1	Year 2	Year 3	Year 4
Premium earned	2,500	2,500	2,500	2,500
Claims expense	2,000	2,000	2,000	2,000
Commission expense	250	250	250	250
Underwriting profit	250	250	250	250
Investment return	270	270	270	270
Profit	520	520	520	520

If Inverness instead used the fair value approach, it would recognize the entire policy premium in the first year, along with all commission costs and the discounted value of the expected claim. It would recognize actual investment returns as earned in the first and subsequent years.

How Do I Assess the Adequacy of My Insurance Liabilities?

If you are an insurer, you should assess the adequacy of your recognized insurance liabilities at the end of each reporting period. You should do this by reviewing current estimates of the future cash flows expected to arise under your insurance contracts. If the carrying amount of your insurance contracts is inadequate in comparison to estimated future cash flows, then recognize the entire deficiency at once in profit or loss.

The estimate of future cash flows should encompass the following items:

+Current estimates of all contractual cash flows
+Related cash flows, such as claims handling costs
+Costs resulting from embedded options and guarantees
= Cash flows to include in insurance liability assessment

If your accounting policies do not require an ongoing liability adequacy assessment that meets these minimum requirements, then you should take the following three steps:

1. *Carrying amount.* Determine the carrying amount of the insurance liabilities, acquisition costs, and intangible assets for which your accounting policies do not require a liability adequacy test that meets the preceding minimum requirements.
2. *Deductions.* Subtract the carrying amount of any deferred acquisition costs and related intangible

assets, not including related reinsurance assets. This is the adjusted carrying amount.

3. *Recognition.* If the adjusted carrying amount is less than the carrying amount that would be required for an accounting provision (see the Provisions and Contingencies chapter), then recognize the difference in profit or loss.

You should conduct this test at the level of a portfolio of contracts that are subject to similar risks and that are managed together in a single portfolio.

 What Is a Reinsurance Contract?

A reinsurance contract is an insurance contract issued by one insurer to compensate another insurer (the *cedant*) for potential losses on contracts issued by the cedant.

 How Do I Account for the Impairment of Reinsurance Assets?

If you are the cedant (see the preceding question) and your reinsurance asset is impaired, then you should reduce its carrying amount and recognize the impairment in profit or loss.

You should consider a reinsurance asset to be impaired only if there is objective evidence that you may not receive all amounts due under the contract's terms, because of an event occurring after the initial recognition of the reinsurance asset. Also, this event must have a measurable impact on the amount you will receive from the reinsurer.

 When Can I Change Accounting Policies Related to Insurance Contracts?

If you are an insurer, you can change your accounting policies related to insurance contracts only if the change makes your financial statements either more relevant and no less reliable to users, or more reliable and no less relevant to users. Here are further comments on specific accounting policies:

○ *Continuation of existing practices.* You may continue to measure insurance liabilities on an undiscounted basis, measure contractual rights to future investment management fees at levels exceeding their implied fair value, and use non-uniform accounting policies for the insurance contracts of subsidiaries.

○ *Current market interest rates.* It is allowable to change your accounting policy to remeasure insurance contracts to reflect current market interest rates.

○ *Future investment margins.* You do not need to change your accounting policies to eliminate future investment margins.

○ *Prudence.* You do not need to change your accounting policies to eliminate excessive prudence, but do not introduce additional prudence if your measurements already incorporate sufficient prudence.

○ *Unrealized gains and losses.* You may change your accounting policies so that a recognized but *unrealized* gain or loss affects your measurement of insurance liabilities, related deferred acquisition costs, and related intangible assets in the same manner as a *realized* gain or loss does. You should recognize the related adjustment to the insurance liability in other comprehensive income only if the unrealized gains or losses also are recognized in other comprehensive income. This change is not mandatory.

How Do I Account for Insurance Contracts Acquired in a Business Combination?

If you acquire insurance liabilities and assets as part of a business combination, you should measure them at their fair values. When presenting this information, you are permitted to use the following split presentation:

○ *Assets.* An intangible asset that is the difference between the fair values of the assumed insurance rights and obligations, and the following liability

○ *Liabilities.* A liability for your insurance contracts, measured according to your accounting policies

How Do I Account for Discretionary Participation Features?

An insurance contract may contain a discretionary participation feature, as well as a guaranteed element. If you are an insurer and issue such contracts, you have the following optional and mandatory accounting requirements:

Requirement Level	Accounting
Optional	Separately recognize the guaranteed and discretionary participation features, with the guaranteed feature classified as a liability. If not, then classify the entire contract as a liability.
	Recognize all premiums received as revenue. If so, then recognize the resulting changes in the guaranteed feature in profit or loss, and also the discretionary participation feature classified as a liability in profit or loss.
Mandatory	If you separately recognize the discretionary participation feature, classify it in either liabilities or equity, using a consistent accounting policy to identify it in either category.
	If the contract contains an embedded derivative, account for it as such (see the Financial Instruments: Recognition and Measurement chapter).

These accounting requirements apply to discretionary participation features in both insurance contracts and financial instruments. If a financial instrument contains a discretionary participation feature, you should use the following additional accounting rules:

- *Interest expense.* If there is a discretionary participation feature, disclose the total interest expense recognized in profit or loss. You do not have to use the effective interest method to calculate the interest expense.
- *Revenue and expense.* You can recognize the premiums for financial instruments as revenue, and recognize as an offsetting expense the resulting incremental increase in the liability carrying amount.
- *Testing.* If you classify the entire discretionary participation feature as a liability, then apply the liability adequacy test described earlier in the question entitled "How Do I Assess the Adequacy of My Insurance Liabilities?"

How Do I Disclose Insurance Contracts?

Generally, you should disclose information about insurance contracts that explains the amounts in the financial statements related to them, as well as the nature and extent of the risk associated with them. More specifically, disclose the following:

- ○ *Assumptions.* The process for creating the assumptions used to measure recognized amounts of assets, liabilities, revenue, and expenses. Also disclose the effect of changes in these assumptions.
- ○ *Claims analysis.* Actual claims compared with previous estimates, going back to whenever the earliest material claim arose for which there is still uncertainty about the claim results, but not more than 10 years. If it is impractical to do this when first applying the International Financial Reporting Standard, disclose that fact.
- ○ *Policies.* The accounting policies for insurance contracts and related assets, liabilities, revenue, and expenses.
- ○ *Recognition.* The recognized amounts of assets, liabilities, revenue, and expenses in the period relating to insurance contracts.
- ○ *Reconciliation.* Reconcile the changes in insurance liabilities, reinsurance assets, and related deferred acquisition costs.
- ○ *Reinsurance.* For a cedant (a policyholder under a reinsurance contract), the gains and losses recognized in profit or loss on buying reinsurance; if there is a deferral of these gains and losses, then disclose amortization for the period and the beginning and ending unamortized balances.
- ○ *Risk concentrations.* How management determines risk concentrations, and the shared characteristics of each risk concentration.
- ○ *Risk from embedded derivatives.* The exposure to market risk from embedded derivatives in an insurance contract, if you do not measure the embedded derivatives at their fair values.
- ○ *Risk levels.* The sensitivity to and concentrations of insurance risk. Provide this information with either of the following disclosures:

  - • *Quantitative analysis.* A sensitivity analysis showing how changes in reasonably possible risk variables can impact profit or loss and equity, as well as the methods and assumptions used to construct the analysis, and any changes in these methods and assumptions from the previous period.

- *Qualitative analysis.* Information about the terms and conditions of insurance contracts that materially affect the entity's cash flows.
- *Risk management.* The objectives, policies, and processes for managing insurance contract risk.

Finally, describe credit risk, liquidity risk, and market risk information, as noted in the Financial Instruments: Recognition and Measurement chapter.

CHAPTER 29

LEASES

 What Is a Lease?

A lease is an arrangement where the lessor agrees to allow the lessee to use an asset for a stated period of time in exchange for one or more payments. A *finance lease* is one in which the lessee assumes substantially all risks and rewards associated with the asset, while an *operating lease* is any lease other than a finance lease. Examples of situations that could lead to a lease being classified as a finance lease are:

- *Additional lease.* The lessee can continue the lease for an additional period at a rate substantially lower than the market rate.
- *Cancellation.* If the lessee can cancel the lease, the lessee pays the lessor's losses associated with the cancellation.
- *Fair value changes.* Gains or losses from fair value changes accrue to the lessee.
- *Ownership.* The lease transfers asset ownership to the lessee by the end of the lease.
- *Present value.* The present value of minimum lease payments substantially equals the asset's fair value at lease inception.
- *Purchase option.* There is an option for the lessee to purchase the asset at a price expected to be sufficiently below fair value on the option date as to make it reasonably certain that the lessee will exercise the option.
- *Specialized nature.* The asset is so specialized that only the lessee can use it without major modifications.
- *Term.* The lease term covers the major part of the economic life of the asset, even if title is not transferred.

The above examples are not always conclusive, so if other features of a lease agreement make it clear that the lease does not transfer substantially all risks and rewards of ownership to the lessee, you should classify it as an operating lease.

EXAMPLE 29.1

The Wilco Radio Company enters into a lease agreement that lasts for nine years. The asset's economic life is ten years. The asset's fair value is €2.3 million, and the present value of future minimum lease payments is €2.1 million.

The lease is a finance lease, because it covers essentially the entire term (90%) of the asset's economic life, and the present value of future minimum lease payments is substantially all (91%) of the asset's fair value.

A *noncancelable lease* can be cancelled only with the permission of the lessor, or if the lessee enters into a new lease with the same lessor, or upon the occurrence of a remote contingency, or upon payment of an amount that makes continuation of the lease reasonably certain.

 ### Can I Change a Lease Classification Later?

A lease can be classified as either a finance lease or an operating lease. If the lessor and lessee agree to alter the lease provisions such that the lease is classified differently, then consider the altered lease to be a new lease for the purposes of reclassifying it.

A change in estimate, such as a revised estimate of residual value or economic life, does not trigger a change in lease classification.

 ### Can I Classify an Operating Lease as an Investment Property?

Yes. If so, the lessee should account for the property interest as though it were a finance lease, and should continue to do so even if the situation subsequently changes, so that the leased asset is no longer an investment property. This situation can arise when the lessee shifts the risks and rewards of ownership through a sublease (and is accounted for by the lessee as a finance lease), or when the lessee occupies the property and then classifies it as owner-occupied property.

What Is the Difference between Economic Life and Useful Life?

Economic life is the period over which an asset is expected to be economically usable, whereas *useful life* is the estimated remaining period over which an entity expects to consume the economic benefits of an asset.

When Does an Arrangement Contain a Lease?

Assessing whether an arrangement contains a lease requires an assessment of whether the arrangement conveys a right to use an asset, and whether fulfilling the arrangement is dependent upon the usage of a specific asset or group of specified assets.

An arrangement contains a right to use an asset if it conveys to the purchaser the right to control the use of the asset. The right of control occurs in any of the following situations:

- *Access.* The purchaser can control physical access to the asset while controlling more than an insignificant part of its output or utility.
- *Operation.* The purchaser can operate the asset in a manner it determines while controlling more than an insignificant part of its output or utility.
- *Output.* There is a remote chance that a third party will take more than an insignificant amount of its output or utility, and the price the purchaser pays for the asset's output is not fixed by the agreement and is not equal to the current market price.

If the supplier is allowed under the arrangement to use assets not specified in the arrangement, then the arrangement does not contain a lease. However, an arrangement permitting the supplier to substitute other assets may not preclude lease treatment prior to the date of asset substitution. If the supplier owns only one asset with which to fulfill the arrangement and it is not feasible to use other assets, then it is assumed that the asset has been specified in the arrangement.

Example 29.2

Aalborg Automotive enters into an agreement with Danish Energy, whereby Danish Energy constructs a wind farm next to the Aalborg radiator construction facility. Under the agreement, Danish Energy will provide a minimum fixed amount of electricity from the wind farm to the facility for the next five years. Danish Energy has ownership of and control over the wind farm, and also is responsible for repairing and maintaining it. Danish Energy could use the wind farm to supply electricity to other customers, but it intends to operate the wind farm solely for the use of Aalborg Automotive. Aalborg Automotive must pay a fixed minimum fee for the electricity, as well as a variable fee if its usage exceeds a specified amount.

This arrangement contains a lease, because it specifically identifies the wind farm and states that the electricity is sourced from the wind farm. Given Danish Energy's intent to devote the wind farm to the Aalborg facility, there is only a remote chance that other parties will use its output. Also, pricing is not based on the market rate at the time of delivery.

How Do I Break out the Lease Elements from an Arrangement?

You should account for as a lease only that portion of an arrangement containing a lease. At the inception of the arrangement, you should separate the payments and other consideration into those for the lease and those for other elements based on their relative fair values. This may require that you estimate the lease-related payments in the arrangement either by comparison to the lease arrangement for a similar asset, or by estimating the payments for other elements of the arrangement and then deducting them from the total payment to derive the lease payments.

If it is impracticable to separate the lease payments in the arrangement, then you should follow either of the following approaches, depending on the type of lease:

○ *Finance lease.* If it is a finance lease, recognize an asset and a liability in an amount equal to the fair value of the asset being leased, and subsequently reduce the liability as payments are made. Also, impute a finance charge using the purchaser's incremental borrowing rate.

○ *Operating lease.* If it is an operating lease, treat all payments as lease payments for lease disclosure purposes, but disclose them separately from the minimum lease payments for other leases not containing nonlease elements, and state that the disclosed payments include nonlease elements.

When Do I Assess Whether an Arrangement Contains a Lease?

You should assess whether an arrangement contains a lease at the earlier of the date of the arrangement or the date of commitment by the parties to its terms. You should reassess whether an ongoing arrangement contains a lease only if one of these conditions occurs:

○ *Asset change.* There is a substantial physical change to the asset.
○ *Asset dependency.* There is a change in the determination of whether fulfillment of the arrangement depends on a specific asset.
○ *Renewal.* The parties agree to renew or extend the agreement.
○ *Change in terms.* The contract terms (other than a contract renewal or extension) change.

A change in estimate, such as for the amount of output to be delivered by the asset, will not trigger a reassessment.

If a reassessment results in the determination that the arrangement has changed to either contain or not contain a lease, then use lease accounting (or not) as of the date when the change in circumstances triggered the reassessment. However, if the reassessment was triggered by an agreement renewal or extension, then use lease accounting (or not) as of the beginning of the renewal or extension period.

What Are Minimum Lease Payments?

Minimum lease payments are those payments that the lessee will be required to make over the term of a lease agreement. This excludes contingent rent and any payments made by the lessee that will be repaid by the lessor or a third party.

From the lessor's perspective, minimum lease payments are the payments that the lessee will be required to make over the term of a lease agreement, plus any residual value guaranteed by the lessee or a third party. If the lessee has an option to purchase the asset at a price so much lower than its fair value at the option date that purchasing is reasonably certain, then the total minimum lease payment is the minimum payments over the lease term until the option date, plus the purchase option price.

How Do I Classify a Lease That Includes Buildings and Land?

If both buildings and land are part of the same lease, then consider them separately for purposes of lease classification. The key factor in favor of treating such leases as finance leases is if title passes to the lessee by the end of the lease term. Since land has an indefinite economic life, a lease is assumed to be an operating lease unless the lessee receives title to the land by the end of the lease term.

EXAMPLE 29.3

Tango Mural Company enters into a property lease that includes both land and a factory building. Tango will obtain title to the factory in 10 years, but not to the land. The fair value of the land is €20 million, and of the building, €50 million. The present value of minimum lease payments associated with the land is €10 million, and with the building, €48 million.

Tango must recognize the land portion of the lease as an operating lease, because title does not pass to Tango, and the present value of minimum lease payments is well below its fair value. Tango should recognize the building portion of the lease as a finance lease, because Tango is effectively purchasing it, based on the passage of title and the high proportion of payments to fair value (96%).

If a combined building/land lease involves a single stream of payments, allocate the minimum lease payments between the building and land elements of the lease in proportion to the relative fair values of the building and land components of the lease. If you cannot reliably allocate the lease payments between the building and land components, then classify the entire lease as a finance lease, unless it is clear that the entire lease should be an operating lease.

If the portion of the lease associated with the land component of the lease is immaterial, then do not break out the land component of the lease. In this case, use the economic life of the building as the economic life of the entire leased asset.

 ## What Types of Residual Value Are Used in a Lease?

The residual value in a lease agreement comprises guaranteed residual value and unguaranteed residual value. *Guaranteed residual value* is that portion of a leased asset's residual value that the lessee or a third party guarantees to the lessor; thus, if the actual residual value declines below the guaranteed residual value, the lessee or a third party will pay the lessor for the difference.

The *unguaranteed residual value* is that portion of a leased asset's residual value for which the lessor has no assurance of realization.

 ## What Are the Gross and Net Investments in a Lease?

The *gross investment in a lease* is the minimum lease payments receivable by the lessor, as well as any unguaranteed residual value accruing to the lessor. The *net investment in a lease* is the gross investment in the lease, discounted at the interest rate implicit in the lease. The *interest rate implicit in the lease* is the discount rate at which all minimum lease payments and the unguaranteed residual value equal the sum of the asset's fair value and any initial direct costs incurred by the lessor. The difference between the gross and net lease investments is *unearned finance income*.

 ## What Is Contingent Rent and How Do I Record It?

Contingent rent is any lease payments not fixed in amount, but rather that is based on the future amount of some factor other than the passage of time. For example, contingent rent can vary with the percentage of a lessee's future sales, future interest rates, or the future cost of living.

Always charge a contingent rent payment to expense in the period in which you incur it.

How Does a Lessee Recognize a Financial Lease?

The lessee recognizes a financial lease at the commencement of the lease term. The lessee recognizes a financial lease as an asset and a liability to pay future lease payments, at an amount equal to the leased asset's fair value or, if lower, the present value of the minimum lease payments. Also, add any initial lessee direct costs to the amount recognized as an asset, such as the costs of negotiating and securing a lease.

EXAMPLE 29.4

Glass Lamination International enters into a five-year finance lease to lease a polycarbonate bonding machine from another party. The fair value of the machine is €200,000. The present value of the minimum lease payments at lease inception is €184,000, and the machine has an unguaranteed residual value in five years of €25,000.

Glass Lamination records the machine asset and lease liability at the minimum lease payment present value of €184,000, which is the lower of the machine's fair value or present value of minimum lease payments. The difference between the €25,000 unguaranteed residual value and the €16,000 difference between the machine's fair value and the present value of minimum lease payments is the present value of the unguaranteed residual value.

Use the discount rate implicit in the lease for the present value calculation. If it is not practicable to determine the implicit rate, then use your incremental borrowing rate instead.

In addition, the lessee should record depreciation expense for the asset. If there is no reasonable certainty that the lessee will obtain ownership of the asset by the end of the lease, then fully depreciate it over the shorter of the lease term or its useful life. See the Property, Plant, and Equipment chapter for more information about methods of depreciation.

How Does the Lessee Record Subsequent Financial Lease Payments?

Whenever the lessee makes a lease payment, it apportions the payment between a finance charge and a reduction of the outstanding liability. The finance charge should result in a constant periodic interest rate on the remaining liability balance.

EXAMPLE 29.5

Amalgamated Munitions leases a munitions loading machine that has a fair value of €250,000. The lease term is four years and involves four equal payments of €75,480, one at the end of each year. There is no assumed residual value. The implied interest rate in the lease is 8 percent, and the present value of the minimum lease payments is €250,000 (€75,480 annual payment × 3.31213 present value factor for an ordinary annuity of 1 per period).

Amalgamated records the lease using the following table:

Payment	Balance	Finance Charge	Payment	Lease Liability
1	€250,000	€20,000	€75,480	€194,520
2	194,520	15,562	75,480	134,602
3	134,602	10,768	75,480	69,890
4	69,890	5,591	75,480	0

Amalgamated records the initial asset acquisition with the following entry:

Leased equipment	€250,000	
Lease obligation		€250,000

Amalgamated records the first lease payment with the following entry:

Lease obligation	€55,480	
Interest expense	20,000	
Cash		€75,480

(Continued)

(Continued)

Amalgamated also depreciates the munitions loading machine. It chooses to do so using the straight-line method, so it records the following entry in each of the four years of the lease term to fully depreciate it by the end of the lease term:

Depreciation expense	€62,500	
Accumulated depreciation		€62,500

At the end of the lease period, the munitions loading machine reverts back to the lessor. Amalgamated has already drawn the lease obligation balance down to zero with its four lease payments. The only remaining step is to eliminate the asset and its offsetting accumulated depreciation, which Amalgamated accomplishes with the following entry:

Accumulated depreciation	€250,000	
Leased equipment		€250,000

How Does a Lessee Recognize an Operating Lease?

The lessee normally recognizes an expense on a straight-line basis for lease payments under an operating lease. It is possible to recognize the expense using other than a straight-line method, if the other method is more representative of the lessee's usage of the asset.

How Does a Lessor Recognize a Financial Lease?

A lessor recognizes an asset held under a financial lease at an amount equal to its net investment in the lease. The lease payment receivable is a repayment of principal, as well as finance income.

The lessor includes initial direct costs in the initial measurement of the finance lease receivable. Direct costs include commissions, legal fees, and internal costs that are directly and incrementally attributable to negotiating and arranging a lease. Do not include in the measurement of the finance lease receivable any of these direct costs if they involve a manufacturer or dealer lessor; in these cases, the lessor charges the direct leasing costs to expense at the same time that it recognizes the selling profit (normally when the lease commences).

The lessor recognizes finance income based on a pattern that reflects a constant periodic rate of return on its investment in the lease. As each lease payment arrives from the lessee, the lessor applies the payment against the gross investment in the lease to reduce both the principal and unearned finance income.

 ## How Does a Manufacturer or Dealer Lessor Recognize a Financial Lease?

A manufacturer or dealer lessor recognizes a selling profit or loss in the period when the lease commences. The revenue it recognizes is the lower of the fair value of the asset or the present value of minimum lease payments (using a market discount rate). The cost of sales is the cost or carrying amount of the asset being leased, less the present value of any unguaranteed residual value.

If the lessor incorporates an artificially low rate of interest in the lease, then it must reduce its selling profit to the amount that would apply if it had charged a market rate of interest.

The manufacturer or dealer lessor recognizes as an expense any lease negotiation and arrangement costs when it recognizes the selling profit or loss.

EXAMPLE 29.6

The Poseidon Boat Company has issued a seven-year lease to the Adventure Yachting Company (AYC) on a boat for its yacht rental business. The boat cost Poseidon €450,000 to build and should have a residual value of €75,000 at the end of the lease. Annual lease payments are €77,000. Poseidon's implicit interest rate is 8 percent. The present value multiplier for an ordinary annuity of $1 for seven years at 8 percent interest is 5.2064. The present value multiplier for €1 due in seven years at 8 percent interest is 0.5835. We construct the initial journal entry with the following calculations:

○ *Lease receivable.* This is the sum of all minimum lease payments, which is €539,000 (€77,000/year × 7 years), plus the actual residual value of €75,000, for a total lease receivable of €614,000.

(Continued)

(*Continued*)

○ *Cost of goods sold.* This is the asset cost of €450,000, minus the present value of the residual value, which is €43,763 (€75,000 residual value × present value multiplier of 0.5835).

○ *Revenue.* This is the present value of all minimum lease payments, or €400,893 (€77,000/year × present value multiplier of 5.2064).

○ *Inventory.* Poseidon's book value for the yacht is €450,000, which is used to record a reduction in its inventory account.

○ *Unearned interest.* This is the lease receivable of €614,000, minus the present value of the minimum lease payments of €400,893, minus the present value of the residual value of €43,763, which yields €169,344.

Based on these calculations, the initial journal entry is as follows:

	Debit	Credit
Lease receivable	€614,000	
Cost of goods sold	406,237	
Revenue		€400,893
Boat asset		450,000
Unearned interest		169,344

The next step is to determine the allocation of lease payments between interest income and reduction of the lease principal, which is accomplished through the following effective interest table:

Year	Annual Payment	Interest Income	Reduction in Lease Obligation	Remaining Lease Obligation
0				€444,656
1	€77,000	€35,572	€41,428	403,228
2	77,000	32,258	44,742	358,486
3	77,000	28,679	48,321	310,165
4	77,000	24,813	52,187	257,978
5	77,000	20,638	56,362	201,616
6	77,000	16,129	60,871	140,745
7	77,000	11,255	65,745	75,000

The interest expense shown in the effective interest table can then be used to record the allocation of each lease payment between interest revenue and principal reduction. For example, the entries recorded for Year 4 of the lease are as follows:

	Debit	Credit
Cash	€77,000	
Lease receivable		€77,000
Unearned interest	€24,813	
Interest revenue		€24,813

Once the lease expires and AYC returns the boat to Poseidon, the final entry to close out the lease transaction is as follows:

	Debit	Credit
Boat asset	€75,000	
Lease receivable		€75,000

How Does a Lessor Account for Unguaranteed Residual Value?

If a lessor has included unguaranteed residual value in its computation of its gross investment in the lease, it should review this value regularly. The lessor should immediately recognize any reduction in the estimated unguaranteed residual value.

How Does a Lessor Recognize an Operating Lease?

A lessor recognizes lease income from an operating lease in income on a straight-line basis over the term of the lease. It is acceptable to use a method other than the straight-line method if it is more representative of the usage pattern of the asset.

Recognize the depreciation associated with the asset over the term of the lease. As with the related revenue, recognize the depreciation on a straight-line basis unless there is another method more representative of actual usage. The lessor should use a depreciation method that is consistent with its normal depreciation policy for similar assets.

If the lessor incurs any direct costs in negotiating and arranging an operating lease, the lessor adds these costs to the carrying amount of the leased asset and recognizes it as an expense over the term of the lease, on the same basis used to recognize lease income.

Can a Manufacturer or Dealer Lessor Recognize a Selling Profit on an Operating Lease?

A manufacturer or dealer lessor does not recognize a selling profit upon initiation of an operating lease, since the transaction is not the equivalent of a sale.

How Do I Account for Incentives Associated with an Operating Lease?

The lessor may grant an incentive to a lessee to enter into an operating lease. Examples of incentives are an up-front cash payment or the assumption of leasehold improvements. You should include all of these incentives in the total amount of consideration for the use of the leased asset.

The lessor recognizes the cost of incentives as a reduction of rental income over the term of the lease. The lessee recognizes the incentive benefit as a reduction of rental expense over the lease term. The lessor and lessee should recognize the incentives on a straight-line basis, unless another method is more representative of asset usage.

EXAMPLE 29.7
Magellanic Company enters into a new building lease arrangement with Norwegian Properties, where it will build custom sea-going rowboats for the fishing industry. Norwegian agrees to give Magellanic free rent for the first year of the agreement as an incentive for entering into the lease. The new lease has a term of 10 years, at a fixed rate of €50,000 per year after the first year of free rent.
The total payment over the 10-year term of the arrangement is €450,000. Both Magellanic and Norwegian should recognize the €450,000 over the full 10-year period, using a standard amortization method.

How Does a Seller-Lessee Account for a Sale and Leaseback Transaction?

A sale and leaseback transaction occurs when an entity (the seller-lessee) sells an asset to a third party and then leases it back. The accounting for this transaction varies depending on the type of lease that results. For example:

○ *Finance lease.* The seller-lessee defers and amortizes over the lease term any excess of sales proceeds over the carrying amount of the asset.
○ *Operating lease.* The seller-lessee can immediately recognize a profit or loss if the transaction is established *at* fair value. If the sale price is *above* fair value, then the seller-lessee defers and amortizes over the lease term the excess amount over fair value. If the sale price is *below* fair value, the seller-lessee immediately recognizes any profit or loss on the sale (the difference between its carrying amount and fair value); however, if a loss compensates for future lease payments that are below the market rate, then the seller-lessee defers and amortizes the loss in proportion to the lease payments over the asset usage period.

The table in Exhibit 29.1 shows the various treatments accorded to a sale and leaseback transaction under different scenarios.

 ## When Do I Merge Multiple Transactions into a Single Lease?

An entity may lease assets to another party and then lease them back for a variety of reasons, including the sharing or shifting of tax advantages. You should link a series of transactions that involve the legal form of a lease when you cannot understand the overall economic effect without reference to all of the transactions. The accounting should reflect the substance of the arrangement. Indicators that an arrangement may *not* involve a lease are:

○ *Option.* The terms include an option that is almost certain to be exercised.
○ *Ownership.* The entity retains the risks and rewards of ownership of the asset, and has the same rights to its use that it had before the arrangement.
○ *Tax goal.* The arrangement is designed to achieve a tax goal, rather than convey the right to use the asset.

Exhibit 29.1 Sale and Leaseback Decision Matrix

Recognition Scenario	Carrying Amount = Fair Value	Carrying Amount < Fair Value	Carrying Amount > Fair Value
Sale Price at Fair Value			
Profit recognition	No profit	Recognize profit upon lease commencement	Not applicable
Loss recognition	No loss	Not applicable	Recognize loss upon lease commencement
Sale Price below Fair Value			
Profit	No profit	Recognize profit upon lease commencement	No profit; recognize loss for the difference upon lease commencement
No loss compensation with reduced future lease payments	Recognize loss upon lease commencement	Recognize loss upon lease commencement	Recognize loss for the difference upon lease commencement
Loss compensation with reduced future lease payments	Defer and amortize loss	Defer and amortize loss	Recognize loss for the difference upon lease commencement
Sale Price above Fair Value			
Profit recognition	Defer and amortize profit	Defer and amortize excess profit; recognize excess of fair value over carrying amount upon lease commencement	Defer and amortize profit, which is the difference between fair value and sale price
Loss recognition	No loss	No loss	Recognize loss for the difference upon lease commencement

If there is a fee associated with multiple transactions involving the legal form of a lease, present the fee in the statement of comprehensive income. You cannot recognize the entire fee as income when received if one of the following indicators is present:

- *Obligations.* There are fee performance obligations or requirements to refrain from significant activities.
- *Restrictions.* There are significant restrictions on the entity's use of the asset.
- *Reimbursement.* There is a nonremote possibility of reimbursing the fee or paying some additional amount.

 ## What Controls Should I Use for Leases?

For a financial lease, the lessee must depreciate the assets acquired under the terms of the lease. If the asset was recorded in the fixed assets tracking module of the accounting system in the normal manner, this likely would result in a system-designated depreciation period. Such a depreciation period is acceptable if the financial lease involves a transfer of ownership. However, if the lessor retains ownership at the end of the lease, the depreciation period must be limited to the lease term. Using a shorter depreciation period will increase the periodic depreciation expense, so this issue has an impact on earnings. Consequently, verification of the depreciation period should be a standard review item in the period-end closing procedure.

The lessor should conduct at least an annual review of the residual value of all leased assets and adjust those valuations downward if there appear to be permanent valuation reductions. Any such adjustment will result in the recognition of a loss, so there is a natural tendency to avoid or delay this step. By including it in the standard schedule of activities, the accounting staff is more likely to conduct it.

A manufacturer or dealer can artificially increase its selling profit on a sale by using an artificially low rate of interest in the lease. To avoid this, have the internal audit staff ensure that a market rate of interest is used when calculating the selling profit on a financial lease.

 ## What Information Should a Lessee Disclose for a Financial Lease?

For each class of assets, the lessee should disclose the following information:

○ *Balances.* The net carrying amount at the end of the reporting period

○ *Contingent rent.* The contingent rent recognized in the period

○ *Future payments.* Total future minimum lease payments and their present value at the end of the reporting period, as well as for not later than the next year, later than one year and not later than five years, and later than five years

○ *Lease terms.* The general terms of all material leasing arrangements, including the basis on which contingent rent payments are determined; the terms of any renewal, purchase, or escalation clauses; and any restrictions imposed by lease arrangements

○ *Reconciliation.* Reconciliation between the total future minimum lease payments at the end of the reporting period and their present value at the end of the period

○ *Subleases.* The total of all future minimum sublease payments that the entity expects to receive under noncancelable subleases

What Information Should a Lessee Disclose for an Operating Lease?

A lessee should disclose the following information for an operating lease:

○ *Future payments.* The total of future minimum lease payments under noncancelable operating leases for not later than the next year, later than one year and not later than five years, and later than five years

○ *Subleases.* The total of all future minimum sublease payments that the entity expects to receive under noncancelable subleases

○ *Current expense.* The amount of all lease and sublease payments expensed in the period, separately disclosing the amounts for minimum lease payments, contingent rents, and sublease payments

○ *Lease terms.* The general terms of all material leasing arrangements, including the basis on which contingent rent payments are determined; the terms of any renewal, purchase, or escalation clauses; and any restrictions imposed by lease arrangements

What Information Should a Lessor Disclose for a Financial Lease?

A lessor discloses the following information for a financial lease:

○ *Bad debt allowance.* The accumulated allowance for uncollectible minimum lease payments receivable
○ *Contingent rent.* The amount of any contingent rent recognized as income in the period
○ *Finance income.* The amount of any unearned finance income
○ *Future payments.* The gross investment in the lease and the present value of minimum lease payments receivable at the end of the reporting period, as well as for not later than the next year, later than one year and not later than five years, and later than five years
○ *Lease terms.* The general terms of all material leasing arrangements
○ *Reconciliation.* Reconciliation of the gross investment in the lease at the end of the reporting period to the present value of its minimum lease payments
○ *Residual values.* The amount of any unguaranteed residual values that accrue to the lessor

Although not required, it is useful to also disclose the gross investment less unearned income in new business added during the reporting period, less deductions for cancelled leases. This metric is a good indicator of growth.

What Information Should a Lessor Disclose for an Operating Lease?

A lessor should disclose the following information for an operating lease:

○ *Contingent rent.* The amount of any contingent rent recognized as income in the period
○ *Future payments.* The future minimum lease payments under noncancelable operating leases, both in the aggregate and for not later than the next year, later than one year and not later than five years, and later than five years
○ *Lease terms.* The general terms of the lessor's leasing arrangements

What Information Should I Disclose for Multiple Transactions Involving the Form of a Lease?

If there are number of transactions that should be combined and treated as a lease, disclose the following information, either individually for each arrangement or in the aggregate for each class of arrangements:

- ○ *Asset.* General description of the asset and any restrictions on its use
- ○ *Fees.* The accounting treatment used for any fee received, the amount recognized in the current period, and where it is located in the statement of comprehensive income
- ○ *Linkages.* The transactions that are linked together, including options
- ○ *Terms.* The life and other significant terms of the arrangement

CHAPTER 30

MINERAL RESOURCES EXPLORATION AND EVALUATION

 How Do I Initially Measure Mineral Exploration and Evaluation Assets?

You should measure assets related to the *exploration* and *evaluation* of mineral resources at cost. This is accomplished most easily by creating a policy to specify which expenditures are to be recognized as such assets, with an emphasis on designating assets based on the degree to which they are associated with locating specific mineral resources. You can alter this policy if the change makes the entity's financial statements more relevant to user needs and more reliable.

Examples of exploration and evaluation assets are:

Acquisition of exploration rights	Mineral extraction feasibility studies
Exploratory drilling	Sampling
Geological studies	Trenching

Consistently classify these assets as either tangible (such as drilling equipment) or intangible (such as exploration rights) assets.

Do not recognize expenditures related to mineral resources development as exploration and evaluation assets.

 How Do I Subsequently Measure Mineral Exploration and Evaluation Assets?

You can either carry an asset at its cost or periodically revalue it to its fair value. In either case, subsequent measurement must include reductions for any accumulated depreciation and impairment losses. It is acceptable to revalue a class of assets on a rolling basis, as long as the revaluation is completed within a short period of time.

If you choose periodic revaluation, then conduct revaluations with sufficient regularity to ensure that the carrying amount does not vary significantly from its fair value. For those exploration and evaluation assets having significant and volatile changes in fair value, it may be necessary to revalue annually. When there are insignificant changes in fair value, a revaluation once every three to five years is sufficient.

Use the following table to determine the proper accounting for an asset that has been revalued:

Asset value increases	Recognize in other comprehensive income and as revaluation surplus in equity
Asset value increases, but reverses a prior revaluation decrease	Recognize as profit to the extent that it reverses a revaluation decrease previously recognized in profit or loss
Asset value decreases	Recognize as a loss
Asset value decreases, but credit balance exists in the revaluation surplus for the asset	Recognize in other comprehensive income to the extent of any revaluation surplus for the asset, with any excess recognized as a loss

For more information, see the Property, Plant, and Equipment chapter.

When Do I Stop Classifying Assets as Exploration and Evaluation Assets?

You should stop classifying assets as exploration and evaluation assets when you can demonstrate that it is technically feasible and commercially viable to extract a mineral resource in the area related to those assets. You also should assess asset impairment prior to reclassifying the assets.

How Do I Determine Whether Exploration and Evaluation Assets Are Impaired?

An entity should have an accounting policy for rationally allocating exploration and evaluation assets to cash-generating units, so that it then can periodically assess the cash-generating units for asset impairment.

Any of the following issues may indicate that an exploration and evaluation asset is impaired:

- *Exploration expiration.* The entity's right to explore has or shortly will expire, and it does not expect to renew the right.
- *No discoveries.* The entity has not discovered commercially viable quantities of minerals in a specific area, and so has decided to discontinue its operations in that area.
- *Terminated expenditures.* The entity does not plan to make substantive additional exploration and evaluation expenditures in a specific area.
- *Unrecoverable carrying amount.* The carrying amount of the exploration and evaluation asset is not recoverable in full, even if further development or sale is likely.

If these issues indicate that an impairment assessment is warranted, see the Asset Impairment chapter regarding how to conduct an assessment.

 ## How Do I Account for Removal and Restoration Obligations?

You can recognize a provision for a removal and restoration obligation associated with the exploration for mineral resources when there is a present obligation resulting from a past event, there is a probable payment required in order to settle the obligation, and you can reliably estimate the amount of the obligation. If the situation does not meet these conditions, then do not recognize a provision. For more information about provisions, see the Provisions and Contingencies chapter.

 ## What Information Should I Disclose about Mineral Resources Exploration and Evaluation?

You should disclose the following information about an entity's mineral resources exploration and evaluation assets:

- *General.* Identification and explanation of recognized amounts arising from exploration and evaluation activities

- ○ *Financial results.* The amounts of assets, liabilities, revenue, expenses, and cash flows arising from the entity's exploration and evaluation activities
- ○ *Policies.* Accounting policies for these expenditures, including how it recognizes assets

CHAPTER 31

RETIREMENT BENEFIT PLANS

 What Is a Retirement Benefit Plan?

A retirement benefit plan is an arrangement whereby an entity provides benefits for its employees either on or after their termination of service. The entity calculates the benefits to be paid, or can estimate the contributions toward them in advance of employee retirement.

 What Is a Defined Contribution Plan?

A defined contribution plan is a retirement benefit plan under which payments by an entity to its former employees are based on the funding entity's payments to a fund, plus any subsequent earnings on those funds. The funding entity's obligation to pay employees usually is discharged by its contributions to the fund.

 What Is a Defined Benefit Plan?

A defined benefit plan is a retirement benefit plan under which payments to former employees are fixed based on a formula that typically incorporates employee earnings and/or years of service. It has no direct relationship to the funding entity's payments to the fund from which payments are made.

 How Do I Account for a Hybrid Retirement Plan?

If your retirement benefit plan contains characteristics of both a defined contribution plan and a defined benefit plan, then account for it as a defined benefit plan.

What Are Vested and Unvested Benefits?

A *vested benefit* is a benefit that an employee has already earned the right to receive, irrespective of continued employment. Vesting typically is based on an employee's completed service time with an entity. An employee does not yet have the right to receive an *unvested benefit*, for which the individual has not yet completed sufficient service time.

 ## What Is a Trustee?

A trustee is a third-party administrator who manages the assets of a fund into which an entity deposits financial assets.

 ## What Is Actuarial Present Value?

Actuarial present value is the present value of payments that an entity expects to pay, under a retirement benefit plan, to its existing and past employees for services already rendered.

 ## On What Salary Basis Do I Calculate Actuarial Present Value?

When calculating the actuarial present value of promised retirement benefits, you can determine the present value based on either current salary levels or projected salary levels. Either variation is acceptable, as long as you disclose which variation you are using.

The reasons for using current salary levels in this calculation are to reduce the number of assumptions in the actuarial calculations, and because the resulting obligation most closely matches the entity's total obligation if the plan were to be terminated or discontinued in the near future.

The reasons for using projected salary levels in this calculation are because not doing so may result in apparent overfunding of the plan when the opposite is the case, and also because one should assume that an entity will continue as a going concern, which calls for the use of salary projections into the foreseeable future.

How Frequently Should I Obtain Actuarial Valuations?

The frequency of a formal valuation process in some countries may be, for example, only once every three years. Thus, if there is no current actuarial valuation as of the most recent financial statement date, then use the most recent valuation as a base and disclose the date of the valuation.

On What Cost Basis Should I Record Retirement Plan Assets?

You should always record retirement benefit plan investments at fair value. If a plan asset is a marketable security, then its fair value is its market value. If it is not possible to estimate fair value, then disclose the reason why you cannot use fair value.

What Information Should I Disclose for All Retirement Plans?

For any type of retirement benefit plan, an entity should disclose the following information:

- *Funding policy.* Description of the funding policy
- *Accounting policies.* Significant accounting policies related to its retirement benefit plans
- *Statement of changes in net assets available for benefits.* Employer contributions, employee contributions, investment income, other income, benefits paid or payable, administrative expenses, other expenses, income taxes, profits and losses on investment disposals and valuation changes, and transfers from and to other plans
- *Statement of net assets available for benefits.* Assets at the end of the period, the basis of asset valuation, details for any investment over 5 percent of the net assets available for benefits or of any security class, details of any investment in the entity, and any liabilities other than retirement benefits

What Does a Statement of Changes in Net Assets Available for Benefits Look Like?

The following is an example of a statement of changes in net assets available for benefits:

Investment income	
Interest income	€25,000
Dividend income	5,000
Net appreciation in fair value of investments	40,000
Total investment income	70,000
Plan contributions:	
Employer contributions	100,000
Employee contributions	25,000
Total plan contributions	125,000
Total additions to net asset value	195,000
Plan benefit payments:	
Pensions	30,000
Retirement lump-sum payments	15,000
Severance pay	5,000
Total plan benefit payments	50,000
Net increase in asset value	145,000
Net assets available for benefits	
Beginning of year	250,000
End of year	395,000

What Does a Statement of Net Assets Available for Benefits Look Like?

The following is an example of a statement of net assets available for benefits:

Assets	
Investments at fair value:	
EU corporate bonds	€75,000
EU equity securities	150,000
U.S. equity securities	75,000
U.S. government securities	100,000
Others	25,000
Total investments	425,000
Receivables:	
Accrued interest	25,000
Dividends receivable	5,000
Total receivables	30,000

Cash:	35,000
Total assets	490,000
Liabilities	
Accounts payable	€25,000
Benefits payable to plan participants	50,000
Accrued expenses	20,000
Total liabilities	95,000
Net assets available for benefits	395,000

What Information Do I Disclose about a Defined Contribution Plan?

If an entity has a defined contribution plan, its financial statements or attached notes should contain the following information:

- ○ *Activity.* Significant activities for the period, the effect of any plan changes, plan membership, and changes in the plan's terms and conditions
- ○ *Performance.* Investment performance for the period
- ○ *Policies.* The investment policies associated with the plan
- ○ *Position.* The financial position of the plan at the end of the period

What Information Do I Disclose about a Defined Benefit Plan?

If an entity has a defined benefit plan, its financial statements or attached notes should contain the following information:

- ○ *Activity statement.* One of the following three statement formats, any of which must differentiate between vested and unvested benefits:

  1. A statement showing net assets available for benefits, the actuarial present value of promised retirement benefits, and the resulting excess or deficit
  2. A statement of net assets available for benefits, showing the actuarial present value of promised retirement benefits, and a statement of changes in net assets available for benefits
  3. A reference to the same information in an attached actuarial report

- *Actuarial valuation date.* The date of the most recent actuarial valuation of plan benefits
- *Assumption changes.* The effect of any changes in actuarial assumptions that have a significant effect on the actuarial present value of promised retirement benefits
- *Basis of calculations.* Whether the actuarial present value of promised retirement benefits is based on current or projected salary levels
- *Reconciliation to promised benefits.* The difference between the actuarial present value of promised retirement benefits and the net assets available for benefits, as well as the entity's policy for funding the promised benefits
- *Significant assumptions.* The significant actuarial assumptions made, and the calculation method used to determine the actuarial present value of promised retirement benefits

If an entity has not prepared an actuarial valuation as of the financial statement date, then use the most recent valuation as a base, and disclose the date of this report.

 ## What Information Do I Include in a Retirement Benefit Plan Report?

The report of a retirement benefit plan contains a plan description. This report can be included in the financial statements, or it may be aggregated as a separate report. A retirement benefit plan report usually contains the following information:

- *Benefits.* Description of the retirement benefits promised under the plan
- *Names.* The names of the employer and the covered employee groups
- *Participant payments.* Whether participants contribute to the plan
- *Participants.* The number of plan participants currently receiving benefits, and the number of other participants
- *Termination.* Any plan termination terms
- *Type.* Whether the plan is a defined benefit or defined contribution plan
- *Changes.* Any changes in the preceding report items during the reporting period

INDEX